Burst Afresh

Also by Larry Frank

Historic Pottery of the Pueblo Indians

Indian Silver Jewelry of the Southwest

The New Kingdom of the Saints

Train Stops (Short Stories)

A Land So Remote (Three Volumes)

Fragments of a Mask

Siftings (Poems)

Burst Afresh

Poems
by
Larry Frank

Edited by Alyce Frank
with an Introduction by Sawnie Morris

SUNSTONE
PRESS

SANTA FE

Sunstone books may be purchased for educational, business, or sales promotional use.
For information please write: Special Markets Department, Sunstone Press,
P.O. Box 2321, Santa Fe, New Mexico 87504-2321.

Book design ✣ Vicki Ahl
Body typeface ✣ Arial Regular
Printed on acid free paper

Library of Congress Cataloging-in-Publication Data

Frank, Larry.
 Burst afresh : poems / by Larry Frank ; edited by Alyce Frank with an introduction by
Sawnie Morris.
   p. cm.
 ISBN 978-0-86534-664-2 (alk. paper)
 I. Frank, Alyce, 1932- II. Title.
 PS3556.R33426B87 2008
 811'.54--dc22
                              2008032444

Published in

WWW.SUNSTONEPRESS.COM
SUNSTONE PRESS / POST OFFICE BOX 2321 / SANTA FE, NM 87504-2321 /USA
(505) 988-4418 / ORDERS ONLY (800) 243-5644 / FAX (505) 988-1025

Contents

Burst Afresh

Preface

"*P*oetry was the thing Larry did when he wasn't busy doing something else; he always returned to it. He is primarily known as a collector and a filmmaker, but he was a poet before he became either of those other things. He was writing poetry when I first met him. I was twenty and he was twenty-five and we were at UCLA making movies. He had started writing poetry when he was in Paris in 1949 and a lot of his poetry was about things he had done before he met me. After he met me, he would write poems to me. The poems were funny and I liked them. Some of those early poems are in his first book. We moved to Taos when he was thirty-five and for the first four years we were still receiving substantial royalties on the films we'd made, so he continued to write poetry and he did that until we had our third child. At that point, he had to make a living for our family. We had three kids, so during the middle part of his life he didn't write poetry nearly as much. Even so, when he did sit down to write, he would do it for three or four months at a stretch. He always showed me drafts of his poems after he finished writing them and I'd comment, make a suggestion about a word or a line. From time to time, he took classes and workshops. During the last few years of his life he wasn't working at making a living so much and he returned in a more focused way to writing poems. He wrote mostly at night on yellow legal pads. He wrote a number of books about pottery or Santos or Native American jewelry, and also a novel and collection of short stories, but for Larry, poetry was always the finest form of expression."

—Alyce Frank, Editor
Arroyo Hondo, New Mexico
August 20

Introduction

I read the poems of Larry Frank for the first time a half hour or so before I met the poet. His wife, Alyce, and I were seated at the Frank's dining room table about to indulge in tea and scones when Alyce gestured toward Larry's first collection of poems, a full-length volume titled, *Siftings,* which lay on the table. Alyce and I had only recently met, but during our brief encounters she had mentioned more than once that her husband was a poet. I had heard of the Larry Frank who was a collector of Santos and Native American iconography, and I had heard of the Larry Frank who railed against the powers-that-be in local town meetings, but the Larry Frank who wrote poems I had no knowledge of, at all.

I opened the book prepared to glance at a poem or two, murmur something polite, and move on. Montale speaks of the poetic moment in terms of song pelting like rain into the breast. I was literally struck by something I hadn't expected in the poems, by the energy of their maker captured in the field of each of the poems. I didn't expect it, and to the moment of this writing cannot entirely account for the experience, except to say: this is what happened and I am grateful. The poems led me to the poet and the poet became my friend.

If poems serve as an intersection between two individual's realities, then what happened that day in the

Frank's living room can be described as a moment of recognition. The voice in the poems of *Siftings* as well as that of *Burst Afresh*, Frank's second and final collection, is at times humorous, at other times scalding, at still other times full of charm—even playfully silly—but, in the end it is honest—"a man speaking to men"—and intimate.

Larry Frank wrote the poems in *Burst Afresh* primarily during the invasion and continued occupation of Iraq by the United States, and that background noise, those "lethal cannons" appear to play a significant role in poems such as "Soldiers March . . . ," "Breathing," "Counterpoints," "Curse," and "Disorder." Frank wrote the poem, "Curse" in response to an assignment I gave in a workshop I taught the first summer we met. The other participants in the workshop were moved by the poem and assumed its speaker to be a prisoner in Guantánamo. Larry was pleased by that reading, but later told me the poem was inspired by Dylan Thomas' "Do Not Go Gently Into That Dark Night," and was an address to Death. Poets are often the last to know the meanings their poems contain. One thing may be consciously intended, while a host of other equally relevant meanings wait to be unleashed by time, circumstance, and insightful readers. Nevertheless, we read the poems in *Burst Afresh* knowing that many were written during the eightieth year of the poet's life, the year that was his last, and that he was grappling with the fact of mortality. His concerns on that score are tenderly and with humor articulated in love poems such as "Breathing," and "Love," as well as the elegiac "We will meet somewhere . . . ," "Circles," and "Your absence from me . . . ," while "Blue Asters," also a love poem, addresses the possibility of the transmigration of souls (it may help the reader to know that Alyce Frank, to whom the poem is addressed, suffered from polio at a young age and walks with a cane). Frank's poems express his vigorous preoccupation with definition and transformation, from the light touch of,

> Wearing black-orange banners
> a glut of butterflies
> engulfs the yellow sagebrush blooms
> and momentarily
> changes their color

to "Fragments," the poem that most exemplifies Frank's philosophical kinship with Whitman, as it meets and is clarified by argument:

> It matters not, doesn't matter
> yet matters I define myself
> exactly as self
> and not as cat, bassoon, void or turnip
> but as thinking instrument

In temperament, Frank resembles one of his poetic heroes, William Blake. There is fury in a poem like "Curse," rage at the fact of death, balanced by concern that a hummingbird may have "tarried too long/to complete/its destined migration." Where Blake's circumstances were largely urban and his concerns included social justice issues, Frank lived in the high mesa desert and was a committed environmentalist. In the poem "Dirge" he spares the reader nothing, "Ant larvae emerge still-born. /And insect packed dirt/dies inert," while " . . . the sky does not lie/ comfortably on our guilt." In a more overt gesture of homage, Frank offers an endangered species response to

Blake's "Tyger." The mythological and imagistic world that so compelled the visionary Blake, becomes the only remaining sanctuary for the big cat in whose symmetry the existence of God is expressed. It is worth noting how Frank blends Blakeian preoccupations with the influence of his other hero, Hopkins. In the poem "Related to Gerald Manley Hopkins," found in *Siftings*, we hear echoes of Blake in the phrase "a green God stirs in symmetry," while in "Curse" Frank at one point addresses Death, as well as Death's executioners, in the sprung rhythms, packed rhyme, and alliteration recognizable as deriving from Hopkins' influence.

All of these factors come into play in the poem "Counterpoints." Its speaker is primal and mythological, articulate and (one senses) ferocious in physical strength, as well as in emotion—fearful, perhaps, of nature in an animal way—yet one with nature, aware of himself as *being* nature. At the same time, perhaps unnerved to discover himself dislocated at the turn of the millennium, horrified by the events, the realities of what it means to be human—what human beings have evolved to become—in particular the alpha human: "a sterling bedecked general/emblazoned in 1998 newsprint/quashing rebellion . . ." It's a philosophical poem, full of energy and intensity. I think of the speaker as a kind of Beowulf, were Beowulf to wake to himself on the vast high mesa desert in 1998. Or, Frankenstein's monster— a being larger than life, and full of a complicated range of emotions, most predominately love.

While "Counterpoints" reflects in a certain way on its maker, so does its alter ego, the beautifully meditative title poem of the chapbook, "Burst Afresh." In it the reader experiences the other side of Frank's richly complex personality: "It is not

I who burst afresh among humming-/birds,/ Nor do I out-race startled running/ deer . . ." the poem begins in a series of broken seven stress lines of negation, that shift, in the second half of the poem, into a run of short affirming enjambments of what the speaker, Frank's everyman, is, and is capable of being. I would ask the reader to look closely at the last two lines, " . . . when the moon's floodlight/ smothers the warp of war." The word "floodlight," when situated near the "warp of war," insists on an image we associate with imprisonment, yet Frank alters it, heralding nature and the feminine as he shifts the source of that floodlight from a dark tower to the moon, thus doing what poetry, incantation, prayer have always sought to do, transform the metaphorical base metal into gold. "Burst Afresh" is a song of praise, humility, and acceptance calling to mind Job. A poem that, even as it lists human creative limitation, delivers typically Larry Frank style images "Neither could I jam into a picnic basket pulsing stars . . . " And even as it recognizes human flaw in "rancid parliaments," quietly announces and confirms, "Yet, I am made holy/ by a natural order of things."

The order and selection of the poems in this posthumously assembled and edited book reflects the continuation of a lifetime of creative collaboration between Alyce and Larry Frank, as does the final determination on all edits.

—Sawnie Morris
Ranchos de Taos, New Mexico
2008

Burst Afresh

Burst Afresh

It is not I who burst afresh among humming-
      birds,
Nor do I out-race startled running
      deer,
While to no avail can I encompass ocean's jelly-
      fish,
Or string mountains into strands of
      pearls,
Neither could I jam into a picnic basket pulsing
      stars.

Yet, I am made holy
by a natural order of things,
like a stream running through
stones touching each other
revealing ancient runes
that shaped our minds;
we will heal when the flash
of incandescent fireflies
cancels corrupted words,
when jeweled oriole's feathers
erase rancid parliaments,
when the moon's floodlight
smothers the warp of war.

Dance of Kachinas, Zuni Pueblos

The walls bedecked with enormous
elk heads—
festooned with turquoise necklaces—
host a giant wingless bird that
clacks his beak. He is
feathered with a black tiara and ruff
dominating
entirely over a ruckus of misshapen
man/beast,
in perpetual movement back-forth
controlling a corner of the firmament.
These are the lords of empowerment
who came from long before
to bestow blessings, fertilizing
fields and animals
through rain and fornication to
multiply
so all spheres brim with an
entanglement
of every form of pulsating life.

Fragments

It matters not, doesn't matter
yet matters I define myself
exactly as self
and not as cat, bassoon, void or turnip
but as thinking instrument
able to push thoughts as rocks
through a gorge strewn with rubble,
rumbling each concrete impulse, drive,
or splash in a puddle of tadpoles
that count individually with their
dark embryonic heads, swimming limbs.
Consumed I am with countless numbers
cast on velvet, feathered, flesh wings
like bats, all unique.
It hurts my surfeited head with knife-sharp pleasure.
So I swim drowning in shattered expanse,
a flotsam of ends, bits, parts, cores, dabs,
each singularly splendid in its splurge
into little kingdoms apart
which breathe, sprint,
foment and settle in my being
spreading and overwhelming
who I am, expanding me larger than
clouds, storms, deserts, chaos
when in unison we triumph
as fragments.

Niche

I seek space, my space
in the edifice built of words,
written poetry
where I can reside.
I don't care how I enter this
Hierarchy,
whether through a hopscotch maze
interminably crazed
or like fish that slip through
labyrinths of coral reefs
changing form, color, size.
I can be a shape-changer
embracing cause, virtue, sacrifice
or play a dumb docile fox.
Will my niche allow me to
squeeze in as a smoking
shadow, or unlikely, a secular
animist?
It only matters that I fit.

Soldiers march,
politicians serve politics,
firemen stem fires,
runners jog, lamplights
pierce fog, so frogs
bleat in bogs,
while I, in harness,
push stray words.

My friend, if you kill your
elk on your impending hunt,
I will no longer regard you
tenderly but as one who
fulfills his manly role as
hunter at the expense of
one less elk which I will miss
tremendously.
Yet, I still value you
beyond the scope of your
hair-triggered rifle
to kill in a will of
bullet-imploding flesh
drenched in a rush of
gleaming hot blood.

Harmony

It is said to be one
with the universe makes
you one with yourself,
but I prefer many
odd realms of self
draped in singular
colors, sizes, shapes
who bump into each other
and apologize with crazy humor
as they perform in
riotous harmony.

Two birds emerge on
my stony turf. I do not
know the names they have
in the bird book, but they
claim their immutable
selves with red eyes and heads on
white breasted, black underbodies
I welcome as males making
an extended visit into
my lonely digs.

Bedrock

To know what is true is
like drilling for water
in beds of fractured rocks
where liquid sluices out
a hundred fold,
hard to trace or define.

Our bedrock cracks into
fractured words we spin
as skeins
tangled with blurred outlines
and pocked centers steeped
in deception.

Duo

She talked with gossamer-
spun words connected
by tiny wires pulsing
her intricate thoughts
so finely wrought in
rapid succession
that one discordant fist
or ugly shout would shatter
her teetering sanity
like crystal.

He spoke slowly,
weighty sounds tumbling
ponderously as he
glossed over them
to underline the coated
data he savored
enormously,
all-the-while, hazing
his way through a background
of rat-a-tat words
his wife machine-gunned
into his skull.

She is a wounded bird.
Injured by her father's
spite, her mother's bile.
She moves warily,
peeping pleasantly,
hardly ruffling her wings.
Still she holds her poise
knowing her differences
from others. I like her.
As we tread around
each other—respectfully—
seeking openings, I think
all of us are wounded.

Fate

"Marry, my daughter," I say,
"to Tom, Dick, or Harry,
don't dawdle or tarry."
"No way," she flips, but I reply
"Don't be wary
and wait too late
with no tempting
morsel on your plate,
for if you contemplate
endlessly
I hate to reiterate
your fate will be to never have
a male primate."

Love

I love my white puppy so
I really don't know
how much love it's possible
to bestow on such a small
fluff of snow as my love
continues to flow over its
chow's black tongue, nose,
apricot ears all in tow.
Yet, there's a woe I face, a
grief I sow as I watch my
puppy grow and grow.

My black-bodied, white-breasted,
red-headed,
spotted-tail bird came
finally back to where I
watched it scoot from bush
to turf, before my window.
My luck.
I thought I had lost
its friendly way.

Breathing

Against the rumble of war,
you beside me in bed,
I hear you hardly breathing,
embracing your slightly rippling
form of tiny fluttering gasps
deeply spread afield in a
meadow of beloved flesh.
Again the din of raging battles
hover through our fragile systems,
fused by love,
ruptured by strewn bodies
whose specter cuts across our
torn dreams severing us apart.
I still hear your breathing over
a barrage of lethal cannons.

Will we meet somewhere
in the heart's hinterland
after many green and gray,
greengray fields we have
trampled, flowered
and flowerless through
sweet bittersweet eras?
May we meet between
the interstices of life lived—
life ending, wedged in place
perfectly as a knot
holding tight its elements.

Blue Aster

When blue asters die they don't
lie down dead. Their souls
rise to heaven, transforming
their faces into white fluffy
puffs equally transient.
So you, my dear, when you
transpire, wish your soul to morph
into a turkey vulture
sweeping the fields with its
huge feathered sails, a phase
hopefully not transient, and
preventing you from changing into
a landlocked turtle.

Circle

With all your care, all your care
I am losing you.
Like a compass failing to
come full circle, I cannot close,
make the sweep of completion.
I am not I, unable to fulfill what
we richly have or to repair
my shredded will
with elements of a higher need—
to consecrate
what part of self I know to you.
I cannot, cannot.
With all your care, all your care
I am losing you.

Counterpoints

Hunkered in dry stretches of
sage, cactus, brush
staunched by mountain sweeps,
I stand stuck in my shoes
combing my hair
held fixedly in place,
yet fluid with frumpy clouds,
moored,
able to splurge on bird wings
purring in my honed space.
Thunderclaps darken grimly
belligerently
inhaling warm air to a hush.
Insects cease—trees
freeze.
I dread the ensuing roar, weigh
immensity on my shoulders.
In my haven—
focusing on grubs,
honeysuckle,
tree-sap—
furtive stirrings   I distill
with one eye open, the other averted
to note
a sterling bedecked general
emblazoned in 1998 newsprint
quashing rebellion
on some un-poetic frontier.

Dirge

From tortured lands where soils
reside in devastation, I speak.
Rich alluvial spreads of loam
now lie in turmoil.
Beneath earth's crust it does
not go well here.
Worms fight in disarray:
water bugs shiver, collapse
unraveled.
Ground dried, robbed of its ooze
is wearily drained.
Snails with cracked shells wield
antennae broken,
ant larvae emerge still-born.
An insect packed dirt
dies inert.
Of bleak arrays of land
I plead.
Above, the sky does not lie
comfortably on our guilt.
Blackened and bird-less it bleeds
on an afflicted turf.

Curse

You black nothingness,
brute darkling of crimes
whose closing walls squeeze
a Python's vice—
defecating, I am prisoner
in your vast cartel.
Roaring hatred, I shred lungs
as you gather your stark
lawless legions who
have never lost a battle
to claim my assassination.
You Bastard!
Am I your corroded toothless saw?
Your wretched minion
finger-retched
on a vile dominion?

Through the void
far beyond your stricken rule
I embrace stars you cannot smash.

In the Kingdom of Flux

Numbers of living forms, once dead
now dying, soon recreated in
myriad variations infinitely
mirrored, not duplicated
was caused, or was before—
there it was,
multiple items:
deer spotted or not, burnt out suns
falling, endless entities ending,
not ended, things sprout, emerge,
give wings to butterflies
converging in nourishing space
from nothingness came,
blacked void
there it was;
why doubt
rather lavishly consume limitless
menus of sweetmeats:
mildewed, frayed clouds
ant rivulets
robust turbines
crenulated mountains puffing ash
armies of gnus now called
wildebeests of encyclopedias;
there it was:
lovers unloved; wealth, poverty,
a duo clutched in horrid embrace;
diverse torrents in motion.

I do not wonder
whether among furtive shrews
or bristling boars
we are distant cousins
with feet and hearts,
nor do I wonder
about myself adrift
with lanks of footless snakes
earthbound
while tracking a
canary's yellowed song
or salmon's climactic
leap into the throes
of survival.
I do not wonder.
With these allies
may I never blunder.

Tiger

Tyger! Tyger! Burning bright

William Blake's sparkling enormous cat—
implanted in our brains—
who prowled along ridges
with its striped stalking bestiality,
will no longer roam in realms
now fatefully shrunk to the margins
of our rapacious civilization.
The endangered brute will be
among those mysterious
magic creatures in our mythic
sanctuary, lingering
as cherished images that dwell
in our jungle-fabled mind.

She said god is a metaphor,
a place and time in the mind's
comfort zone where we create forms
like friendly fish to nestle with,
but not like the real scaly ones
with fins and jelly eyes.
She likens the weight of
god to dreams she nurses
and coaxes as metaphors
real to her but to no
one, no where else.
She craves metaphors.

Trolling deep into the zone of memory
I reel in my line a ragged soul
festooned with pearlescent
barnacles.
I wonder if it is mine.

Unrecognizable
my old friend who had become
my foe I saw finally
again   we sniffed
coldly   warily
I uttered his name:
island
twenty years extinct.

Questions filtered through
him as a prism of
refracted light, tangled:

always a writer
he was is a novel
in an agent's hands
a plethora of paintings
in a gallery
of marriages askew.
He grew overly flocked
he hulked
a flagship of corroded time
ripe contrived
condescension
and blustery geniality.
We stood
ancient friends
sucked dry
by erosion of disuse.

I barely see the small bird—
enveloped in a tightly
skeined sagebrush bush—
so contentedly immersed
in its natural cage
that I pretend it would
choose not to leave
denying me comfort.

Last September's hummingbird
fed from my feeder starkly alone
igniting in me fear
unknown to it—
whether it tarried too long
to complete
its destined migration.

In the night I saw a skunk's
black body run across the
road with its stripe spanning
its back undulating as if a
white rivulet rambled past me.

Wearing black-orange banners
a glut of butterflies
engulfs the yellow sagebrush blooms
and momentarily
changes their color.

I will laugh again, but rarely;
no reason to splurge beyond
ridges of acute contempt.

My fingers creak,
my toes tweak,
and I squeak.

Everything's just going to be
just like it's going to be
she said, perched on her head.

A streak of charged humming-
birds scissoring space
between tree branches
ignites a feathered explosion.

The fat moon in orbit
grows lean
as the fat wears away
my mood changes.

Your absence from me
endlessly extended
I now realize cuts
horribly across
the face of my days.

Cleaving wild fields of flowers
preying winds seize
their painted faces,
shredding them
and spreading the gore
of all the fragile savages
around-the-world.

And even if the reign of death
reigns everlastingly
we can tamper with its rule
temper it
more than less,
for birth is death.

www.ingramcontent.com/pod-product-compliance
Lightning Source LLC
Chambersburg PA
CBHW020516100426
42813CB00030B/3264/J

Mick Lynch

Manchester University Press

Mick Lynch

The making of a working-class hero

Gregor Gall

Manchester University Press

The right of Gregor Gall to be identified as the author of this work has been asserted in accordance with the Copyright, Designs and Patents Act 1988.

Published by Manchester University Press
Oxford Road, Manchester M13 9PL
www.manchesteruniversitypress.co.uk

British Library Cataloguing-in-Publication Data
A catalogue record for this book is available from the British Library

ISBN 978 1 5261 7309 6 hardback

First published 2024

The publisher has no responsibility for the persistence or accuracy of URLs for any external or third-party internet websites referred to in this book, and does not guarantee that any content on such websites is, or will remain, accurate or appropriate.

Typeset
by Cheshire Typesetting Ltd, Cuddington, Cheshire

To my mother, Alisan, for all her love, care and attention down the years

Contents

Preface

Given the patent and palpable public interest in Mick Lynch and his association with workers, unions and strikes, I have written this book to be more accessible than the average academic study. I deploy critical analysis but in a way that is relatively jargon-free. Crucially, I use the phenomenon of the 'working-class hero' to shine a light on the issue of turning 'power to' (disrupt) into 'power over' (bargaining opponents). The book is an independent piece of research and writing, not affiliated with the RMT itself or any faction, group or individuals within (or outside) it. Those who gave testimony for the research are not responsible in any way for the analysis put forward. This book takes account of and analyses developments up to early October 2023. This was before the national dispute with the Train Operating Companies was concluded.

My thanks go to the TUC Library, George Binette, Tomás Cassidy, John Kelly, Leandro Moura and Keith Richmond for providing help for this study.

Abbreviations

ACAS	Advisory, Conciliation and Arbitration Service
AEEU	Amalgamated Engineering and Electrical Union
AEU	Amalgamated Engineering Union
AGM (RMT)	annual general meeting
ASLEF	Associated Society of Locomotive Engineers and Firemen
BALPA	British Airline Pilots Association
BMA	British Medical Association
BSG	Blacklist Support Group
CAC	Central Arbitration Committee
CFDU	Campaign for a Fighting Democratic Union
CoE (RMT)	Council of Executives
CWU	Communication Workers Union
DOO	driver-only operated
EEPTU	Electrical, Electronic, Telecommunications and Plumbing Union
EiE!	Enough is Enough!
EPIU	Electrical and Plumbing Industries Union
EPS (RMT)	European Passenger Services branch
FBU	Fire Brigades Union

Abbreviations

IASOS	industrial action short of striking
JIB	Joint Industry Board
LBC	London Broadcasting Company
LSE	London School of Economics
MSF	Manufacturing, Science and Finance union
NEC (RMT)	National Executive Committee
NEU	National Education Union
NGA	National Graphical Association
NUJ	National Union of Journalists
NUM	National Union of Mineworkers
NUR	National Union of Railwaymen
PCS	Public and Commercial Services Union
PDE	means of production, distribution and exchange
RCN	Royal College of Nursing
RDG	Rail Delivery Group
RMT	National Union of Rail, Maritime and Transport Workers
SGM	special general meeting
SOGAT	Society of Graphical and Allied Trades
SWP	Socialist Workers Party
TGWU	Transport and General Workers' Union
TOCs	Train Operating Companies
TSSA	Transport Salaried Staffs' Association
TUC	Trades Union Congress
TUSC	Trade Unionist and Socialist Coalition
UCATT	Union of Construction, Allied Trades and Technicians
UCU	University and College Union
UDM	Union of Democratic Mineworkers
USDAW	Union of Shop, Distributive and Allied Workers

Introduction

In Britain, in the early summer of 2022, a straight, white, 60-year-old bald man from London became a 'working-class hero'.[1] The immediate cause was a series of television interviews he gave in which he came across to audiences as a compelling character. This man was a union leader and not a politician – neither a left-wing Labour MP like Jeremy Corbyn nor a leader of a radical left-wing political party like George Galloway or Tommy Sheridan.[2] Within the space of a few weeks, he went from being virtually unknown among the wider public to having a national profile and being instantly recognisable. His demolition of established media operators – people who were supposed to have the professionally honed skills to take down, if necessary, their impertinent interviewees – was a joy for countless thousands to watch many, many times over (see Inset 1 for excerpts). In the 'hot strike summer' of 2022, this union leader became the undisputed 'man of the moment' for all those angry and aggrieved at the Conservative government and the unequal economic and social status quo in 'broken Britain'. For the first time in many decades, a strike wave saw the return of widespread industrial action to Britain. This man rode that wave.

The man was Mick Lynch, the General Secretary of the National Union of Rail, Maritime and Transport Workers (RMT). In defending the right of RMT members to strike, he told the media: 'What else are we to do? Are we to plead? Are we to beg? We want to bargain for our futures. We want to negotiate ... I don't want any working-class people in this country to have to beg their employers for a decent living.'[3] With fewer than 100,000 members, the RMT is a minnow of a union compared to the likes of Unison and Unite, each with more than a million members. But Lynch was articulate and assertive, forthright and frank. He became a voice for the voiceless – a tribune for those whose interests were not represented, much less served, by the political process. Lynch was able to effectively espouse not only his members' grievances but those of a much wider number of workers. He was able to fashion what were specifically sectional demands into a more popular phenomenon where the strikes – as shields of self-interest – became signifiers of 'swords of justice', seen to be wielded by one group of workers on behalf of many other groups of workers. A columnist in the *Independent* opined that 'Mick Lynch has done more for workers in two days than Starmer has in two years',[4] while a Twitter user tweeted 'I assume I am not the only one tonight wishing Mick Lynch was the leader of the Labour Party'.[5] And so Lynch became a working-class hero. Although this was much more for what he said than what he did, in the absence of effective opposition from the Keir Starmer-led Labour Party inside and outside Parliament, this mattered not. There was popular demand for credible and clear-cut opposition to the Conservatives. And very quickly it became apparent that the establishment in Britain could not ignore Lynch. Like his RMT predecessor Bob Crow, he appeared on the BBC's *Question Time*, *Newsnight* and

Inset 1: Excerpts from videos that went viral

Piers Morgan Uncensored (TalkTV), 17 June 2022

Piers Morgan: Let me show you what I believe is your Facebook page. I want you to confirm or deny if this is your Facebook page. It's a picture of 'The Hood' from *Thunderbirds*.

Mick Lynch: Yes, can you see the likeness?

PM: Well, I'm just wondering where the comparison goes because he was obviously an evil, criminal, terrorist mastermind described as the world's most dangerous man.

ML: That is a joke amongst me and my friends and you can see the likeness if you like.

PM: So, you're not denying that you are comparing yourself to 'The Hood'?

ML: I'm not comparing myself to anyone. I'm me.

PM: You've literally made your profile picture 'The Hood' and I'm simply saying ... he was the most dangerous person in the world.

ML: He's the most evil puppet made out of vinyl in the world. Is that the level your journalism's at these days?

Good Morning Britain (ITV), 21 June 2022

Richard Madeley: You've been accused severally in the last few weeks of being a Marxist. It happened again last night. A backbench Tory MP said you were a Marxist with no interest in anything other than trying to tear down the government. Now are you or are you not a Marxist? Because if you are a

Marxist then you're into revolution and into bringing down capitalism. So, are you or aren't you?

Mick Lynch: Richard, you do come up with the most remarkable twaddle sometimes ... I'm not a Marxist. I'm an elected official of the RMT. I'm a working-class bloke leading a trade union dispute about jobs, pay and conditions of service, so it's got nothing to do with Marxism. It's all about this industrial dispute.

Sky News (Sky), 22 June 2022

Kay Burley: I'm guessing that some of your members will still stay on the picket lines. What will they do if agency workers try to cross those picket lines?

Mick Lynch: Well, we will picket them. What do you think we'll do? We run a picket line and we'll ask them not to go to work. Do you not know how a picket line works?

KB: I very much know how a picket line works. I'm much older than I look. What will picketing involve?

ML: Well, you can see what picketing involves. I can't believe this line of questioning. Picketing is standing outside the workplace to try and encourage people who want to go to work not to go to work. What else do you think it involves?

KB: I just wondered what else it might involve because I very well remember the picket lines of the 1980s.

ML: Where are you going with your questions?

KB: I'm asking you what your members would do.

ML: Which picket lines are you talking about?

> **KB:** The miners' strike.
> **ML:** Does it look like the miners' strike? What are you talking about? You've gone off into the world of the surreal. Your questions are verging into nonsense.

Have I Got News for You television programmes, adding to his reputation and popular profile.

Lynch achieved this feat because of his quick-witted, straight-talking and often sardonic – even sarcastic – responses to journalists who thought they could bludgeon him back to where he came from with their reactionary, right-wing talking points. Though the media spoke of springs, summers, autumns and winters of discontent, drawing on the negative narrative of the 1978–79 'winter of discontent', Lynch's media performances turned 2022 into something of a 'glorious summer' for the union movement.

This book examines the process by which a working-class hero was made in the figure of Mick Lynch. It tells the tale of how and why all this happened, as well as what portent it has for radical, progressive politics in Britain. It tells the story of what Lynch did and how others – people, politicians and the press – reacted and responded, in the process making him a working-class hero for many and a bogeyman for others. This study explains how Lynch's persona and politics made up one half of the equation that led to this phenomenon; it also explains how the other half of the equation was made up of a particular political period, along with the potential power of the railway workers. In doing so, a number of counterfactual questions need to be asked and answered. Prime amongst them are: why Mick Lynch and the RMT rather than another general secretary and another union; why a union leader and not a politician; and why now and not before?

Accordingly, this study is both a celebration and a critique of Lynch. A celebration because politics, economics and society in Britain have for too long lacked authentic and influential working-class representatives as the hold of neo-liberalism has tightened and reinforced the power, material interests and ideology of the ruling class. Margaret Thatcher began this project to push back the advances of the working class in the post-war period in order to solve the crisis of capitalism current at the time. It was continued by subsequent governments involving Tories, Labour and Liberals. In this context, working-class heroes and working-class heroines can be seen to be badly needed in order to be able to effectively espouse and campaign for equality, fairness and decency, whether couched in terms of social democracy or socialism. Unfortunately, they have been few and far between. And it can be ventured that they are especially needed as, while unions unfortunately still remain somewhat enfeebled, the organised radical left has also not been able to break out of its marginalisation on the edges of society.

But this is not a starry-eyed, rose-tinted study. It does not romanticise the process by which Lynch became a working-class hero (which, according to John Lennon, 'is something to be'). So it does not suspend its critical faculty on account of the situation that gaining representation of working-class people and their interests still seems to be a somewhat desperate task. If we are to understand how popular left-wing leaders emerge and flourish and, critically, how they can play a part in advancing a wider collective struggle, we must be hard-headed enough to examine all the angles and not duck any difficult issues by glossing over them. This is the sense in which this study is also a critique. Therefore, among the issues are the need to understand how to turn 'power to' disrupt into 'power over' bargaining opponents, and how leaders develop socially and politically. Some skills and traits can be taught but others cannot, being generated organically. Classroom lessons and mentoring cannot substitute for the experience of being hardened in the heat of battle. Within this, it is important to appreciate that one of a leader's major tasks is imparting confidence and certainty to followers – the confidence to fight collectively and the certainty that the battles can be won – in order that an understanding of how this happens can be ascertained. But this must be done in a way that is realistic and does not become full of bombast, bluster and bravado. Accordingly, this study is one of leadership but also of followership. If positing that 'we are all leaders' is to be anything more than an empty platitude, it must be recognised that leadership can take different forms at different levels and at different times. But this does not get away from the manifest reality that being a national leader of a union with mass appeal outside of one's own union requires certain skills and attributes as well as windows of opportunity.

Structure of the book

Chapter 1 lays out the intellectual approach and analytical framework used for this study, with an assessment of what is meant by the term 'working-class hero' in Chapter 2. Chapter 3 goes on to examine Lynch's formative years and considers his initial union activism before and after joining Eurostar. Chapter 4 recounts and assesses Lynch's period working full-time for the RMT. In Chapter 5 his tenure as RMT General Secretary is examined, while Chapter 6 considers him in terms of working-class herodom. Chapter 7 assesses Lynch on the issues of membership power and participation, and the penultimate chapter gives an analysis of Lynch's political world view. Finally, in the Conclusion some of the wider issues for union renewal that arise from studying Lynch are considered. Appendix 1 provides information on the sources and materials used for this study.

Conclusion

Chronologically, there were two crucial components in the process by which Lynch became a working-class hero: his path to becoming RMT General Secretary, and then being RMT General Secretary at the time of the battles over the 'cost-of-living crisis' and 'rail modernisation'. But as the glory days of 'soft power' in the early summer of 2022 faded into the distance as the two national rail disputes dragged on into the spring and summer of 2023, this study examines the changing dynamics of the processes and outcomes associated with the figure of Lynch and the RMT strikes. Critically, it looks behind the phenomenon of the 'working-class hero' to see what it might mask and mystify. Most importantly, this concerns whether the RMT's strategy and tactics were capable of turning 'power to' (disrupt) into the 'power over' (bargaining opponents) and what role Lynch's leadership played in this.

1

Approaching Lynch: the framework

This book is both biographical and sociological. Issues of social class and power, material interests and ideologies are necessarily examined, through the prism of Mick Lynch and the RMT. I draw on insights from research in industrial relations, sociology and political science. My two primary aims are to explain how Lynch developed to the point where he became eligible to be a working-class hero and then the process by which he finally became one. Speaking chronologically, the first of these concerns Lynch's development up to the spring of 2022, and the second the period from the summer of 2022 onwards. To put it another way, the first is about what was necessary to become a working-class hero without being sufficient, and the second covers what was sufficient to become a working-class hero after securing what was necessary. 'Accidents of history' played a part in both. Lynch benefitted from a constellation of circumstances. However, this is only the first layer of the analytical framework I use to study him. Beneath it lie three components: power, material interests and ideology. In order to help anchor matters of industrial relations to these three components, I use a three-fold schema called the 'frames of references'. Under these components is another layer, termed the four 'P's: persona, politics, period and potential power. The final layer concerns the functions of leadership. This chapter then begins to operationalise these different layers of analytical framework by discussing the issue of 'power to' (disrupt) being turned into 'power over' (bargaining opponents).

Power, material interests and ideology

In his final speech in Parliament on 22 March 2001, long-standing left-wing Labour MP Tony Benn sought to ask five powerful, pointed questions: 'What power have you got? Where did you get it from? In whose interests do you exercise it? To whom are you accountable? And how can we get rid of you?' He continued: 'If you cannot get rid of the people who govern you, you do not live in a democratic system.'[1] Though good questions, they essentially only address half of the equation. They are questions for the powerful about their power, and not questions for the powerless about how they might create their own counter-power. Moreover, being able to 'get rid of people' speaks to a limited notion of democracy, for it indicates a particular form – an indirect, representative conception. Instead, radicals should be more concerned about creating direct forms of expanded democracy covering the economy, polity and society as an alternative to parliamentary liberal democracy. Here, the mass of 'ordinary' people would begin to exert increasing control over their lives in terms of market, state and society through both state and civil society organisations. Consequently, there is a need to recognise the different forms power takes. According to the sociologist Steven Lukes's radical conception, power comprises 'three faces': decision-making, non-decision-making and ideological. These can be understood as political power, legitimised agenda setting and limiting world views.[2] In the field of international relations, power can be thought of in other ways, as 'soft', 'hard', 'smart' or 'sharp'.[3] 'Soft power' concerns framing issues, 'hard power' coercion, 'smart power' the combination of 'soft' and 'hard', and 'sharp power' manipulation. However, both conceptualisations need to be expanded on for the study of unions and union leaders.

Writers such as Eric Batstone, Erik Olin Wright, Beverly Silver, Christian Lévesque and Gregor Murray, Stefan Schmalz and Jane Holgate have broadly identified the resources of power in terms of being associational, structural, institutional, coalitional and ideological or discursive.[4] Associational power concerns collective banding together, while structural power is about strategic positions in the economy and society. Institutional power relates to laws and regulation, while political power concerns instituting laws and regulations, and moral and discursive power is about the framing of issues. The first two involve the power to disrupt. For example, Wright and Silver have argued that structural power arises from labour's position in the economic system in terms of its ability to disrupt capital accumulation in the workplace or the labour market, while associational power results from collective actions of workers.[5] Batstone has classified the resources of power as disruptive capacity, scarcity of labour and political influence.[6] However, with a few partial and limited exceptions (for example Holgate), little attention has been paid to the important issues of how, where, when and why 'power to' can and does become 'power over'. Even though Lévesque and Murray have stressed the importance of both understanding the resources of union power and having the strategic capacity to advantageously apply them (based on strong internal solidarity and membership participation, a compelling narrative which frames issues accordingly and a capacity for organisational learning),[7] this still does not directly address the $64,000 question of turning the 'negative' of disruption into the 'positive' of outcome. Indeed, whether power is conceptualised as the ability, capacity or capability to effect a desired change in an opponent's behaviour, power is ultimately not made manifest until it leads to gaining one's bargaining objectives as a result of concession or compromise from the bargaining opponent. This study will illuminate this key point.

Material interests are the economic, financial and monetary interests which are found in owning the means of production, distribution and exchange (PDE). Ownership gives benefit, primarily through profits, as well as control. These means can take the forms of land, property like buildings (offices, shops, factories), plant and machinery, infrastructure (communications, transport) and shares and investments in all of these. To paraphrase Karl Marx, money is not a thing as such, but rather a relationship. It flows in vast quantities from owning the PDE, allowing its transformation into a usable mechanism with which to buy and sell. For those that own these means, they produce the resources to defend them as well to benefit from them, including the capture of the state.

An ideology is a world view about what form society should take and how it should run – considerations of politics and economics, morality and philosophy are mere subsets of this. Ideology is not only an after-the-fact validation and justification of the way existing society is organised, but also a positive, before-the-fact rationale of the purpose and nature of society. Consequently, ideology has an organising aspect, where it is the foundation stone of intentions, processes and outcomes. It is, then, not contentious to state that capitalist societies are class-based societies, organised and structured on the principle that the ownership of PDE by a minority of those in society, usually known as the ruling class or ruling elite, is argued to be right and proper by them and their acolytes. With that legitimacy comes authority, because coercion – through force of violence or threat of immiseration – is not enough to ensure control. Equally, it is not contentious to state that those who do not own the PDE are required to sell their labour to those that do. They then have different interests to those that do own the PDE. As a result, they lack their own power, are subject to the power of those that own the PDE, and suffer accordingly. But they can create a counter-power to pursue a counter-ideology to defend and advance their material interests, beginning with associational power and ideologies like social democracy and socialism. Social democracy is the use of the means of the state to intervene in the processes and outcomes of the market and neo-liberal capitalism, to ensure some rudimentary fairness and equality, without abolishing capitalism and its classes. By contrast, socialism sees the abolition of capitalism, so there will no longer be competing social classes.

These issues will be explored more fully in Chapter 8. However, it is necessary to stipulate here that the current ideology of the capitalists and ruling class is neo-liberalism. Neo-liberalism is more than just a reiteration of classical liberalism as per 'the market knows best'. It is about using the levers of the state to organise capital in a more productive way for the benefit of capitalists and capitalism overall. Consequently, it favours not so much no regulation but deregulation, so that regulation remains but it is less onerous for capital and is attuned to the needs of capital.

Another part of this neo-liberal state action is to open up areas of society and the economy to the market in ways that did not exist before. This, then, is more than just privatisation as per denationalisation. However, the one actor the neo-liberal state is keen to further regulate is the collective organisation of labour – primarily unions. So, while labour markets are deregulated and employment rights of workers weakened, there is more regulation, and more stringent regulation, of organised labour. One of the many effects of the ideology and practice of neo-liberalism has been to strengthen the psychological and physical power of capital to dominate and resist labour.

Frames of reference

In the field of industrial relations, there are commonly three 'frames of reference' used for studying the actors, their interests and intentions, and the processes and outcomes of exchanges between them. Following Alan Fox, these are 'unitarism', 'pluralism' and 'radicalism'.[8] Though best understood as ideal types, the three frames seek to articulate and apply external ideologies and world views within the arena of industrial relations. 'Unitarism' best describes employers as having – and believing in the right to have – the sole source of authority and power in organisations and enterprises where their unilateral actions are deemed legitimate. This situation is predicated on there being a symmetry of interests between capital and labour. By contrast, 'pluralism' recognises, if not quite celebrates, the manifest reality that the interests of capital and labour are not synonymous with each other, and that conflict between the two is legitimate and to be expected within certain bounds, where management's right to manage – the managerial prerogative – is not fundamentally undermined and eroded. In other words, there can be something of a negotiated peace between capital and labour. So, whereas unions would be resisted and regarded as illegitimate under 'unitarism', this is not the case with pluralism. Here, unions become part of the institutional architecture of industrial relations, so that 'responsible behaviour' is expected and encouraged. 'Radicalism' is based on the perspective that not only is there a high degree of incompatibility of interests between capital and labour, but capital seeks to exploit and oppress labour. Marxism is one variant of radicalism, suggesting there is a complete incompatibility of interests. But radicalism is not the sole property of Marxism, given that Marxism seeks the abolition of the capitalist employment relationship (as well as capitalism per se). Other radical positions of heavily curtailing the rights and power of capital exist, whereby deliberative state action is believed to be capable of creating an equilibrium of interests and power between capital and labour.

The four 'P's

The four-fold schema of persona, politics, period and potential power provides a perspective where Lynch's own persona and politics are examined in the setting of both the politics of the early 2020s and the potential power of rail workers.

The persona – the outward public face – that Lynch presents is one of being self-assured and authentic in a quiet and calm manner, so that he comes across as eminently reasonable and reasoned. He communicates using plain language that is easily understandable to many. He is also a fairly private person so that his personal life has not become a distraction when prosecuting the office of RMT general secretary. Further contrasts with his predecessors, Bob Crow and Mick Cash, enable the traits of his persona to be drawn out. Indeed, if Cash had been leading the RMT during the strikes, his humdrum, somewhat ineloquent manner would have become obvious and would not have made the RMT's case so persuasive and powerful. In sum, Lynch has been able to use what is called 'framing' to do this, indicating that he understands the discursive power of narratives. But equally important is the content of this framing, which is derived from his political world view.

Lynch's politics are oppositional and progressive; he is best characterised as a left-wing social democrat of the Corbyn mould, thus supporting 'tax and spend' legislation as a means of wealth redistribution, rather than being characterised as a 'communist' or 'Marxist'. Overall, Lynch's politics therefore provide him with more than just a gut or moral sense of what is right and wrong. Consequently, he has the intellectual tools to critique the conditions of workers in order to make an attribution of who and what is wrong as well as give a sense of what is needed to right these wrongs.

The period in which Lynch led the RMT is critical to understanding how and why his persona and politics have come together in a fulsome and forceful way. Put starkly, if Lynch had not had the 2022–23 rail strikes on which to pronounce, he would be much less of a national figure, if one at all. As General Secretary, the summary sacking of 800 P&O workers in March 2022 did not allow him to emerge in the way he subsequently did – highlighting the fact that defeat is not a fertile ground on which to operate. But there are other factors also at play. Along with rising anger against the Tories for their 'inept' economic management while also becoming more reactionary, with plans to even further restrict the right to strike, the rail workers' battle is more generalisable than most. It concerns the railways, which are a key part of the national infrastructure and constitute a situation where the Train Operating Companies (TOCs) are neither fully private nor fully public companies because of public subsidy and government control. The other side to this is that Labour under Keir Starmer has not filled the vacuum that Lynch has for many. There are also no other significant figures from the left in Labour, with Jeremy Corbyn and John McDonnell no longer front-line politicians.

Finally, in contrast to RMT cleaning and catering members, RMT rail workers (especially those on Network Rail) have the resources of associational and structural power to supplement their institutional power, as well as the political, moral and discursive powers of their national union, exemplified by and through Lynch. Consequently, their action is effective in closing down rail services. Save for other transport workers and refuse collectors, this degree of immediate and massive disruptive effect from strikes is not true for most other workers, so care must be taken with platitudes of 'If the rail workers can do it, so can we!' This contextualisation also highlights the fallacy of any 'great man' version of history. However, the limits of this power are also evident. The 'power to' disrupt is not necessarily synonymous with the generation of 'power over' one's bargaining opponent. This could highlight, among other things, a mismatch between the strike strategy and the union's bargaining demands; a situation where the battle cannot be fully won within the confines of the rail sector when the government is the ultimate employer, so that coordinated, generalised strike action by other similarly aggrieved unions has potential purchase; and a state of affairs where extra-parliamentary political action is required to supplement industrial action.

Functions of leadership

There are six essential functions of leadership relevant to unions, and especially applicable to the position of a general secretary, as the organisation's most senior employed officer. These are i) agenda setting and framing of arguments; ii) public speaking and communicating; iii) negotiating; iv) strategising and strategic planning; v) caucusing and alliance building; and vi) managing people and organisational resources. Any union leader needs to perform well in all these areas, not least because they are all interrelated. For example, agenda setting and framing of arguments requires communication, strategising and caucusing. Implementing agendas requires communicating, negotiating, alliance building, and managing people and resources, among others. Underpinning all these functions must be a *modus operandi* of listening so as to gather the necessary information, which is the quintessential foundation on which to be able to then act, having collated and assessed the information. The listening is to members, comrades, colleagues and the like. It is a responsibility of leadership to then know what to do with the information and how it informs the way the six functions are carried out. However, none of these leadership functions are performed in a vacuum, so the forms and processes of union democracy and any associated factions are critical components in accounting for how effective the leadership of a general secretary is.

Ramifications of rail workers' potential power

To deepen the discussion about power and the distinction between 'power to' and 'power over', it is worth noting that – with the exception of the Associated Society of Locomotive

Engineers and Firemen's (ASLEF) train driver members, the British Airline Pilots Association's (BALPA) airline pilot members or Unite's fuel tanker driver members – RMT rail workers have more potential disruptive power than most other workers. This results from having the associational power to utilise their structural or strategic power. But there is no fast or straight line between creating disruption and winning bargaining demands, for 'power to' is necessary but not sufficient to deliver 'power over'. This is because much depends on the strategy and tactics deployed to generate the required leverage. Much also depends on the wider political situation, because rail strikes are more political strikes than they are economic strikes (see pp. 22–27).

But before delving more deeply into those issues, understanding the foundations of associational power is pertinent. Associational power is built on, in the first instance, high or near total levels of union membership (called union density). Then, with this union membership comes the expectation that when a mandate is gained for striking and is implemented, all union members will heed the call to strike. Any strike breakers will not, then, be union members. On top of this, substitute sources of staff like managers or agency workers should not be able to substitute for striking staff. Not all RMT members yet have this potential power. Indeed, the course of a number of strikes over driver-only operated (DOO) trains amongst TOCs in the 2000s and 2010s suggests that not all guards and conductors were RMT members or abided by the strike call, because the number of services still running on strike days was sizeable (see pp. 24–26). This led to a situation of long-drawn-out strikes that were far from victorious.

Turning to the issue of structural strategic power, rail strikes have strategic leverage because they have an immediate impact on large numbers of citizens by stopping the operation of a service, in a situation where few alternative means are readily available and the journeys they wish to make are of a perishable nature (where more often than not they must be made on that day and around that time). Added to this is the fact that public transport remains a public good despite privatisation and because of the continuing public subsidy given to it. Consequently, deliberate disruption to public transport can be thought of as capable of generating political leverage on both employers and the government. It is not merely that public transport is used by millions of citizens, but that it is also central to the operation of a capitalist economy and governments are still, in large measure, held responsible for it. So when a national public transport strike happens, it affects not only the employer but also the public and the economy.

Even if other RMT members like seafarers, or catering or cleaning staff on overground and underground rail services, have potential associational power, they may still not have the strategic power which other rail workers might have. P&O's summary sacking of 800 seafarers in March 2022 indicated this. Once the seafarers had been forced off the ships and put to shore, they had no strategic bargaining leverage,[9] and en masse reluctantly accepted their enhanced redundancy terms.[10] RMT signalling staff members working for Network Rail do have this strategic power if they choose to exercise it. Very few services can be run without their labour. Like signallers, conductors and guards also have a critical safety role which can provide them with strategic leverage as a result of railway regulations, but it has proven to be less effective.

Next, we must consider how the combination of associational and strategic power is deployed. This is especially important because even strikes involving signalling staff are not necessarily won quickly or easily.[11] The 1989 rail strike over collective bargaining machinery and pay, by the RMT's predecessor union, the National Union of Railwaymen (NUR), involved six one-day strikes by all these British Rail members. These were held almost weekly between late June and late July (with ASLEF train driver members striking on one of the same days in their only strike action in the dispute).[12] In the circumstances of a tightening labour market, it is interesting to note that the strikes, according to the officially commissioned RMT history, 'did not achieve all the union's aims'.[13] This puts a rather different slant on the recollection that: 'The 1989 NUR strike won [on pay] in *just* six days because the government were already a bit on the run from other pay strikes and wanted to try put a cap on the action.'[14] Then in 1994, after privatisation, RMT signalling members undertook sixteen strikes amounting to nineteen days of action over three months from mid-June to late September. Again, what they gained was not all they wanted. Labour was unsupportive, not all signal workers were RMT members, RMT signalling supervisor members voted against striking and loss of wages was steep, with relatively more trains running each strike day as the dispute wore on.[15] As I have noted elsewhere, at a time of a weakening Major-led Tory government, even for such a strategically placed group of workers, the strikes were not especially effective.[16] Moreover, Railtrack, the newly established organisation in control of the rail infrastructure, was a private company and could be expected to experience a dent in its profits.

Both the 1989 and 1994 strikes indicated that even though the strikes were effective in creating widespread disruption, nonetheless on their own they did not generate sufficient leverage to gain the union's bargaining demands. In both cases, Tory governments stood steadfast in not succumbing despite the disruption. They prized not being beaten more than any other outcome. This suggests that one-day and two-day strikes are insufficient to quickly and decisively win disputes when the employers and government are resolute in resisting. The same is true for ASLEF, whose members arguably have more strategic or structural 'power to' as a result of the critical role its members undertake and an extremely high level of union density of over 90 per cent over the last few decades, providing associational power. In 1955, ASLEF members struck against British Railways for seventeen days in a pay dispute.[17] Then, on 4 July 1982, ASLEF drivers began an all-out strike which lasted until 18 July 1982 (preceded by a series of one-day strikes, totalling seventeen days, in January and February) over pay and flexible rostering, but which ended in defeat.[18] Without any strike pay, the loss of income in both strikes was considerable. In the 2022–23 industrial dispute, ASLEF members had taken fourteen one-day strikes and six single weeks of overtime ban by early October 2023, with the same type of pay offer made to them by the Rail Delivery Group (RDG) as for the RMT, namely a 4 per cent pay rise for 2022 and another 4 per cent for 2023 in return for a diminution of terms and conditions.

Economic strikes, political strikes and hybrid strikes

Strikes are conventionally thought of as being economic in nature: the intention is to hurt the employer in the pocket by disrupting their operations to such an extent that the process of capital accumulation – that is, making profits – is dented or stopped. Where the employer is not a capitalist profit-seeker – often called a private employer or private sector employer – the intention is still to create disruption but the arena in which the disruption takes place is primarily the polity and society and not the economy. Here, the intention amongst those on strike in public sector and third sector organisations (like housing associations and charities) is to create embarrassment and discomfort because services and operations are not available to users as they would normally be, thus undermining the *raison d'etre* of those organisations, and hence their legitimacy too. Of course, this includes government at local, regional and national levels. In this, public support for the strikers is more critical than in the private sector, for in these non-profit sectors one of the main ways in which embarrassment and discomfort are created is through the public showing support by recognising and then questioning the inability of the employers concerned to provide their services and operations to users. However, matters are far less straightforward and simple when the private and public sectors merge, as they increasingly have, due to contracting out, marketisation and privatisation. In these cases, private sector companies provide public services. They do so for profit-making purposes, although public authorities are still ultimately responsible for the provision of those services as the contract awarder. In this sense, strikes in these cases can be both economic and political, hence they are then called hybrid strikes.

But the railways in Britain provide a particularly peculiar example of the foundation for hybrid strikes. Since 2002, the network's infrastructure (stations, tracks, signalling) has been publicly owned through Network Rail, while TOCs provide the passenger services after winning franchises, mainly from the Westminster government (via the Department for Transport). Though TOCs pay to gain the franchises, they are subsidised by the government with public money. According to the annual UK rail industry financial information reports of the Office for Rail and Road, this subsidy amounted to £2.4bn in 2015–16, £2.5bn in 2016–17, £2.5bn in 2017–18, £3.3bn in 2018–19, £2.3bn in 2019–20, £10.2bn in 2020–21 and £10.9bn in 2021–22. In only the first three of these years did TOCs pay more to the government than they received back in subsidies (to the tune of £0.6bn per annum on average). The franchise contracts also indemnify TOCs against losses (ticket sales) during strikes. The RMT has suggested this indemnity has run into tens of millions, if not hundreds of millions, of pounds during the 2016–19 strikes[19] and £318m in the 2022–23 strikes as of early January 2023.[20] By July 2023, the RMT estimated this was approaching £1bn.[21] In terms of profitability, RMT analysis in January 2023 indicated that TOCs made £310m profit between March 2020 and September 2022,[22] with this predicted to rise to £412m by September 2023.[23]

The level of public subsidy, ensuring high levels of profitability, and the strike indemnity especially, mean that, contrary to the expectations of many observers,[24] RMT rail members actually have less power than they are often assumed to have, with the consequence that RMT strikes by conductors, guards and signallers are far less effective than is commonly believed to be the case. More recently, and under Bob Crow's leadership, there were some long-drawn-out battles where RMT members lost considerable amounts of pay through striking, and the RMT was shown not always to have the potency to its power that was found elsewhere.[25] These included, for example, taking fourteen one-day strikes at Virgin CrossCountry in 2006. Then, between 2016 and 2019, the RMT engaged in multiple long-running disputes involving mostly one-day strikes over working hours and DOO.[26] The TOCs affected included Southern, South Western, CrossCountry, Greater Anglia, Merseyrail, Scotrail, Arriva Trains Northern, West Midlands Trains and Great Western. For example, CrossCountry and Greater Anglia were affected by eight days of strikes, Scotrail by twelve and Merseyrail by fifteen. Meantime, the South Western dispute lasted four years with seventy-four days of strikes, the Arriva Trains Northern dispute lasted three years with forty-seven days of strikes, and the Southern dispute lasted three years with forty-eight days of strikes. Only in the cases of Greater Anglia, Scotrail, West Midland Trains and Merseyrail were bargaining objectives clearly gained. As the transport scholar Tom Haines-Doran noted of the Southern railway dispute, 'the weakness of the guards' position led them to signing contracts to become "on-board supervisors", effectively ending the strike'.[27] Haines-Doran believes that strikes across eight different franchises amounted to 153 days of strikes, though the aforementioned figures for seven franchises indicate that the number of days of strikes was just over 200.

These strikes took place while Lynch was Assistant General Secretary without specific responsibility for any of the TOCs, but he took the position in a joint meeting with sister union ASLEF (which was also in dispute with the company) of saying: 'Guards, conductors, on-board supervisors – I don't fucking care what they are called, I just want to save their jobs.' Prioritising 'jobs first' was a theme that would recur later on, as was the phenomenon of long-drawn-out industrial disputes, which continued under and during Lynch's leadership as Senior Assistant General Secretary, Acting General Secretary and as General Secretary. RMT figures supplied in its annual return to the

Certification Officer show, for example, that in 2021 there were 112 ballots for industrial action (strikes and industrial action short of striking (IASOS)). Of these, eighteen did not pass the 50 per cent majority turnout threshold for a lawful mandate (under the Trade Union Act 2016), with five others not passing the additional threshold of those voting for action equating to 40 per cent of all those entitled to vote.[28] Of the eighty-five lawful mandates, twenty-three were implemented, leading to strikes and IASOS. There were fifteen disputes with strikes. Of these, five disputes saw ten or more days of strike action taken (10, 19, 21, 26 and 34) and these were overwhelmingly one-day actions. Hull Trains, East Midlands Trains, Scotrail and Caledonian Sleeper were among the TOCs affected. There were also eight instances of IASOS, with five of these seeing action like overtime bans and work-to-rules taken for over thirty days (32, 78, 98, 107, 137).

One assessment of these extended actions would extol RMT members for their fortitude, resilience and determination. Here, the act of resistance was to be commended and celebrated. Another assessment would question whether, on a cost–benefit analysis, what was eventually gained in terms of a negotiated settlement – assuming there was one – outweighed the sacrifice of lost wages. Most obviously, this analysis could be carried out on a monetary basis, even though that is not the only possible criterion (with other outcomes being the effects on membership levels, participation levels, membership morale, employer perceptions of union bargaining power, etc.). A further assessment would suggest that the RMT, as a national union with a limited hardship fund, could only help financially sustain a small number of such industrial actions, simultaneously or sequentially, where relatively small numbers of members were involved.[29] Notwithstanding the absence of the use of (prior) strategic planning to generate significant funds to facilitate national industrial disputes (see pp. 160, 205–13, 257), the implication of this is that a larger number of concurrent long-running disputes with greater numbers of members involved would not be so easy to sustain financially (as was the case in the two national disputes of 2022–23, where nearly 50 per cent of RMT members engaged in prolonged strike action). But behind all this, and in contrast to RMT signalling staff, one of the key issues that emerges is to ask whether the RMT had the membership density (associational power) amongst guards and conductors, and whether they had a sufficiently strategic role (structural power), to stop services running. Although managers and strike-breakers played a role, the evidence suggests that they did not have this power (or certainly not in sufficient quantity).

Conclusion

Both the intellectual approach and analytical framework used to study Lynch draw on the same radical perspective previously used to study Bob Crow.[30] This is a broadly Marxist perspective where power, material interests and ideology under capitalism are held to be the most important components for analysing capital's drive to accumulate – making profits through labour exploitation – and the consequent struggle between the contending competitive and conflicting social classes. Using the same perspective to study both Crow and Lynch helps facilitate comparative analysis. However, in this study the analytical framework has been further developed compared to that used to study Crow. For example, the persona, politics and potential power troika has become a quartet, and has been added to with further layers so that the different dimensions of a union's potential power and the role of leaders and followers can be more fully assessed. The next chapter examines what is meant by a 'working-class hero'.

2

What is a working-class hero?

This chapter establishes the providence and the provenance of the appellation of working-class hero given to Mick Lynch. This entails examining how Lynch was perceived by various parties and people. It then lays out a definition of a working-class hero and considers some of the complexities and contradictions involved.

Media motifs and popular perceptions

There are two sources that provide the evidence that Lynch became a working-class hero. The first is the mainstream or traditional media, which is the preserve of professional journalists. The second is social and alternative media, where so-called 'ordinary' people and political activists are able to give their opinions on matters.

Looking mainly at the mainstream media, in the two months from 24 June to 26 August 2022, the *Mirror*, the *i*, the *Evening Standard*, *TaketoNews*, the *New Statesman*, the *National* and *Nevermind Media* all published articles where they called Lynch a working-class hero, as did the far away New Zealand *Standard*.[1] The *Independent* went one further, calling him a 'working-class superhero'.[2] Of course, there were detractors too. For example, the *Daily Express* stated Lynch was 'no "working-class hero"'. It was joined by the *Daily Mail* and *Daily Telegraph* in defiantly rejecting Lynch's working-class hero status.[3]

Turning to social media, Twitter and Facebook were quickly awash with references to Lynch being a working-class hero. LauraLeastLikelyTo was one example of many on Twitter.[4] Within weeks of his first media appearances, the FanGrrrl website was offering 'Mick Lynch "working-class hero"' mugs and tote bags as well as 'Mick Lynch: "You're a working-class hero"' greetings cards, while the Etsytees website had produced 'Mick Lynch you're a working-class hero' t-shirts.[5] This was all taken to be evidence of what 'male-focused publisher' *Joe.co.uk* called 'Mick Mania', because, as one of its interviewees put it, Lynch spoke not just for RMT members 'but also for the entire working-class of Britain'.[6]

For some, many of these characterisations could be dismissed as nothing more than the musings of a distant, middle-class commentariat and not the close-up perceptions of the working-class proletariat.[7] But this is to heap scorn on what is an identifiable and manifest social phenomenon when taken alongside evidence from other commentators, journalists and writers, as well as how Lynch was greeted by other union members and activists and those on the political left (see below).

Then there are other appellations associated with heroism of a radical sort which were given to Lynch. The paper *par excellence* of the captains of capitalism in Britain, the *Financial Times*, called Lynch 'A new folk hero for Britain's working-class' and 'a left-wing hero'.[8] *The Times* chimed in with Lynch being regarded as 'a folk hero – a Robin Hood for the social media age'.[9] In Ireland, Lynch was called a 'new folk hero' in the *Sunday Independent*, while in Scotland, the *National* declared him a 'folk hero', as did the *Christian Science Monitor*.[10] Earlier, *The Times* called Lynch 'a hero of our times', while *Dazed* declared 'Mick Lynch is the hero we need right now' and the *Scotsman* and *Herald* opined that Lynch was 'a new hero for our times' and 'a folk hero for our times' respectively.[11] The *New York Times* dubbed him 'an unlikely national hero'.[12] Others simply called him a 'hero'.[13] The letters pages of different newspapers saw Lynch characterised as a 'hero'.[14]

The appellation of 'working-class hero' contrasts with that of 'folk hero'. A folk hero is a hero of the people, which is a non-class categorisation. Those people could be of any and all social classes and the hero does not have to be of or from the working class. However, there can be ambiguity if the term 'the people' is taken to mean, as it sometimes is, workers in general and the *hoi polloi*. Nonetheless, it is important that Lynch has been primarily labelled a working-class hero because of its clearer meaning and overtones with workers and their class position. By contrast, the connection between the appellation of simply 'hero' and the working class is ambiguous, even if it remains clear that the description is due to being anti-Tory and anti-establishment. Lynch was also frequently labelled a 'legend' in different media, with his media performances being 'the stuff of legend'.[15] The same points pertain to this appellation: namely, not clearly being associated with the working class but not necessarily entirely unconnected to it either.

Alongside the manufacture of 'working-class hero' mugs and the like, 'man of the people' t-shirts, hoodies and mugs were also produced. At the annual fixtures in the union calendar such as the Durham Miners' Gala, Tolpuddle and

Burston rallies, and Trades Union Congress (TUC) and Labour conferences in 2022, Lynch was greeted as a conquering hero, unable to move about freely for the demand for handshakes and selfies from admiring socialists and trade unionists. The same was true when Lynch visited other unions' picket lines and spoke at rallies and marches in the 2022–23 'Winter of Discontent'. By this point, his nomenclature as a working-class hero was still in evidence in the mainstream media. For example, the *Herald* declared he was 'a hero defending the interests not just of his members but of the working-class', while the *Mirror* called him a 'working-class hero' again.[16] Into January 2023, a TikTok vlogger called thereluctantaccountant posted a video called 'Mick Lynch is the working-class hero we needed!'[17] It was viewed 65,000 times within five days of being posted.[18] Meantime, David Lumley, a former classmate of Lynch, contacted LBC (London Broadcasting Company) to say: 'Could you please tell him how proud I am of the stand he's making for working people [and to] keep up the fight?'[19] while *Socialism Today* recognised Lynch's 'hero status'[20] and a YouTube video called 'Working-Class Hero Mick Lynch At His Really EPIC Brilliant Best?' was watched 21,000 times within a day of being uploaded in April 2023.

Even where the 'working-class hero' label was not specifically used, associations with leading the working class were evident. For example, *Joe.co.uk* asserted that 'People have called Lynch a hero, a real representative of the working class and the first person to feel on "their side" in a long time', while *Jacobin* wrote of Lynch being the 'figurehead ... voicing the revival of class consciousness' with his 'no-nonsense, straight-talking articulation of class politics' so that 'the impulse of class consciousness Lynch has captured across the country eclipses any individual dispute'.[21] Earlier, family doctors urged their fellow BMA (British Medical Association) union members to 'channel our inner Mick Lynch' in preparation for balloting for industrial action[22] and the *Big Issue North* called Lynch a 'trade unionist for our times'.[23] At the end of the year, *Tortoise Media* called him 'A union leader for our times'.[24] Into 2023, BBC radio *Hardtalk* called him a 'working-class warrior',[25] and even though very few RMT members were to strike on the day of coordinated action on 1 February 2023 (see p. 98), the *Metro* previewed the day on its front page with the headline 'FEB 1 STRIKE HELL: IT'S ONE OUT, ALL OUT' and a photograph of Lynch.[26] This was 'illustrative of the totemic position Lynch, and the RMT, have come to occupy in the strike wave'.[27] And the *Mail on Sunday* opined in May 2023 that: 'To his followers, he is a hero. To his opponents, he is a troublemaker'.[28] In addition to the continual accusations of being a 'fat cat' union baron intent on bringing down a democratically elected government, the brickbats were also still being thrown by the *Sun* and Tories at the end of 2022 – Lynch was the 'Grinch that stole Christmas' and a Tory poster attacked Lynch as Labour's 'nightmare before Christmas'.

Away from newspaper headlines, it was amongst a certain constituency that Lynch was likely to be found a working-class hero. For example, Google searches for 'Mick Lynch' rose by 1,400 per cent in late June 2022,[29] and three instances of polling by YouGov and Savanta in December 2022 on 'Do you have a favourable or unfavourable opinion of Mick Lynch?' showed 22–29 per cent had a 'very favourable' or 'somewhat favourable' opinion while 28–31 per cent had a 'somewhat unfavourable' or 'very unfavourable' opinion (with the remainder expressing no opinion). Within the former milieux were likely to be those union members that were most active and ideologically committed to a radical world view, and who would likely see Lynch as a working-class hero.

This collation indicates that there is a substantial body of evidence to suggest that Lynch was quite widely seen as a working-class hero in the summer of 2022. It also indicates that though the dynamics and rhythm of the national rail disputes changed thereafter, there was still significant evidence that Lynch was regarded in this way many months later. So, in the minds of many, Lynch has been able to transcend the intra-class segmentations of the working class such as trade, occupation and industry to become a class-wide working-class hero. And, while recognised as the General Secretary-cum-leader of the RMT union for rail workers, Lynch was also recognised as a leader for the working class as a whole, thereby transcending sectionalist mentalities. As now to be discussed, he was assisted in this by the leaders of other unions not being constituted as rivals to his 'crown' due to the configuration of certain components in his case and theirs.

Why Lynch and not others?

Dave Ward of the Communication Workers Union (CWU) is also a straight, white, bald male of a similar age, 63, from London. As General Secretary of the CWU, he led his members in the Post Office, Royal Mail and British Telecom in taking extensive strike action over pay and job security in 2022. Indeed, in Royal Mail, though the strikes began later in the summer of 2022, the number of strikers was nearly three times the number of RMT strikers in Network Rail and the TOCs, and by the end of 2022 the number of days of strikes taken was higher than those taken by these RMT members.[30] And yet Ward was never called a working-class hero.

Why was this? One reason was that Royal Mail was no longer as central to society and the economy as it once was when it had a virtual monopoly on delivering letters and parcels, before privatisation and the rise of electronic communications (such as email).[31] Compared to the railways, this meant Ward was not afforded the airtime and column inches Lynch was, because the CWU strikes were not so disruptive and high-profile as those by RMT members. Another reason was that when Ward was given airtime, he did not generalise politically in the way Lynch did about the then current Conservative government, Labour Party, media, employers and capitalist society.[32] In turn, this meant Lynch was in much greater demand for interviews with social and non-mainstream media outlets than Ward was. Consequently, Ward did not speak to a much wider constituency than his own members, as Lynch did. Part of this was because Royal Mail was owned by private shareholders and not the government. Moreover, it was not subsidised by the government either, as TOCs were. Therefore, there was less of a solid political basis to generalise from.[33] In addition to this, Ward was more of a stereotypical leader with a belligerent style (like Bob Crow) whereas Lynch was calmer and more collected, so that he came across as more reasoned and reasonable. Both were born working-class Londoners – Ward in South London and Lynch in West London – so it was not a matter of accents. There were also several other factors at play. One was that the RMT, with Lynch at its head, was by far and away the first union into battle with national strike action against the cost-of-living crisis. By contrast, the CWU's first strike at BT since 1987 did not take place until 29 July 2022 and at Royal Mail until 26 August 2022. Therefore, Lynch was able to fill the void before anyone else had the chance, even though there were no other credible candidates to do so.

But it was not just Dave Ward who was not called a working-class hero in 2022. The general secretaries of the three biggest unions – Sharon Graham (Unite), Gary Smith (GMB) and Christina McAnea (Unison) – were not called heroes of any sort, working-class or otherwise, and certainly not in the mainstream media. Though representing much smaller, and often more specialist, memberships, the leaders of others unions like Jo Grady (University and College Union (UCU)), Mick Whelan (ASLEF), Mark Serwotka (Public and Commercial Services Union (PCS)) and Matt Wrack (Fire Brigades Union (FBU)) were not accorded this accolade in 2022 either.

The discussion of Dave Ward helps highlight some of the complexity involved in understanding these whys and wherefores. In the most obvious cases of Wrack and Serwotka, the explanation cannot be because they were not well-known radical, left-wing figures, and cannot be because they had not led previous national strikes. It is likely to be more concerned with an issue of timing in 2022, with PCS members not striking until December 2022, and only doing so selectively, and then in greater numbers in early 2023. FBU members did not conclude their industrial action ballot until the end of January 2023 and then were able to obtain, with the threat of industrial action, an improved but still less than the rate of inflation pay offer, which was then accepted in a membership ballot in early March 2023. There may also be the issue that both Wrack and Serwotka represent particular groups of workers, firefighters and civil servants, so that being seen as representatives of workers more widely might be difficult. Even though firefighters are sometimes seen as working-class heroes, they are a small and specialist group of workers providing an emergency service, while civil and public servants are not held in the same regard as nurses because of the work they do. This kind of point is pertinent for Whelan. As the general secretary of a union covering a small number of relatively well-paid and highly skilled workers, the leader of a specialist occupational union was not in a position to exert such a claim on this basis, should he wish, to be a working-class hero. Though Grady represented over five times the number of members Whelan does, the same point was again salient.

Yet this is not true of Graham, Smith or McAnea. In the case of Graham, since being elected in August 2021 as General Secretary, she has led 900 disputes involving 200,000 members and of which 80 per cent were won, putting £400m more into members' wage packets at the cost of £32m in strike pay.[34] Under her leadership, Unite has almost been alone in winning double-digit pay rises for some of its members in the likes of air and road transport and refuse collection.[35] However, despite often being in the strategically important sector of transport (airports, buses, road haulage, ports), few of these disputes received any extensive media coverage. This was not just because other strikes occurred at the same time but because only a tiny number of these strikes – like at Felixstowe port – had the potential economic and societal impact on a national scale that the rail strikes had. Part and parcel of this was that Unite had thousands of different bargaining groups with separate sets of collective bargaining negotiations, compared to the two in Network Rail and RDG (representing TOCs). This fragmentation meant any Unite leader would have needed to coordinate their disputes together to make an overall sizeable impact on the economy and society. So there was less demand for Graham to be interviewed on national media and she also seemed less willing to be interviewed.[36] In the case of the leader of the GMB some of the same issues are involved, but with Unison the lower level of strike propensity of many of the biggest blocks of its members (such as local government in England) was more of a factor, as was the fact that in other areas Unison was not the lead union by dint of membership numbers (as in the education and health sectors).

Star of social media

Lynch's predecessor but one, Bob Crow, was a working-class hero in another age. It was one where television, newspapers and radio as well as mass meetings and rallies had different connotations. Two decades on from when Crow was elected General Secretary, YouTube, TikTok, Twitter, Instagram and Facebook are firm fixtures in the architecture of popular, mass communication. Though Facebook was launched in 2004, YouTube in 2005, Twitter in 2006 and Instagram in 2010, they did not come to be widely used until the 2010s. The RMT did not have a Twitter account until 2009 (Crow died in early 2014). In 2016, TikTok was added to their number. Behind them lies a technology that allows people not just to make public pronouncements to friends and followers, but also make and share videos. No longer are people reliant on hearing or watching an interview at the time it was originally broadcast, and they can upload their own excerpts to these platforms or share those uploaded by others. No longer do people have to attend a rally or public meeting in person to hear the speeches, because these can be livestreamed or recorded for subsequent distribution on social media. The interactive nature of these mediums allow users to legitimise and agree with comments and postings by liking them as well as conversing with others. The mobile phone, laptop and tablet are the accessible, easy-to-use and widely owned tools here.

This technology and these platforms help to explain the extraordinarily rapid rise of Lynch to become a working-class hero. Although entirely self-selected[37] and not constituting a representative measure, for example 46m views were made of the ten short clips of Lynch on TikTok by early February 2023, with 409,000 accompanying 'likes'. By the same time, ninety short clips of Ward had been watched only 1.4m times, while seventeen short clips of Graham had only been watched 114,000 times. Meanwhile, individual podcast interviews were watched and listened to by hundreds of thousands each on YouTube within a few weeks of being posted. Here, the first fifteen displayed videos on YouTube of Lynch being interviewed were watched well over 4m times by late September 2022. By late July 2023, the fifteen most watched videos of Lynch on YouTube had been watched over 10m times. There were many other hundreds of thousands of views, collectively running into many millions, of the same and other videos of Lynch on other platforms, including those of the original broadcasters. These viewing figures were no doubt facilitated by the RMT's social media reach, with the *Guardian* reporting early on that Lynch 'has garnered a cult following online'.[38] Other than the FBU and ASLEF, with half and a quarter of the number of members the RMT has respectively, the RMT (albeit by a far greater ratio of 2:1) was the only major union that had – as of late 2022 – more Twitter followers than members when compared to the Unite, GMB, CWU, Unison, NEU (National Education Union), NASUWT, Educational Institute of Scotland, PCS, USDAW (Union of Shop, Distributive and Allied Workers), Prospect and UCU unions.[39]

Of course, the content and context of the communications are just as critical as the technological capabilities. And we do not know what all the viewers/listeners thought or what they then did differently having watched and listened. We can, however, reasonably assume that most were favourable to what Lynch argued given the extensive sets of comments on social media about the clips or those left underneath those clips on the likes of YouTube.

Heroes

There is no formal or recognised process by which to judge whether a person can become a working-class hero – no application process, no adjudication committee, and no use of referees or references. However, a set of criteria can be established for making a judgement, based on recognising the social construction of the phenomenon and then examining its key aspects.

Starting with a hero, this is a person who is widely and publicly admired and lauded for their courage, achievements and attributes. Above all else, heroes are those that are seen to be able to do things that most others cannot or will not do or say for themselves or others. They are seen to be leaders of sorts. Those things that are done and said are highly valued in different ways and for different reasons, meaning that not all heroes are heroes for the same reasons to the same people. That people, as individuals and even en masse, look to particular individuals as heroes testifies to a friction between individual and collective agencies and identities. Heroes and heroines are those there is a desire, implicitly or explicitly, to emulate, even if this is ultimately believed to be unattainable. As such, this represents an unfulfilled wish. But if those wishes were to be fulfilled, particularly en masse, the status and speciality of heroes and heroines would be diminished, if not destroyed, for it is their peculiarity as having traits and skills that others do not have which makes them stand out and wish to be emulated. The notion that 'We can [all] be heroes', as David Bowie sang on his 1977 song 'Heroes', would undermine the very basis of heroism, even if that was 'just for one day'.

Charisma is a useful though not an essential component for individuals to become heroes and heroines, even in the present media-driven age of widespread use of video recording and sharing. Charisma implies that the candidate concerned will carry a greater connection than the individual without charisma. This is because herodom is about what is done and said, and critically how this is held by the receiver/perceiver. The medium by which the information is derived, and from which a judgement is made, may be indirect and second-hand – as in the written word of the candidate for herodom or a piece of text written by a third party about the candidate. Through such mediums, charisma would not necessarily be obvious. Indeed, it may not be obvious at all given that where charisma does exist, it is not conveyed well through such mediums. That said, with the now widespread usage of video recording and sharing, it is much easier for charisma to be conveyed – or certainly detected by the receiver/perceiver.

But applying this rudimentary understanding to the working-class hero means something quite specific. John Lennon, in his 1970 song 'A Working-Class Hero', sang: 'A working-class hero is something to be ... If you want to be a hero, well, just follow me'.[40] Lennon popularised the appellation more than any other figure, and did so at a time when he himself was becoming radicalised with left-wing politics, when the working class in Britain was at its strongest, especially in the form of mass membership of unions and worker militancy. The working-class hero Lennon sang of was a person who stood up and fought not only for his or her fellow workers but also did so en masse and as part of a class – defending and advancing their economic and political interests. Then communist, Jimmy Reid, primary leader of the 1971–72 Upper Clyde Shipbuilders (UCS) work-in that humbled the Edward Heath-led Tory government in a fight over jobs,[41] was such an example from Lennon's time.[42] Indeed, Lennon sent the work-in a sizeable financial donation. Others from this time would be Vic Turner, one of the five jailed Pentonville dockers, Dessie Warren and Ricky Tomlinson[43] of the jailed 'Shrewsbury Two' flying pickets of 1972, Arthur Scargill during the 1972 and 1974 miners' strikes (and before being elected President of the National Union of Mineworkers (NUM) in 1982), Jayaben Desai, leader of the Grunwick strike of 1976–78, and Derek 'Red Robbo' Robinson, union convenor of British Leyland Longbridge in the late 1970s. All these examples highlight that one of the few general secretaries of the time to be called a working-class hero then (or even subsequently) was Transport and General Workers' Union (TGWU) leader, Jack Jones, who previously fought in the Spanish Civil War on the republican side with the International Brigades, and latterly campaigned in retirement for pensioners' rights.[44] The other was Scargill during and after leading the NUM through the year-long miners' strike of 1984–85.[45]

Other working-class heroes were those proud to be working class and to represent their class in more cultural rather than political terms. Examples of the time include footballer George Best and football managers Bill Shankly, Brian Clough and Jock Stein, as well as comedian Billy Connolly. They were seen by many as working-class heroes. Others included sportsmen such as boxers as well as some actors. Yet these heroes were working-class individuals who rose out of their class to become wealthy celebrities in another class, something that many working-class people might admire or be envious of but could never hope to emulate. This aspect sets them apart from those given the appellation of heroes and heroines of the working class who were leaders in unions, and who often rose with their class as that class engaged in significant class struggles.

If we move away from the period of the 1970s in Britain, the appellation working-class hero is commonly given to individuals within particular occupational groups such as firefighters,[46] as well as to socialists such as James Connolly of the Easter Uprising in Ireland,[47] and the likes of radical folk singers such as Woody Guthrie in the United States in the 1930s, 1940s and 1950s.[48] In Poland in the 1980s, union leader and anti-Stalinist Lech Wałęsa was designated a working-class hero. Bob Crow was also seen as a working-class hero, as was Tommy Sheridan for a decade and more after the anti-poll tax revolt.[49] Left-wing Labour MPs Dennis Skinner and Tony Benn were also called working-class heroes.[50] A more recent example is footballer and anti-child poverty campaigner Marcus Rashford. Nonetheless, in such a pantheon, working-class heroes are pretty much all white males. Working-class heroines are few and far between, although left-wing activist Betty Tebbs was given the title when her biography was published by Unite in 2019.[51]

Though the term 'working-class hero' is commonly used in journalism and is quintessentially an artefact of subjective social construction, in works of non-fiction – especially studies of popular culture rather than political science – it is seldom defined or elaborated on. Bryan Garman, author of *A Race of Singers: Whitman's Working-Class Hero from Guthrie to Springsteen*, is one of the few to do so, but only in terms of protecting the interests of the constituents and extending their rights through cultural reproduction (and not economic struggles). Meanwhile, other authors who have written on the topic are far more numerous in not providing any definition or conceptualisation.[52] This is because the meaning is somehow held to be self-evident. But providing a definition, even a rudimentary one, is critical. In the first instance, it is crucial to determine whether a working-class hero must not only be *for* the working class but also necessarily *from* and *of* the working class. Being for the working class suggests taking a political position of opposition to the capitalist status quo, and consequently a rhetorical position of also being for the interests of the exploited, downtrodden and dispossessed. However, it does not imply much in the way of deliberate and effective action. Whether 'working-class heroes' must also objectively be from and of the working class is relatively more complex. Being a tribune of the working class without being working-class is possible, as the likes of Marx, Engels, Lenin and Trotsky indicate. However, the authenticity and credibility of being for the working class can be heightened if the individual is originally *from* the working class – even if no longer so, as in the case of professional footballers – or is still *of* the working class. This gives rise to the aforementioned issue of whether working-class heroes are those that rise with their class (in forms of struggle) or they are those that rise out of their class and into another one. The latter suggests that the working-class hero is a hero because they defiantly and determinedly managed against the odds to achieve a lifestyle and standard of living which many working-class people want but can only aspire to.

In the second instance, the question arises of what degree of class consciousness is most appropriate to being a working-class hero. Is it one which espouses the interests of the working class as a whole, including its subsections such as the lumpenproletariat? Or is it one which espouses only the interests of the most downtrodden and dispossessed sections of the working class such as the lumpenproletariat, or some vaguer overall notion like the common good which is not class-bound? And to what extent is a working-class hero required to merely express sympathy for – and empathy with – the working class or its subsections, or be far more strident, wide-ranging and radical – even revolutionary – by promoting an alternative to the capitalist status quo such as socialism? In this regard, it is interesting to note that Bryan Garman believed a working-class hero should 'be radical [but not] too damn radical' in order to be credible to the widest number of workers possible.[53]

In the third instance, what are the actions of a working-class hero? At the most basic level, is this just to make anti-establishment comments that then become well known and which are seen to represent the working class in broad cultural terms? Or, at a more advanced level, is it to reveal truths about the conditions of the working class, and to articulate the righteous anger that springs from the exploitation and oppression that characterise those conditions? Doing so could be termed undertaking acts of propaganda against capitalism. At an even more advanced level, would it be not only to espouse a counter-morality to that of the capitalist status quo but give a strong sense that righteous anger can lead to the hope of change and the collective action necessary to achieve it? For many, this would mean not only a socialist ideology but acts of agitation and campaigning.

In the fourth instance, union organisers and leaders are amongst the more obvious contenders to be working-class heroes and heroines because their role is to advance and defend the interests of their members, even if this is done in a sectionalist way. Yet opportunities to generalise their union's struggles to those of others do provide the occasion to frame their own union's struggles in ways that speak to the wider union movement and the working class as a whole. Compared to leaders of labour or social democratic parties, union organisers and leaders have a more direct and intimate connection with workers – as workers rather than as citizens or consumers – and their struggles.

In the fifth instance, as with herodom, charisma is not an essential component for an individual to become a working-class hero, even in the present media-driven age of widespread use of video recording and sharing. However, it is certainly conducive to conveying charisma. For the perceivers/receivers, it is a medium that allows them to experience more directly the charisma of the candidate for working-class herodom because the balance between the written word and the moving image has tilted in favour of the latter.

Contextual considerations and controversy

Lynch will be assessed against these aforementioned criteria in this study. However, there are several other contextual considerations that need to be contemplated. Firstly, even if unintended, the line 'If you want to be a hero, well, just follow me' in Lennon's 'Working-class hero' lyric also alludes to a hierarchy of heroes. The desire to be a 'hero' might lead to followership of heroes, but at some point the follower must then also become a 'hero' leader, and the two are not necessarily compatible. Indeed, they could be in conflict through competition. However, this tension could be resolved if the hero is a national union leader encouraging his or her followers to become workplace, local (branch or district) or regional leaders, prior to any considerations of these individuals becoming national union leaders (see pp. 211-13 on transformational leadership style). How these subleaders might see themselves and be seen by others could be through the prism of heroism.

Secondly, when union leaders are called working-class heroes, it is not normally or necessarily by their own members. Rather, it is by members of other unions, because union members tend to see their own union leaders in a more direct manner, as their highest representative and negotiator, and speaking for their union rather than unions or workers as a whole. By contrast, members of other unions can see a leader of another union as representing themselves and their interests in a less direct manner – not through collective bargaining but through political discourse and narratives. However, if union members' general secretaries transcend the parameters of their own unions to a considerable extent and at a time of heightened struggle, thereby playing a role for the wider union movement, then union members may recognise the validity of the appellation even if they choose not to use it themselves for the aforementioned reason. This was the case with Lynch, as testimony will show.

Thirdly, winning battles and struggles for, and on behalf of, the working class may be thought of as a crucial component of union leaders who are seen as working-class heroes. This would be mistaken, for popular perception can be based on mere articulation of working-class interests as much as on the role played in achieving positive material outcomes for the defence or furtherance of working-class interests. Indeed, articulation of interests may be viewed as crucial to doing that. This is all the more so when considering not just sectional battles of particular unions but class-wide battles and how objectively sectional battles are subjectively perceived by others. Moreover, the perception of being seen to 'fight the good fight' is important even if that fight is not won, and especially so when there are few fights and many are lost, with unions and the left therefore having a habit of celebrating 'glorious defeats'. Thus, fighting is often seen as more important than winning because the decision to fight is, at least, in the hands of particular individuals choosing to do so, while the outcome of the fight is not. In other words, the willingness to resist by fighting is valued in itself.

But of course matters are not quite so simple. Unions are collective bodies comprised of members who, in strikes, have withdrawn their labour. They are organised and directed by workplace activists as well as more senior lay officials and officers employed by their national union. At the apex of unions are the general and deputy or assistant secretaries, national presidents and NEC (National Executive Committee) members. In the case of the RMT, NEC members are seconded full-time. This means it is not always self-evident what the precise role of the general secretary is in winning – or losing – a particular industrial dispute. That said, and although there are different components to winning a dispute, the key one is the members' actions. Yet, what it takes to get the members to take action, how their motivation is created and sustained, and what strategy and tactics are deployed via the members' actions do allow for the key contribution of the upper echelons of the union, and in particular the general secretary. One would have to have been an RMT NEC member – or a fly on the wall in their many meetings – to have a concrete, corroborated sense of which particular individuals played key roles at particular points. This would be in terms of setting the strike strategy, resisting initiatives from others to change course and the like.

Fourthly, for some, heroes – though not so much heroines – are viewed as anathematic and abhorrent because herodom creates hierarchy and prevents the development of others as leaders. In essence, heroes are seen to be not just poor substitutes for collective actions but barriers to generating them where individuals are counterposed to collectives. Here, the Redskins' 1986 song 'Take No Heroes!', with its chorus line of 'Take no heroes, only inspiration', is apt. The implication in the song is that it should be the ideas of the person that should inspire and not the person themselves: 'And if you learn nothing from his life / Learn this from his death / The man may die but his dream survives'. But there is an element of inspiration to be taken from heroes, and people commonly do so. Indeed, one of the roles of heroes is to inspire, and it is often easier for people to take inspiration when individuals are regarded as heroes.[54]

Context is 'king'

In the summer of 2022, unemployment was at its lowest level since 1974, but this tight labour market did not mean any easy wins on the pay and conditions front for unionised workers. The value of real wages continued to fall as very few pay agreements, even after striking, matched or exceeded the rate of inflation. Even those that did, did not help make up for the fall in the value of real wages before late 2021 when the cost-of-living crisis began. All this indicated that union revitalisation, back to the membership levels and militancy of the 1970s, was badly needed. In 2022, after some slight rises from 2017 onwards, density fell back for a second year to 22.3 per cent: just 12.0 per cent in the private sector and 48.6 per cent in the public sector.[55] Within this, in 2022 younger workers continued to be non-unionised, with only 20.9. per cent of those aged between 25 and 34 being members of unions. Even amongst older workers the figures were not encouraging: 35.7 per cent for those aged between 35 and 49. It is this palpable sense of powerlessness and hopelessness as a result of non-unionisation and de-unionisation that provided one of the key contextual factors explaining the rapid rise of Lynch as a working-class hero.

Focussing on strikes themselves, the years before 2022 experienced the lowest levels of strike activity since records began. This provided another key contextual component in accounting for Lynch's emergence as a working-class hero, because, more than any other measure, the low level of strikes shows that workers, especially unionised workers, could not or would not engage in collective workplace struggle to the degree they had done before. Take the year 2018, the latest year for which full data is available: there were just 273,000 working days not worked due to strikes, the sixth-lowest annual total since records began in 1891, with just 39,000 workers involved, the second-lowest figure since records for workers involved began in 1893, and just eighty-one strikes, the second-lowest figure since records for strikes began in 1930. The figures for 2017 were 276,000, 33,000 and seventy-nine respectively. The number of working days not worked in 2019 due to strikes was 234,000. And although the state of (working-) class consciousness cannot be read directly off strike statistics, for various reasons of economism and sectionalism,[56] the figures do nonetheless provide some indication of it being at a low ebb. Together, the poor state of striking and (working-) class consciousness help contextualise and explain Lynch's emergence as a working-class hero – first, during a low point in workers' collective struggle and self-confidence compared to others like Reid and Scargill before; second, as an indication of workers looking more strongly for representation of their interests by others rather than by themselves, as in periods like the 1960s and 1970s; and third as a significant revival in strike activity, if not also oppositional working-class consciousness, was underway from the summer of 2022 onwards. The year between June 2022 and May 2023 saw 3.93m days not worked due to strikes.[57] Critically, the messages Lynch espoused found a ready audience because they gained traction as a result of not just popular anger over pay, but also because of high hopes that some kind of fightback was underway, exemplified by the rising strike level after such a historical low. This ranged from baristas and barristers to dockers and doctors, cleaners and carers, with many others like rail and postal workers in between. Most importantly, being first to the fight – to fight back – coming out of a period of stupor for striking, gave Lynch the edge. Consequently, context was 'king' because a constellation of components came together in a conducive way.

There was also continual pressure to cut costs in the rail sector. Both Labour and Conservative governments had commissioned reports – McNulty of 2011 and Williams of 2021 respectively – to examine how and where costs could be cut in order to reduce government subsidy to Network Rail and TOCs. The majority of 'savings' were to be the result of productivity gains, which the RMT rightly assessed as meaning fewer workers doing more and with worse terms and conditions of employment. This pressure was further heightened by the pandemic, where massive subsidies were given to TOCs in order to keep trains running, but with hugely reduced passenger numbers and thus revenue. For Lynch, this meant another 'accident of history', for it was he – and not Cash – who was the General Secretary when this particular train came rolling down the track in the post-pandemic period, and which the RMT sought to make hit the buffers. Lynch recognised this, saying: 'I didn't want that timing – it just came on top of me.'[58]

Conclusion

Back in 1977, in the song 'No More Heroes', *The Stranglers* asked: 'Whatever happened to all the heroes?' The phenomenon of Lynch as a working-class hero helped answer this by showing that even though heroes and heroines were in short supply in Britain in the twenty-first century, there was at least one well-known one. Lynch's demonisation by much of the media at a time of growing popular anger against the Conservatives, the establishment and the cost-of-living crisis created one part of the equation of becoming a working-class hero. Another part was Lynch's popular and polished media performance. But, as already argued, the process and the outcome of becoming a working-class hero are more complex than this. This is because they rest on concoction and context. And if the term 'hero' is troubling for some, there are other terms such as 'lodestar' – a person that serves as an inspiration or guide – and 'lodestone' – a person that is the focus of attention or attraction – as well as 'talisman' – a person regarded as representing and inspiring a particular group. Lynch was all three, but however he is characterised cannot take away from the leadership role he was perceived to have played for many in the organised working class.

Lynch became, as already emphasised, a working-class hero for many because of what he said rather than what he did. But having become a working-class hero, what were the expectations thereafter? And were they realistic? Would 'fighting the good fight' be good enough? Would words rather than deeds suffice? And for how long could words suffice? These are issues that we will come back to in Chapter 6 when we return to an assessment of Lynch's leadership.

3

Sparks fly! Boyhood and blacklisted but back again

This chapter first considers Mick Lynch's formative years, covering his recollections of his family background, childhood and young adulthood. What comes through strongly is the combined influence of his parents and the community his family lived in for helping shape his values and beliefs. The chapter then covers his life from the mid-1980s to late 2000s. As Lynch was a 'spark' – a colloquialism for electrician and the Electrical and Plumbing Industries Union (EPIU) had a publication called *The Spark* – it was apt that he began work on Eurostar, which was an early example of a fully electrified railway line. But there was a darker aspect to this. Being blacklisted in the construction industry for his growing union activity, he had little option but to 'fly' to another sector looking for work.[1] Only years later would light be shone on his blacklisting. The endpoint of this chapter is represented by 2009, when Lynch was elected to the RMT's Council of Executives (CoE).

Birth and beginnings

Michael (Mick) Lynch was born in January 1962 to an Irish Catholic family in West London. He was the youngest of five children (three other sons and one daughter).[2]

His father, Jackie Lynch (1922–78), was from Cork in Ireland, and his mother, Ellen 'Nellie' Morris, was from a farm outside Crossmaglen in Northern Ireland.[3] Both emigrated to Britain during the Second World War, in 1941 and 1942 respectively, in search of work.[4] Moving to America – as many Irish people had in the past – was not an option at this time. Jackie worked as a building labourer, engineering worker (where he was a shop steward) and postal worker (who was on strike for seven weeks in 1971), while Nellie was a domestic servant at first, then a shop worker and cleaner. They met in the dance halls of North-west London in Kilburn and Paddington and Cricklewood.

Lynch grew up in Paddington, West London, in what he has described as 'rented rooms that would now be called slums [with] the old tin bath and shared toilet with other families' and then a council flat in an area called the Warwick Estate.[5] He characterised this as 'real poverty'.[6] Of the council housing, he said: 'People had come out of housing that had been condemned. I thought [our flat] was okay, but a lot of people now would be shocked. It was freezing, there was no heating. You had a coal fire in the sitting room, but the rest of that flat was freezing.'[7] Yet he also ventured:

> [People] were quite glad that they had been rehoused, which is completely understandable if you knew what Paddington, or west London, was like in those days ... I don't want to get dewy-eyed or sentimental about it, but when I was growing up people were glad to be living in council-provided housing which they could afford, according to their wages.[8]

Of his parents, he told the *Sunday Independent*: 'We were always well-fed and decently turned out, as you would expect from an Irish mother, but we didn't have any "spare" money. We never had a family holiday together, for example. Sometimes a couple of us would go back to Ireland now and again, but we never all went back together at the same time. It was difficult to manage with five kids.'[9] Lynch said his family 'did all the traditional Irish stuff: Catholic primary school, Catholic secondary school. There was a lot of Irish people in our community, but it was very diverse as well.'[10] The diversity came from people from the Caribbean, Italy and Poland, who were also Catholics. Though he was raised as a Catholic, Lynch has long since stopped being one. He said of his parents:

> My dad was a shop steward. He wasn't a massive activist, but he was an opinionated fellow ... with Labour Party values. I don't want to make out that we were raging activists – we weren't, but we did like a decent debate ... We were always Labour supporters, socialists with a small 's'. [My parents] weren't theoretical people. They just knew what their values were, which was always to stick together ... My father wasn't ... academic in any way. He was a bloke who liked to go to the pub. He wasn't uneducated, but he wasn't ... academic – he was a labourer.[11]

Elsewhere, Lynch recalled: 'There was an awful lot of conversation in our house about current issues, not just about celebrity culture or frivolous stuff, but about what was going on [in the world] all around us'[12] and that 'Our family was a left-wing family, but we weren't in active groups. I don't want you to get the wrong impression, because we were a devoutly Catholic family as well. We didn't have posters of Chairman Mao or Che Guevara ... The most important thing was going to Mass. Holy Days of Obligation, going to confession on Saturday night, and the pub. Our family was always a bit left-wing, but Catholic at the same time.'[13] His father was a Labour Party member.[14] Elsewhere, Lynch described being a Catholic in his childhood as 'not a lifestyle choice as it is nowadays'.[15] Overall, Lynch described not being taught his politics by his parents as such, but 'develop[ing] ... and absorb[ing]' what he experienced and, though his parents were both 'socially conservative, Labour voters', growing up in an Irish Catholic community gave him a 'sense of social solidarity'.[16] Earlier, he put it this way: 'The values of solidarity and trade unionism are what I was brought up on. A lot of those values came from my Catholic background. I'm not a believer, but it was a solid base and I think people have lost a lot of that.'[17]

Teenage years

Lynch's twin passions as a teenager were football and music. He was more interested in them than school, because his Catholic secondary schooling was 'strict', meaning he 'didn't enjoy school'.[18] Lynch liked the music of The Clash, Gang of Four, Three Johns, The Cure and The Smiths.[19] Asked whether he was a punk, Lynch responded: 'No, I was what they called a New Waver. We used to wear Harrington jackets, Levis and Dunlop Green Flash [trainers] – that was people on the edge of punk, who weren't quite brave enough to face their mum about dyeing their hair or having their ears pierced. So, we just drank a lot of lager instead and listened to dodgy bands.'[20] Lynch still follows Irish sports, and is a fan of Cork City Football Club, saying: 'When it comes to Cork City, I'd support Cork in anything, even in tiddlywinks if they had a team',[21] along with also supporting Brentford and Chelsea football clubs. And from this period, he formed lifelong friendships: 'If I get a chance, [I like] to ... go out with a few mates of mine that I've known for 40 years or more and just have a few pints.'[22]

Just at the time that Lynch was taking his O-levels, in May 1978, his father died. He gained five O-levels, and shortly afterwards, at the age of 16, Lynch left school and began a period of being 'on the tools', as he likes to put it, that would last for thirty-seven years. From a choice of three apprentice-ships he was offered, he trained as an apprentice electrician for four years, becoming a qualified electrician at a company making, exporting, installing and servicing printing machin-ery. Starting at the same time were eight other apprentices, five of whom came from the same school. Lynch joined the Electrical, Electronic, Telecommunications and Plumbing Union (EEPTU) on his first day at work. This, he explained, was nothing out of the ordinary:

Unions were part of working-class life. You wouldn't find many people that weren't in the union. It was just part of your life like paying tax or going to Mass. It was just what you did. So, when I left school, I joined the union because that was what people did. A decent job was seen as a union job ... Unions would be part of the works committee [of an employer].[23]

We were always in unions, it's just what we did. For us, it was the same as going to Mass. Being a union activist was the same as being from west London.[24]

West London, where I lived, was full of engineering – Park Royal, the Great West Road, it was all engineering and manu-facturing plants. So, all of that community had the idea of shop stewards, or people who were convenors – people knew about all that instinctively ... So I thought it was very natu-ral when I saw that there was a virtual closed shop where I worked. There were five trade unions there, [two] print unions, [two] engineering unions and the electricians' union, which I joined. The day I started they came up to me and said, 'here's your form, we want it signed by teatime' – and I just signed it. And if I had waited to ask my mum or dad 'should I sign it?', they would have said, 'You should have signed when you got it. Don't bring it home here, make sure you're in it'. That's the attitude we had.[25]

With portent for over forty years later, when Lynch argued the labour movement needed to rekindle its cultural side (see pp. 168–69), he remembered that because unions 'used to have social clubs, sports clubs, cultural activities, art clubs, outings, holidays – all sorts of stuff ... people just expected to have a more community lifestyle.'[26] But there was a rub to joining his first union: 'the electricians' union wouldn't let me in for a year. They said "You've got to finish your probation. When you come out of probation and you start your electrical training, then we'll let you in the union."'[27] Lynch added: 'The electricians' union at that time was the most right-wing union in the country, but even the most right-wing electrician, if you went to another site, would say "where's your union card?". Even a Tory-voting electrician wouldn't accept that you could be an electrician without an electricians' union card. And that was true of many of the trades, they wouldn't accept you on site. That was the attitude.'[28]

In addition to politics 'around the [family] dinner table', Lynch recollected:

> The first politicians I remember were [Harold] Wilson and [Dennis] Healey and all those characters in the 1970s, and trade unions were just part and parcel of what we were ... From when I was very young I was a TV addict ... [T]here seemed to be a tremendous number of historic events in the 1960s and 1970s, both at home and abroad. The colonies were being disbanded, and ... [national] liberation struggles were going on – and not just in the British empire, the French empire was also being disbanded. And the US was asserting itself, and so were the Soviet Union and the Eastern bloc. All that was going on, and you couldn't help but be stimulated by it, no matter what your views were. I think that was a very interesting upbringing. I am probably one of the only people here who can still remember the trade union leaders' names from then – Vic Feather, Jack Jones ... I thought these people were very important.[29]

Lynch also remembered: 'A lot was going on in the news back in the day between the Vietnam War and Northern Ireland and there were lots of radical things happening. I was the youngest of five. So, there was always discussion in the house, whether it was religion, politics, and music. It was quite an articulate house [and] loud, like most Irish houses and the community was like that too. There was a pub culture and you learn a lot in that environment; arguing your point or winding people up. That carried on into the workplace.'[30] And, Lynch also recalled reading *The Ragged Trousered Philanthropists* by Robert Tressell at an early age of 14, later saying: 'It informed ideas that were already welling up in me instinctively through all those conversations and arguments we had at home and in the pub. It put some theory and some knowledge behind it and it still informs me now'[31] and that it 'made perfect sense ... [but] the issue is what you do about it'.[32] He called it his favourite book.[33] Tressell was the pen name of Robert Noonan, an Irish nationalist and socialist. At the RMT 2023 Young Members Conference in Hastings, appropriately, Lynch commended the book, which was based on Tressell's experience of working there as an underpaid painter and decorator. Later in 2023, and given his Irish heritage, national profile and interest in the author, Lynch addressed the Robert Tressell Festival at Liberty Hall in Dublin.

All aboard the union express

Though Lynch attended EEPTU meetings and spoke at them, he was not an activist as such, and did not hold an elected lay position until the mid-1980s. By then he had left the printing machinery manufacturer because he felt there was a danger of 'becoming institutionalised' and employment prospects were not as good in this sector as they had been.[34] He moved into the construction sector, becoming far more active in his union there. Asked why he became active then and not before, he put it down to the desire to 'express myself and [my] ... beliefs'.[35]

Lynch's first baptism of fire was not simply his blacklisting but rather it being co-joined with the founding of the EPIU on 5 September 1988 as a split from the EETPU.[36] That day, led by Eric Hammond,[37] the EETPU was expelled from the TUC for signing agreements with employers that it would be the only union recognised, contrary to TUC rules.[38] Such agreements were also often effectively 'no-strike' agreements. The cases in point were two companies (Orion Electronics and Christian Salvesen),[39] and the unions which took the EEPTU to the TUC Disputes Committee over these were the GMB and TGWU. Several thousand EEPTU members formed the EPIU in order to remain in the mainstream union movement, as well as to embody politics that rejected such collaboration with employers. Indeed, though this was the specific trigger for the creation of the breakaway union, tensions within the EEPTU had been bubbling away for many years. There were infamous incidents like accepting government money to organise union postal ballots for industrial action, contrary to TUC policy; Hammond calling the striking miners led by Scargill 'lions led by donkeys' at the 1985 Labour Party conference, to which the retort from the TGWU leader, Ron Todd, was 'I'd rather be a donkey than a jackal';[40] and the willingness of the EEPTU leadership to help Rupert Murdoch castrate the NGA (National Graphical Association) and SOGAT (Society of Graphical and Allied Trades) print unions at News International's Wapping newspaper plant before, during and after the year-long dispute from 1986 to 1987. But within the EEPTU, the main 'beef' against the leadership was the signing of what many felt was a 'sweetheart' agreement with employers and contractors in electrical engineering who were members of the Joint Industry Board (JIB). Though set up in 1968, EEPTU membership in the JIB sector was falling to such an extent that JIB employers and contractors agreed in 1975 to pay the union subs of their employees through a 'check-off' system, amounting to what was believed to be around £1m per annum by the early 1990s. This gave grist to the mill for those left activists like Lynch, and especially those in the EEPTU Broad Left, with its newsletter, *Flashlight*. Many of these activists would become key figures in the EPIU. On its expulsion, some on the left in the EEPTU argued to stay and fight for reaffiliation to the TUC, but many felt this was a battle that could not be won.[41]

Under the leadership of John Aitkin as General Secretary, the EPIU applied for TUC affiliation in 1989, but was rejected because the EPIU was not deemed to be an independent union as TUC rules required. This situation arose because initially the EPIU had no structure and was unable to represent its members, or even accept their membership payments. As a result, five other unions (including the NUR) represented its membership, on a temporary basis, using what were called 'holding sections'. Only in 1991, when the EPIU was put on a sound basis and gained a certificate of independence from the Certification Officer, was the application to affiliate then accepted. In 1989, EPIU records showed it had 3,000 members, rising to 4,200 by 1991. The main business of the EPIU in its first few years consisted of the hard tasks of establishing its structures and seeking to gain union recognition from employers, rather than conducting collective bargaining. It was opposed in this latter task by the EEPTU.

Lynch was active in leaving the EEPTU and forming the EPIU, and although he was not its executive councillor for London, he was the London convenor for the EPIU at its formation. This was surprising given his young age, being in his mid-twenties at the time, and when many other EPIU activists were older with longer track records of union activity. Despite his relative youth, EPIU members had faith in his leadership abilities, and Lynch had the time to carry out the work required as, being blacklisted, he had no employment (though he did undertake a full-time university degree). Lynch was a member of the London Electrical Branch, attending and speaking at EPIU annual conferences. For example, in 1992 he spoke on the danger – as he saw it – of the still nascent EPIU union seeking a JIB-type 'check-off' agreement rather than undertaking the harder, longer-term task of developing the union's site organisation of shop stewards and health and safety representatives.[42] In 1995, the EPIU merged into the TGWU, indicating that such a small union was not viable as either an agent of collective bargaining or an organisation itself. By 2007, when the TGWU merged with Amicus to form Unite, the remnants of both the EEPTU and EPIU were reunited (via the EEPTU merging with the AEU (Amalgamated Engineering Union) to form the AEEU (Amalgamated Engineering and Electrical Union) in 1992, and the AEEU merging with MSF (Manufacturing, Science and Finance union) in 2001 to form Amicus). In retrospect, Lynch said the EPIU was 'probably a big mistake'.[43]

According to the *Financial Times*, Lynch was 'blacklisted for joining a breakaway union'.[44] This is unlikely, because Lynch was probably already on the blacklist before joining the EPIU or, if he was not, it was not the act of joining the EPIU that would have marked his card here but rather that he was an active EPIU member who sought to represent his fellow workers, to the chagrin of employers and contractors, for as he said: 'that made me a big target'.[45] Sometimes, this also involved attending the actions of the inter-union grass-roots body, the Joint Sites Committee, in London in the early 1990s. For Lynch, the main lessons learnt, from the EPIU experience especially, were not just the hard tasks of union organising in challenging circumstances but also undertaking a middle-level leadership role at the regional rank, marking him out as a 'player' rather than a 'mover and shaker' as he was later to become. Such tasks included making and carrying arguments and framing issues so as to promote a sense of grievance or injustice amongst workers by persuading them that they had a 'just cause', encouraging a high degree of work group cohesion and identity, which encourages workers to think about their collective interests in opposition to management, and then advocating the appropriateness and legitimacy of collective action to prosecute these interests.

The Blacklist Support Group (BSG), formed in 2009 with the help of unions like Unite, GMB and UCATT (Union of Construction, Allied Trades and Technicians), took up the civil claim cases of the blacklisted workers, eventually winning financial compensation for many of those who had been identified, amounting to some tens of millions of pounds, possibly running into hundreds of millions.[46] Among them was Lynch, who received a settlement of compensation of £35,000 in the form of a cheque which he has on the wall in his General Secretary's office in the RMT's headquarters.[47] Lynch told the *Guardian*: 'As an electrician looking for work, you'd ring the labour manager, they'd phone this company, and he'd go on his Rolodex and pick your name out, and say don't hire him, he was seen on that demonstration, he took part in that strike. Some people were out of work for years ... I knew I was blacklisted but you can't prove it, because it was all secret.'[48] This was the situation where he could not get a 'start', but there were other types of post-'start' victimisation too, as Lynch experienced: 'We're letting you go because your references are no good.'[49] The company was the Consulting Association, based in Droitwich, and run by Ian Kerr. It was subsequently shut down as a result of the blacklist being discovered by the Information Commissioner's Office, which served an enforcement notice against it under the terms of the Data Protection Act in 2009. Of the victory, Lynch later said: 'They sent me a letter [in 2009]. They held the blacklist on a database, and they sent me this thing about the companies that had blacklisted me. We took them to court in the end, and I got this cheque.'[50] However, in the BSG campaign for an apology, admittance of guilt and financial compensation, Lynch was not particularly active, as he admitted 'I wasn't very active in it',[51] with Steve Hedley, Lynch's later fellow but senior, Assistant General Secretary, being much more so.[52]

Student days

Between 1988 and 1991, Lynch studied full-time for a BA in Medieval and Modern History at the London School of Economics (LSE). The department was the Department of International History, and the cohort starting in 1988 numbered just twenty-two students, of whom half were mature students and most were left-wing (including members of the Revolutionary Communist Party and Socialist Workers Party (SWP)). Without employment due to being blacklisted, and the availability at that time of government student

financial support,[53] Lynch decided to further his interest
in the study of history. He attained an upper second class
(2:1) degree. A fellow student and an acquaintance from
those times and afterwards into the later 1990s remembers
Lynch as a serious and engaged mature student who was
quietly self-assured and respectful of the views of others,
but 'generally quite a quiet guy'. He 'was already going out
with Mary, maybe even living with her, but not yet married
[to her]'. Though the Students' Union was the LSE's hub of
political activity, on account of his other time commitment
to the EPIU and the age gap with most students, Lynch
was not involved in it. With portent for the future, another
acquaintance from those days recalled that: 'In a remark-
able coincidence I bumped into Mick on Monday evening
[15 January 2023] in a pub after the RMT-initiated rally in
Whitehall against the Tories' latest legislative attack on
the unions. To my amazement, though we'd probably not
spoken in person for more than thirty years, he remembered
me. I guess a good visual memory [of people] is a consider-
able asset for politicians and senior union officials.' Lynch
has since maintained his interest in and knowledge of his-
tory by being an avid reader: 'If I get a chance, [I like] to read
a few books.'[54]

RMT union activist

Lynch explained his emergence as an RMT activist and
organiser after joining Eurostar as 'the gift of the gab took
over', 'If you see a ball, you ought to kick it sometimes'[55]
and being 'a bit of a motormouth'.[56] Along with this, his
convictions through his family upbringing and his experi-
ence of being blacklisted led him to found and build the
Eurostar branch into one of the biggest in the RMT, even

though he said: 'I got the job to get a bit of real money and keep my head down'[57] and 'I went into Eurostar to hide and earn some money for six months.'[58]

As secretary of the RMT European Passenger Services (EPS) branch for those workers employed by and associated with Eurostar, Lynch played two main roles. First, he was involved in the protection and advancement of members' interests. For example, this included organising a ballot for industrial action amongst the 500-odd members in 2004, which was successfully used to gain a higher pay rise following a 'yes' vote for action. Second, on a number of occasions, Lynch helped organise and support fellow workers in operations associated with Eurostar. One example was the case of the International Currency Exchange staff at the stations used by Eurostar, where these workers approached Lynch to be organised as RMT members. Another example was in 2005, when Lynch helped support the RMT's members working for Chubb Security in their strike and dispute to gain union recognition at the stations used by Eurostar.

Participating in the RMT's democratic processes

Lynch was a fairly frequent delegate to the RMT's annual general meetings (AGMs). For example, in the first decade of the 2000s, when Crow was General Secretary, Lynch attended the 2002, 2003, 2005 and 2006 AGMs (but not those in 2004, 2007 or 2008) as the (sole) delegate for the EPS branch. At this time, his job title was Engineering Senior Team Member – which was not, according to Lynch, a promoted, supervisory, chargehand or managerial position[59] – and he and his family lived in a modest, three-bedroom semi-detached house in West Acton in London.

At the 2002 AGM, his branch brought forward motions on producing and distributing targeted campaigning materials because, as the motion stated, the union 'cannot rely on sponsored MPs to influence transport policy'; on travel facilities for members; on motions passed at AGMs taking immediate effect and being implemented no later than four weeks later; and on seeking RMT representation at the senior levels of the newly created Network Rail not-for-profit public company. All were passed, most unanimously and with little amendment. As Lynch was the EPS branch secretary, he wrote the motions and spoke for them. The RMT monthly magazine, *RMT News*, carries extensive coverage of the union's AGMs so Lynch was featured in terms of selected quotes, sometimes with a photo of him. He also spoke on issues which his EPS branch did not have motions on, such as pensions. At the 2005 AGM he spoke in support of Palestinian national liberation but was unsuccessful in seeking election to the Standing Orders Committee, winning seven out of forty-five votes, but his branch's motion on reviewing the role of the union's regional councils was passed. Although not involved in any prominent way in the debates over disaffiliation from Labour and support for left-wing parties (like the Scottish Socialist Party) from the early 2000s onwards, he did proffer at the 2006 AGM that trying to set up yet another new socialist party when so many already existed and 'pointlessly contest elections' was a fool's errand.[60] Instead, he stated: 'I carry the current RMT policy into the voting booth and vote for the candidate closest to this union's policy.'[61] This would have meant a vote for a Labour candidate in all likelihood. Unsurprisingly, he never sought to be a candidate for the Trade Union and Socialist Coalition (TUSC) or No2EU in any of the elections these parties stood in.

Marriage and children

Lynch's wife, Mary Waldron, has been an NHS nurse and union member since 1984. Together, they have three children, Róisín, Connie and James (who works on the railways). Lynch met Mary when she was a student nurse. Her family came from Ballyhaunis in County Mayo, Ireland. According to HM Land Registry, their property in Howard Close in West Acton was sold for £400,000 in 2008. They now live in a four-bedroom Victorian terrace in Ealing, West London, valued at 'approaching £1million',[62] though *The Times* valued its worth at £730,000.[63] Lynch commented that his ability to buy a property was down to 'always ha[ving] a decent wage along with [that of] my wife'.[64]

Conclusion

The influence of his parents is apparent if not overwhelming, but put together as part of an Irish, Catholic working-class community in West London during the 1960s and 1970s, Lynch's social democratic politics (see Chapter 8) had their germination. These views, values and beliefs have remained a constant throughout his life, where unions, the Labour Party, community and the social democratic state were the lynchpins. Some working-class people are keen to clamber out of their class, disassociating themselves from it along the way. Lynch was proud of his working-class roots so one of the constants from these days became his psychological attachment to being 'working-class', something he often referred to as a senior official of the RMT from 2015 onwards. And his continuing psychological attachment from these early days to Irish republicanism and anti-imperialism was indicated by holding an Irish and not British passport. Though he graduated from the LSE, Lynch also graduated from the 'school of hard knocks' by dint of his extensive period of being blacklisted. The move to Eurostar, though motivated by financial desperation, did allow Lynch to apply what he had already learnt about union organising to a new environment. It was from here that his rise to the top of the RMT can be first traced. There were bumps and diversions along that road but the path was aided by assorted 'accidents of history'.

4

Working for the union

This chapter covers Mick Lynch's next baptism of fire, this time as a national officer of the RMT during an internal union dispute between 2020 and 2021. Although Lynch did not start working as an employee of the RMT until 7 April 2015, he did work for the RMT as a fully seconded, full-time CoE member for two periods,[1] from 1 January 2009 to 31 December 2011 and 1 January 2015 to 6 April 2015. Because of the nature of this CoE position, which is almost tantamount to being a union officer, although technically a lay position, it is dealt with in this chapter. Citing his working-class credentials, Lynch frequently liked to say prior to being elected Assistant General Secretary in 2015: 'Thirty-seven years I was on the tools.'[2] But another way of looking at this is to say that for a quarter of his working life, Lynch has been a union officer. Before looking at these aspects of his work as a union officer, this chapter briefly considers the RMT as an organisation.

The RMT

By membership size, the RMT is only the eleventh-largest union affiliated to the TUC. Yet what it lacks in quantity, it may be thought to more than make up for in quality. In 2014, the year before Lynch was elected Assistant General Secretary, RMT membership was 82,278. It rose to 83,854 in 2015 before falling back to 79,113 in 2016. Thereafter, it rose almost continually – to 80,391 in 2017, 80,103 in 2018, 81,494 in 2019 and 82,204 in 2020 – before falling back again to 81,197 in 2021. Some 1,500 new members joined during the early period of its industrial action of 2022, so it remained to be seen if these would represent a net gain. On 31 December 2021, the vast majority (86 per cent) of members worked on the railways (overground and underground), with much smaller numbers found in road transport (6 per cent) and shipping and offshore energy (7 per cent).[3] In 2021, 83 per cent of its members were male, compared to 86 per cent in 2015. And 91 per cent of members contributed to its political fund in 2021, compared to 95 per cent in 2015.

The RMT has had a militant reputation for many years, being seen as militant in its demands and in the action taken to secure them. The number of industrial action ballots[4] organised by the RMT in recent years varied from 89 in 2018, 126 in 2019, 49 in 2020, 112 in 2021 and 164 in 2022. This was an overall rise from the years under Crow (2002 to 2014) and the earlier part of Mick Cash's first term of office as General Secretary (where there were 76 in his first year and 53 in his second year). Ballot results were somewhat mixed. In 2018, nine did not attain a 50 per cent turnout and eight more did not have a majority voting for action that also equated to 40 per cent of all those entitled to vote. In 2020, eleven did not make the first threshold and four more did not make the second threshold. In 2021, eighteen did not make the first threshold and five more did not make the second threshold. The figures for 2022 were nineteen and eleven. In terms of the industrial action following from these ballots, in 2021 there were 143 days of strike action and 618 days of IASOS.[5] The figures for 2022 were 406 and 92 respectively.

Unlike many other unions, the sixteen members of the RMT National Executive Committee (NEC) – twelve from the general grades, four from maritime grades – are full-time members. That is to say, when elected for a period of three years, they leave their workplace to work full-time as NEC members, with their salaries paid by the union. The NEC elections are staggered so that not all are elected at the same time, being roughly on a 33 per cent basis per year over a three-year cycle. Once they have served a term of office, they cannot stand for re-election until a period of three years has elapsed. The only exception is where a former member becomes the president following the end of a term of office. The president sits on the NEC and chairs it. At annual general meetings (AGMs) and special general meetings (SGMs), annual and special conferences respectively, only delegates can vote (they number around just seventy). The same is true of the NEC – only its members can vote in its scheduled and special meetings. This means the general secretary (and other assistant general secretaries) can attend and speak but not vote at these meetings.

Senior lay representative

In 2005, Lynch stood unsuccessfully for the CoE seat for Region 9, the South East of England, securing only his own branch's nomination. This was the first indication that Lynch had ambition to seek a national role in the union. In late 2008, Lynch again sought election to the CoE, this time for Region 10, London and Anglia, securing ten branch nominations in the process (against the six of his rival). He was elected, serving his first term from January 2009 to December 2011. Lynch did well to be elected for this seat given that it served London, where competition for the seat was often stiffer as a result of the significant concentration of RMT members in and around the capital (though this did not include London Transport, consisting of overground and underground trains). Lynch was paid by the RMT for attendance and lodging allowances for serving on the CoE: £40,585 (2009), £37,388 (2010) and £40,687 (2011). These allowances are, in effect, the wages CoE members would have earned had they stayed in their employment rather than serving on the CoE.[6] A former CoE member recalls of the time served with Lynch:

> He was intelligent, competent, articulate and thought for himself, which I'm afraid to say made him stand out from most of the others … No one on the RMT Executive is right-wing, but Mick was on the right-wing of the Executive. He seemed keener on settling disputes than starting them. And while everyone in the RMT's leadership will say that they believe in the union being 'member-led', in practice, many uphold the bureaucratic ways in which the union operates, and Mick was one of those.

Around the same time as he campaigned for branch nominations for election to the CoE, he also became the President of the union's credit union, which at the time had some 1,000 members. Following the end of his first term on the CoE, and while still chairing the union's credit union,[7] Lynch then sought election as the union president in late 2012. Standing against Peter Pinkney, both secured twenty-one branch nominations, with Pinkney winning. Pinkney stood as a self-proclaimed Marxist,[8] pledging that the RMT 'will fight for the abolition of capitalism and to replace it with a socialist system'.[9] Meantime, as Lynch's election address leaflet showed, he highlighted his experience as an organiser and negotiator while making general and somewhat bland statements like 'The RMT must listen and back the members' and 'Our members must be our first concern'. Standing for the position of president is not always or necessarily an indication of further ambition for higher office, but it often is. Those who have held this office, such as Alex Gordon, John Leach and Sean Hoyle, have subsequently stood for the position of RMT general secretary. In recent times, Lynch has been the only one – albeit unsuccessful in his bid to be president – to do so and then be successful.

Of his election victory, Pinkney commented of Lynch: 'He ran a fair and hard campaign and I think we both raised major issues that need to be addressed. The graciousness that Mick has shown in defeat is an example to us all. It is easy to be magnanimous in victory, but much harder in defeat. I am sure there will be *further opportunities for Mick*, and I wish him well, and look forward to working with him in the future.'[10] Little did Pinkney know how prophetic his words would turn out to be – and how quickly so. The unexpected and untimely death of Bob Crow on 11 March 2014 opened up windows of opportunity and set in train a series of events that were critical for the emergence of Lynch on the national stage as a working-class hero. That is not to suggest there was anything inevitable or mechanical about the interplay of consequence and sequence, but that opportunities were created that would not otherwise have existed. And it is evident that it took Lynch's acumen and skills to turn these opportunities into outcomes. The first part of this was that Lynch was elected again to the CoE, serving from January 2015 onwards. Before that, and while attending the RMT's 2014 AGM, he told delegates that while Britain, the

US and other imperialist powers had no right to interfere in Syria, in forming its policy, the RMT had 'got to be careful because we're not dealing with a band of saints, on the one hand, and a band of sinners, on the other'.[11]

Elected Assistant General Secretary

Lynch's second CoE term was cut short because on 31 March 2015 he won the election for the post of Assistant General Secretary, beginning his five-year term of office on 7 April 2015. Lynch's pitch for the post when he launched his election campaign in October 2014 was, as his @MickLynch4AGS Twitter profile put it: 'Our union must remain strong, militant and united'. On being elected, he commented: 'We need to continue the work of Bob Crow and build a fighting, democratic trade union to defend our members. To do that we need to stay united and strong.'[12] The vacancy arose because Cash won the general secretary-ship to succeed Crow. Cash was the sitting Senior Assistant General Secretary, and vacated this position, to which the incumbent Assistant General Secretary, Steve Hedley, was then appointed (as is standard procedure in the RMT). Hedley's elevation then created a vacancy for the position of assistant general secretary. In terms of branch nominations, Lynch secured seventy-six against those of his two rivals, Alan Pottage (sixty-two) and John Tilley (twelve). Pottage was the union's long-standing National Organising Co-ordinator, and had contested the election to replace Crow in 2014,[13] while Tilley was a regional organiser for North West England. More than any other single development, Lynch's victory in this election began a series of events providing the route for Lynch to become General Secretary in 2021. It was something that Lynch recognised himself.[14] But along the way, there were two other major developments which built Lynch's profile prior to him standing for the top position. The first concerns Steve Hedley. His suspension in 2020 (see p. 80) meant Lynch moved up temporarily to be Senior Assistant General Secretary in July 2020, giving him a higher profile. The second concerns Cash's period of ill health where, as Senior Assistant General Secretary, Lynch filled in for Cash as Acting General Secretary.

As Assistant General Secretary, Lynch took responsibility for the RMT credit union and became the lead officer for buses, cleaners, freight and logistics, Network Rail, engineering grades and railway pensions. He was also in charge of the 'internal structures review' based on a branch consultation but which, according to a former CoE member, resulted in 'only proposals that the leadership agreed with being presented to the AGM'. Figures published in *RMT News* show Lynch's salary for his first full year (2016) as Assistant General Secretary was £76,028, with the subsequent years being £77,810 (2017), £80,879 (2018) and £83,335 (2019), with pension contributions of £18,586 and then £19,410 (2017), £20,193 (2018) and £21,553 (2019), and other benefits of £1,444 and then £1,548 (2017), £1,600 (2018) and £1,566 (2019). For 2020, the figures were £85,282 salary and £22,175 pension contributions with no other benefits given. For 2021, the figures were £90,222, £24,418 and £2,860, when Lynch was both Assistant General Secretary and General Secretary. For 2022, the figures were £89,961 salary and £27,900 pension contributions with no other benefits given. Even though the media conflated the salary and pension contributions together as one to suggest a six-figure salary from 2018 onwards, it is problematic to suggest these salaries are commensurate with being working-class even though the salary was set by the RMT AGM (see pp. 115–18).

Along with Cash and Hedley, Lynch supported reaffili-
ation to Labour, which culminated in an SGM in May
2018 but the meeting narrowly voted against reaffiliation.
The branch and regional meetings prior to the SGM revealed
a 'slight majority ... voted in favour of reaffiliation, but those
voting against represent a slightly larger proportion of the
membership ... [but such meetings] were attended by less than
0.5% of their memberships'.[15] In July 2020, Lynch opposed the
majority decision of the NEC (10:4) to support the resump-
tion of the Trade Unionist and Socialist Coalition's (TUSC)
electoral activity. At the RMT's 2021 AGM, he opposed a
motion calling for support for Corbyn to stand independently
in the next general election, also opposing motions to back
'pro-trade union, anti-austerity candidates in local and gen-
eral elections' and to approach the disaffiliated Bakers, Food
and Allied Workers Union and the critical but still affiliated
Unite union to organise a conference to discuss the possibil-
ity of a new union-based party.[16] Lynch also spoke strongly
in favour of a motion withdrawing the RMT from the TUSC
steering committee 'if TUSC wishes to continue as a politi-
cal party standing in elections'.[17] This was consistent with
his actions in May 2018. Nonetheless, in 2022 he admitted:
'my union is not affiliated to [Labour] anymore, and won't be
getting affiliated'.[18]

Mick Cash

'We want our Cash back', the slogan of the campaign to re-
elect Cash as General Secretary, did not come to fruition
for very long. Cash won his re-election on 27 August 2019,
defeating former president Sean Hoyle by 9,312 votes to
6,372 on a turnout of just under 20 per cent. But in the space
of little more than a year, Cash gave notice of his de facto

resignation on 3 November 2020. Cash returned to work on 15 September 2020 after a period of sickness absence caused, Cash said, by a mental health 'meltdown'[19] and a 'breakdown'.[20] This period of absence began on 19 June 2020. On his return to work, Cash thanked Lynch for covering in his absence because he 'stepped in at a moment's [notice] and worked tirelessly'.[21] In a letter of 15 September 2020 to branches, regional councils, regional organisers, NEC members and RMT staff, Cash charged: 'the lack of support and hostility I have been receiving from a majority of the union's National Executive … has made it impossible for me to do the job of General Secretary properly'. He went on to accuse these NEC members of not accepting his election twice to the general secretaryship, trying to force him out in order to install their own candidate in a fresh election, of acting as a 'faction' and 'elite', and in doing so creating a 'toxic culture'.

Of his de facto resignation, announced at the 2020 AGM, Cash stated that 'factional groupings within the union have seized every opportunity to undermine and frustrate my efforts to keep the organisation focused on delivering for our members regardless of the consequences. That campaign of harassment has come to a head at this AGM to the point that my authority has been systematically destroyed to such an extent that I can no longer deliver the RMT rule book functions of the General Secretary and have no option but to announce my retirement.'[22] Shortly before, the Campaign for a Fighting Democratic Union (CFDU) issued a release called 'RMT NEC statement on union democracy', stating: 'On the contrary, the NEC has backed the General Secretary on key issues this year, such as our campaign to retain guards, the handling of the COVID-19 lockdown, and complaints made against SAGS Hedley. But he does not have a NEC vote under our rules and he is required to act on the majority decision of the NEC.'[23] The spur to Cash's resignation was that the AGM, meeting virtually, voted to overturn the NEC's decision to issue a disciplinary sanction to Steve Hedley (see below). Cash's resignation was characterised by many as a 'retirement'[24] even though Cash stated: 'I had made it clear during the AGM while we were discussing internal matters that if the delegates found themselves unable to back me that they would put me in a position where I had no option but to announce I was moving on and clear the way for an election. The AGM made its decision in the full knowledge of my position.'[25] Cash's resignation had its historical parallel in the resignation of previous (NUR) General Secretary, Sidney Weighell, in 1982 as a result of losing the support of the then NEC.[26]

Factional fighting and suffering stress

During Cash's period of absence, when Lynch was covering for him, Lynch also went off sick due to stress in early September, saying to then President Michelle Rodgers:

As I perceive it, this Union is currently beset with seemingly intractable problems that have created an intolerable, toxic atmosphere which makes a good relationship between myself and the NEC impossible. I regard the current stance of the NEC as overbearing, harassing and bullying towards myself as an elected national officer and I am of the view that the same continued stance has caused the long-term illness of our elected General Secretary. The constant hounding of senior officers by the members of the NEC has made it impossible for the Union to be managed properly, efficiently or professionally in the way that established precedent, working arrangements, the rule book, AGM and previous NEC decisions have provided for. The stance and attitude of the NEC goes beyond their duties and responsibilities under the constitution of the Union and has had the effect of undermining the role of General Secretary itself and the individuals that have been carrying out the role. In 42 years as a trade union activist, I have never seen a union so divided as this one now – dominated by petty squabbling over matters that are not important to the mass membership. The current environment is having a detrimental effect on my health and wellbeing, as it has on the General Secretary before me. I now consider it best for me to take some time off work due to stress related ill-health created by this situation in order to recover and consider my future with the Union.[27]

The Press Association reported: 'Lynch said he believed the root cause of the troubles was the continuing refusal of some elements in the union, including within the NEC, to accept the results of the general secretary election a year ago, and their desire to have Mr Cash, and now him, removed.'[28] Later Lynch recalled what he told the NEC: 'If you don't support me, I'm not going to carry out the functions [of my office].'[29] Following Lynch's leave of absence, Steve Hedley, the Senior Assistant General Secretary, had his suspension lifted in order for him to cover for Cash. Hedley was suspended by the union's NEC on 11 April 2020 for two years after being accused of saying on social media that he would throw a party if Boris Johnson died of Covid-19, and was appealing the decision at this time.

Given not least the statement on the RMT's website that 'The "supreme government of the union", the Annual General Meeting, meets for one week in the year. So, what happens for the other 51 weeks? The union is run by the National Executive Committee ... which consists of the president, the general secretary, two assistant general secretaries and sixteen representatives',[30] the majority of NEC members charged that the NEC's constitutional role is precisely to lead the union between AGMs. These members believed the NEC should act on motions from the likes of branches, regional councils, industrial organising and advisory committees and conferences, while the general secretary and assistant general secretaries are servants of the NEC, and the NEC has the constitutional power to set its own agenda. The complication arose because the RMT rulebook states that the NEC shall 'administer the business and affairs of the Union; oversee the work of the General Secretary and the work of other officials and employees of the Union through the General Secretary' and that 'The General Secretary shall obey the instructions of the NEC.' But it also states that the general secretary has a role in managing staff and officers as per 'through the General Secretary'; 'The General Secretary shall be responsible for all the functions of that office' with assistant general secretaries 'acting under the direction of the General Secretary and the NEC'; 'The National Secretary and the Assistant National Secretary shall work under the direction of the General Secretary'; and regional organisers shall 'act under the direction of the General Secretary and the NEC'. At the core of the dispute were different conceptions of union democracy and how it should operate, with the axes being between the union being led by elected lay representatives (primarily the NEC) on the one hand, and elected but employed union officers on the other; and the friction being between a lay activist-dominated union and one where employed union officers lead on behalf of the members, as managers of resources. One of the specific aspects concerned the management of staffing. To the charge that the union was already democratic and member-led, critics in the union retorted that it was not democratic and member-led enough. By contrast, the RMT Broad Left believed: 'We are already proud to be the most democratic, fighting [and] campaigning union in the country ... Our grassroots democracy is the envy of the trade-union movement.'[31]

Intra-union factionalisation

The CFDU was formed in 1991, but imploded with the election of some of its supporters like Crow and Pat Sikorski to senior positions in the union in the mid- to late 1990s,[32] when it was seen as consequently being surplus to requirements. Subsequent attempts to refound it came to little, with the last attempt in 2018 foundering as a result not just of energies being taken up with the presidential and general secretary elections in 2018 and 2019, but also because the basis on which it tried to organise was more formalised and wide-ranging, so becoming contentious compared to earlier incarnations. Nonetheless, a loose association of far-left NEC members did exist. One indication of the traction of this tendency was that Michelle Rodgers was elected President in late 2018 – as the first woman officer to hold the post – to serve a three-year term from January 2019 to December 2021 in a clear-cut victory of 7,198 votes against Steve Shaw (4,598) on a 15 per cent turnout. Shortly afterwards, Shaw co-founded the RMT Broad Left. Rodgers's platform was based on holding union officers to account and ensuring grass-roots views were accorded primacy at the highest levels in the union. The RMT Broad Left was established on 9 November 2019 in Wigan by members of the Communist Party[33] and left-wing 'old Labour' Labour Party members and supporters. Its establishment was a response to what it saw as the growing internal strife within the union's senior echelons, where it sought to act as a counterweight to what it saw as other counterproductive left-wing elements at senior levels in the union, especially the CFDU, Rodgers and Socialist Party NEC members. Specifically, it was to support Cash. Arguments about the CFDU-influenced majority on the NEC 'selling out' members by agreeing particular deals on terms and conditions came later.

To give an indication of the depth of animosity at the time, the RMT Broad Left accused some NEC members of 'attempting to distract our union with incessant internal strife in pursuance of their own aims'.[34] Meantime, in an article in its *Newsletter* entitled (with capitalisation in the original) 'STOP THIS COUP', the RMT Broad Left, itself a faction, accused 'some ... NEC members [of] abusing their powers to pursue personal vendettas and factional agendas through destabilising attacks on RMT's nationally elected leaders ... Now an organised, self-appointed "elite" are [sic] focussed on undermining the national officers who are members elected only last year ... They promote their own sectarian interests.'[35] And, in its 8 November 2020 newsletter, the RMT Broad Left attacked the CFDU as 'sectarian', a 'clique' and an 'unprincipled faction' with a 'desire for personal advancement', and cited the Socialist Party and Alliance for Workers' Liberty as the main culprits.[36] Lynch dubbed some of them as Crow wannabees: 'Some people thought they are Bob Crow. Some people thought they could be', as well as suggesting that 'some of them take their orders from bodies outside my union'.[37]

The organising skills of the RMT Broad Left – dubbed the 'Narrow Right' by some – were comprehended and credited by its critics:

With the election of Alex Gordon, a member of the Communist Party of Britain's Executive Committee, as National President [in late 2021], the Broad Left faction ... has further consolidated its power within RMT's structures. Its favoured candidate, Mick Lynch, won the General Secretary election, and its candidate Eddie Dempsey was recently elected Assistant General Secretary. Broad Left supporters and fellow-travellers hold numerous full-time officer and staff positions in the union, and several seats on the union's rank-and-file NEC. Its existing base within the union bureaucracy gave the Broad Left a significant platform, but it is not just a bureaucratic shell. [It] has succeeded because it has organised consistently over several years ... [Oppositional] activists [have] failed to organise, and [have] often actively opposed the idea of organisation.[38]

and

The general secretary, senior assistant general secretary, president, numerous NEC members, and several regional organisers are all affiliated with the Broad Left ... Hats off to them, frankly; although they began with a pre-existing base of supporters within the bureaucracy, they have mostly won their current position of influence by out-organising their opponents in a series of elections. Those of us who oppose their political and strategic perspectives would do well to learn the lesson that we need to organise more effectively.[39]

But with the election of Lynch and then Dempsey, where Leach was then the junior of the three senior national officers, the RMT Broad Left became almost inactive from November 2021 onwards. Its main mode of public operation, its Facebook page, had no new posts from that date until well into late 2023, even though there was a smattering of activity in early 2022 on its Twitter account. There are four reasons for this inactivity. Consistent with previous experience, there was little need to be actively organised as the RMT Broad Left because its members and supporters now dominated the union in formal and actual terms through holding officer positions. For the RMT Broad Left to continue to be active in this situation would be to duplicate activities and consume additional resources of time and energy. But there was also the factor that the leading lights of the RMT Broad Left were heavily involved in preparations for winning the ballots for industrial action in the spring of

2022 and then organising the strikes from June 2022, along with deciding on responses to the actions of the government and employers. Moreover, to have used the platform of the RMT Broad Left to criticise Lynch (and Dempsey) for their handling of negotiations would have caused considerable further internal ructions. Lastly, the oppositional left amongst the likes of the CFDU did not coalesce into a more coherent force after the factional fights, so there was no need to counter an 'enemy within' in the eyes of the RMT Broad Left. For example, an initiative taken by Rodgers to establish with others a Left Platform in May 2021 came to nought, with both candidates associated with the non-Broad Left failing to secure the presidency (which Gordon won against Hoyle) and the first assistant general secretaryship (which Dempsey won against Pottage).

Conclusion

This chapter has traced Lynch's elevation to the senior levels of the RMT, involving him as a 'mover and shaker' in a period of severe internal turbulence. Though he was critical of the far-left (see also pp. 173–74), he did form a working relationship with the RMT Broad Left. This would be an important part of his election victory as General Secretary, seeing Lynch complete his rapid rise to the top of the RMT. The internal struggle showed Lynch had developed the capabilities to fulfil many of the six functions of leadership. Again, these would be put to good use as General Secretary to shape what the RMT did according to Lynch's agenda and style.

Becoming General Secretary

A year before Mick Lynch experienced his third baptism of fire at the hands of the media during the 'hot strike summer', he was elected RMT General Secretary. But there was a precursory development, when hundreds of RMT seafaring members were summarily sacked in March 2022 by P&O and replaced by cheaper, agency labour in what Lynch dubbed the 'St Patrick's Day massacre'. Notwithstanding the weakness of employment law, the RMT was left pretty powerless to exert any leverage over the employer, highlighting the critical issue of creating and wielding collective union power beyond expressing righteous anger and indignation. Fortunately for the third baptism, the potential to generate power was easier but the outcome by no means assured. So this chapter covers Lynch's election and his first year in office before the maelstrom of media attention was unleashed with the national rail strikes of 2022–23. Lynch characterised his path to becoming General Secretary as not 'by design but ... [not] an accident either. When the vacancy came up, I was asked to stand ... It wasn't by design or a career path. It was more about tackling the tasks in front of us ... and then being pushed to the fore.'[1]

The election

In late 2021 to early 2022, Lynch received 148 branch nominations compared to far, far fewer for his rivals, Steve Hedley (thirty-one), John Leach (fourteen) and Gordon Martin (thirteen). These rivals were all to the left of Lynch. Lynch's platform was effectively to be the continuity candidate to Cash, with Lynch and his supporters stressing his competence and experience in previous senior posts, making him the best qualified candidate. Indeed, his campaign slogan was 'Experience you can trust'. Leach was the then London Transport Regional Organiser and Martin an RMT Scottish Regional Officer. Come the casting of votes, Lynch was elected with 7,605 on a 19.4 per cent turnout. Hedley, Leach and Martin won 4,352, 2,944 and 1,628 votes respectively, amounting to 8,924 votes. As with Cash's first election in 2014,[2] if the left had put forward a single candidate, it is possible the outcome could have been different. This may be considered another 'accident of history', with the lesson in 2019 of a straight fight between Cash and Hoyle proving to be only a temporarily learnt one. Supported by the RMT Broad Left, including future Assistant and then Senior Assistant General Secretary, Eddie Dempsey, Lynch also had the advantage of almost being the incumbent, as in mid-2020 he became the Senior Assistant General Secretary and then in this position filled in for Cash when Cash went on sick leave. Along with being responsible for some of the biggest bargaining groups in the union, these two developments further elevated Lynch's legitimacy and profile.[3] The extent of Lynch's branch nominations, while not a guarantor of victory, nonetheless indicated he was likely to win. Intriguingly in terms of why he stood and his attitude towards union democracy, Lynch later recalled: 'In the event [of the internal turmoil caused by the

NEC], I went to the members and I won and my style of trade unionism is what governs the RMT, with the support of the members and our various conferences. They voted for me very heavily [and] against the people that opposed me.'[4]

On taking up the post on 4 May 2021, Lynch said:

> [M]y ambition ... [is] to grow the union and make sure that every worker is a member, every member is an activist, everyone is covered by an RMT agreement – and all are ready to support the union's position when it comes to engaging with the employer, up to and including industrial action. I think we are in a good position to make those transitions – but it won't be a one-off: we must constantly be able to adapt to deal with whatever is in front of us, and that means all members being informed on all of the issues in front of them.[5]

> The unions have got to make a militant stand – and use the strike weapon wherever it's appropriate.[6]

He also made it clear he would not seek the reaffiliation of the RMT to Labour:

> We will support the Labour Party when it does good things and we will be critical of it when it does bad things – but I am very concerned about its direction of travel. Clearly, it is in the interests of everyone in the working class to have a strong and powerful Labour Party, even if we don't support everything it does ... On a class basis, we need people who can defend our interests in the town halls, in the parish councils, and all the way through the regional and national assemblies, the new mayoralties and in Westminster [with] permanent principles [around] public ownership and public housing, ... the education system, the welfare state and the NHS and oppos[ing] privatisation and imperialist war. Those four or five things are permanent positions that should be on a permanent pledge card: do that, and you can build on the particulars in any period to put the detailed policies out.[7]

To RMT members, he said: 'I am personally proud that you have given me the honour of *leading this trade union from the front.'*[8] The pledge to 'lead … from the front' saw him stamp his authority on the union with 'one of his first acts as general secretary [being] to place before the National Executive a unity statement, which was endorsed unanimously by its members and by all the union's officers'.[9] Although some of the NEC members he found troublesome had, in his words, 'moved on'[10] and 'others … changed their ways',[11] the repercussions of the internal strife continued after he was elected as General Secretary.[12] Following a 2021 AGM vote to overturn an NEC ruling, the AGM was ended a day early after RMT staff members providing the AGM's administrative support walked out over concerns about their treatment by some RMT members at a 'picket' of RMT headquarters over Cash's decision to make compulsorily redundant the union's Learning Rep coordinator, Petrit Mihaj. Then from January until June 2022 there was again a 'picket' of the RMT's headquarters over this staffing matter (where Mihaj was reinstated by Lynch but then suspended and dismissed by him over allegations about his conduct in opposing the redundancy). This 'picket' comprised some ugly and violent incidents and led to the temporary closure of the headquarters.[13] Allegations were made by Mihaj and his supporters that RMT officers and staff, including Lynch and Alex Gordon but not Steve Hedley, had crossed a picket line, thus breaking the so-called 'eleventh commandment' of the union movement. On entering RMT headquarters for the first time as General Secretary, Lynch dismissed the 'picket', saying 'There is no picket line here' and referred to it as no more than a protest. While there was a continuing protest by supporters of Mihaj, there was no collective employment dispute or strike, and no picket line, unofficial or otherwise, of any union representing RMT staff members.[14] It was only after the election of the new assistant general secretaries – Dempsey and Leach[15] – as well as the preparation for the strikes in 2022 that 'peace broke out' at the top of the RMT, at least in relative terms.

Another of Lynch's initial acts as General Secretary was to commission an internal paper looking at the issues of RMT organisation and membership.[16] The paper suggested the RMT was an underperforming union with major dysfunctions in terms of membership, union density and strength as well as in the coherence of its internal organisation, where it spent more than it received in income from members, bringing into doubt the long-term future of the RMT as an independent union. Indeed, the paper pointed out that the RMT was essentially just a rail union: '86% of RMT members are working in Rail and Metro [rail services].'[17] The solution put forward was to seek to manifestly become an industrial union for all transport workers. The author of the report was Lynch himself. He argued to the NEC on 6 May 2021 that as he had just been elected on this platform, which included this diagnosis and prognosis, the union was obliged to progress this agenda. Ironically, in recognition of the NEC's sovereignty as the union's highest body in between AGMs, he asked the NEC to commission the paper from him. It may be that little progress was made on this reform agenda due to the beginning of the long-running national disputes. However, the report was not well received in branches and regions, for a number of reasons. Among them was that the RMT had always sought to be an industrial union, with former General Secretary Cash, for example, stating: 'We are at our best when we stand united and focussed as an industrial trade union',[18] and that some believed the underlying thrust was a move towards a more centralised and managerial, and less participative, form of unionism.[19] What the report did highlight, however, was how little substantive change had come out of the union's own internal structures review in 2015, the point at which Lynch became a national officer.

As General Secretary, Lynch's salary for 2022, his first full year in post, was £84,100, as he mistakenly told listeners on LBC, adding: 'I am very happy with my salary.'[20] Though his salary was actually nearly £90,000 (see p. 76), and even after his request for a 20 per cent pay reduction was accepted by the 2022 AGM, he was still very well paid. Without the reduction, and based on Cash's salary (excluding pension contributions) for his last full year (2020) of £109,542, Lynch's salary would have been well in excess of £100,000 for 2022. And although Lynch's General Secretary salary in 2022 was less than his salary as Assistant General Secretary in 2020, such salaries put him in the band of senior managers, if not quite those of company executives. All this meant that Lynch was personally protected from the ravages of the market and the deleterious diktats of government policy, unlike members of the working class.

Conclusion

Lynch showed himself to be confident in his own abilities within the RMT, especially as General Secretary. This is not to suggest he was egotistical, 'out for himself', that he put himself first and before others, or that he had always sought the position of the highest office in the union. Indeed, he stated: 'I didn't have any ambition [to become general secretary]. I was on the tools for 37 years. I was never an officer of the union ... And then Bob Crow died ... Mick Cash won the election to become general secretary ... and then he retired last year, and I was asked to stand for his position. But I never had any ambition.'[21] Almost a week later the

Guardian reported: 'Lynch had no great ambition to lead the RMT, he says. "I didn't want Bob [Crow] ... to pass on, and I didn't want Mick Cash to have to retire last year, but he did. So, we're here. I didn't become an officer in this union till I was 54. I didn't have a trade union career. I was out doing my shifts. I was on the tools for 37 years, as an electrician."'[22] Rather, it was obvious he felt that he had leadership abilities that others did not possess, and these leadership abilities were essential in order to make a critical contribution to achieving the union's bargaining objectives and running the RMT as an efficient and effective organisation. In this, the RMT Broad Left concurred, for it called on RMT activists to be 'supportive of the leadership' and to unite 'behind our elected leadership'.[23]

6

A working-class hero is made

Amongst the ranks of working-class heroes, the summer of 2022 saw a new one made in the minds of many. This chapter begins by recalling the praise Mick Lynch won in the early summer of 2022 as he broke into the mainstream media and the national consciousness. He emerged as the victor and not the vanquished. But as Chapter 7 highlights, this did not necessarily equate to the RMT winning its struggles with him at the helm. 'Soft power' did not generate 'hard power'. But before examining that, this chapter considers Lynch's communication capabilities, his self-deprecating demeanour and comparisons with Crow, Cash and Corbyn. Finally, the chapter considers whether Lynch as a working-class hero was not just a 'hero' *for* but also *of* and *from* the working class. The other criteria concerning candidature for being a working-class hero, such as charisma, consciousness and leading collective actions, are considered in the following chapters.

The one-man working-class lynch mob

In the 'summer of solidarity', as unions regained some of the moral high ground in 'broken Britain', the shock of the new was apparent on the airwaves and elsewhere. Lynch led the way in putting the case not just for pay rises during the cost-of-living crisis, but for a rebalancing of the interests of contending social classes. Lynch's media performances were praised for various qualities: quickness, deftness and wittiness;[1] a clear and understandable message;[2] being incisive and fearless,[3] clear and direct;[4] a straight-talking, no-nonsense, unflustered style;[5] straightforwardness and eloquence;[6] giving simple answers and quick-witted retorts;[7] deploying shrewd arguments;[8] being calm, plain-speaking, never verbose and never raising his voice or appearing ruffled;[9] and being frank and straightforward.[10] In a rare comment, *RMT News* observed that Lynch operated with his 'usual urbane style'.[11]

Even the *Sun's* former industrial correspondent, Mark Solomon, wrote articles for what the *Evening Standard* called the 'Tory in-house bible',[12] namely the *Spectator*, entitled 'In praise of Mick Lynch' and 'The secret of Mick Lynch's success', in which his straight and plain talking and calm composure were lauded.[13] But it was more than just how he said what he said, for there was the no small matter of what he said. So, while not all of those that praised his delivery and demeanour also praised his politics, quite a few did. Thus, he was also praised for 'speaking truth to power',[14] presenting 'a socialist perspective on current events',[15] 'articulating what millions are thinking'[16] and 'articulat[ing] in a very clear, simple way how everyone's feeling'.[17]

Communicative capabilities

Lynch showed he possessed various spoken communicative capabilities which reflected different aspects of his persona in mainstream media interviews, at rallies, in alternative media interviews as well as within the RMT.[18] The skills of composition and confident delivery are necessarily to be taken alongside the content of what was conveyed (see Inset 2). His mainstream media skills have been covered already, but it is worth stressing that even his harshest internal RMT critics acknowledged, in their own words, that he had 'done brilliantly well with the media' and 'done a good job of communicating the union's basic case in the media, and of expressing a broader, pro-worker, pro-union perspective', while admiring RMT activists pointed out, in the words of one, that he had 'not ... been seduced by the demands of celebrity' and had succeeded in 'get[ting] across the message that [the attack on rail workers' jobs and terms and conditions] ... was an attack on the public services and the RMT was not simply acting in its own naked self-interest'. Another commented: 'He speaks in the working-class language we can all understand with a touch of eloquence about it. He proves that [the] working class are not stupid.' Lynch also possessed a very good command of his brief and subject matter, which was evident when interviewed by parliamentary select committees from 2018 onwards. Indeed, in mainstream media interviews he dialled down on any of the grandstanding he was prone to elsewhere, and was much more focussed on the details of the dispute on the railways.[19]

Turning to rallies, like Crow before him, Lynch could deliver a rousing speech at public meetings or demonstrations, complete with grandstanding in terms of the language used. He tended to speak without much in the way of notes, instead having prepared 'just a framework', according to his wife,[20] and using the same or similar phrases where he sensed they worked and were appreciated. Among those he used and popularised were 'We refuse to be poor any more'

Inset 2: Lynch's lexicon of memorable turns of phrase

On Network Rail contracting out: 'We've got a structure that gives us officers in the army but no soldiers.' (*RMT News*, August 2017)

On P&O: 'Gangster capitalists should not be rewarded for their appalling employment practices; they should be punished with the full force of law.' (RMT press release, 5 May 2022)

'The world is made up of two sets of people, and it's the workers who create all the wealth in any society. They have got to get their share. Most of the problems in any society are based on unequal distribution of wealth.' (*Sunday Independent*, 26 June 2022)

'It's profit that is causing inflation ... tax is the means by which you create equality.' (*BBC Newscast*, 21 July 2022)

'Wages are chasing prices, not the other way around. If you keep wages low, more value goes into profit.' (*LBC*, 24 July 2022)

'Companies [are] living on state benefit because that's what pays for their employees' in-work benefits ... the state is subsidising companies' low pay.' (*PoliticsJOE*, 11 August 2022)

'It's legalised corruption and skimming of the public purse, and that is going on all over this society ... these so-called providers who don't provide anything, they just take over existing services and put a logo on it and skim money out of the pot and keep it for themselves, and when they can't make the appropriate skim they say you can have it back now, we don't want it.' (*PoliticsJOE*, 11 August 2022)

On the Tories: 'If Noddy was running this country it would be better than this lot.' (Liverpool dockers' picket line, 26 September 2022)

'The Tories have declared class war against us and we need to fight back.' (*Morning Star*, 3 October 2022)

'The proliferation of private agencies and contractors, often employing casual staff on zero hours contracts is rapidly dragging us back to the edge.' (RMT press release, 5 October 2022)

'We have had a summer of solidarity, now we're having an autumn of action.' (*RMT News*, November 2022)

'We are challenging the paradigm – as the posh people call it – the way society is set up and the way we are being treated.' (*Times Higher*, 30 November 2022)

'The Tories … are consistent in pursuing the needs of their class. They are famous for it and they do it every time they get into power. We need a set of politicians that are consistent in supporting the needs of working people … and you don't need to be a radical to do this.' (*Soundings*, 6 December 2022)

'This is the struggle of our life time, our generation. And if we don't succeed in freeing ourselves from these shackles, not just the anti-trade union laws that already exist but the ones they are proposing, we will go into terminal decline as a working-class movement.' (*Soundings*, 6 December 2022)

'Democracy has decayed in this country. We have left it to a professional class and that has been to our detriment.' (*Tribune*, 5 January 2023)

'Public sector workers are not on strike because they want to break the system. They're on strike because the system is broken.' (Aberdare, 21 January 2023)

'[The Tories are] about making working-class people poorer in order to maintain profit in our system ... They are deliberately trying to make people poorer.' (*Wales Online*, 22 January 2023)

'Meek compliance with this legislation is the road to oblivion for this movement. Nobody remembers those who comply with oppression. People remember the Tolpuddle Martyrs ... Chartists ... 1926, and the miners' strike. Not because they gave in, but because they fought back. That's what we have to do.' (*Novara Media*, 12 September 2023)

and 'The working class is back'. For example, at the Durham Miners' Gala on 8 July 2022 he stated: 'We are back! The working class is back ... We refuse to be meek, we refuse to be humble and we refuse to be poor any more.'[21] And at the Enough is Enough! (EiE!) London rally on 17 August 2022, he pronounced: 'We're in a class struggle ... They act in their class interests, it's time for us to act in ours ... The working class is back. We refuse to be humble. We refuse to be poor any more. We will organise every sector in our class.' Then

at the EiE! protest at Kings Cross in London on the group's
1 October 2022 'national day of action', he told assembled
protestors: 'We refuse to be poor anymore. We are going to
fight for our class. We are going to lift up our hearts ... apply
our brains. We are going to create a mass movement of work-
ing people and we're going to change this country and we're
going to win.'[22] Meanwhile at the anti-Minimum Service
Levels Bill rally at Westminster on 16 January 2023, he told
the crowd: 'The working class is back now and we are going
to fight for our rights. If we are together, if we are united, if
we build our movement for ourselves, we will be an unstop-
pable force in this country.'[23] A few days earlier, a meeting in
Wigan hosted by the local RMT branch and supported by the
local Trades Council heard Lynch tell the audience: 'This is
the fight of our generation and it is the fight of our lives and
it is the fight of our class and it is up to our class to deliver
change, to deliver a change in the way we think, a change in
the way we act and a change in what we achieve.'[24]

On 1 February 2023, the biggest single collection of
strikes since the one-day public sector pension strike of
26 November 2011 took place. It was dubbed 'walkout
Wednesday', with some 500,000 workers on strike including
a small number of RMT train driver members. At a rally on
the day in London, Lynch told the crowd: 'We are the work-
ing class, and we are back. We are here, we are demanding
change, we refuse to be bought, and we are going to win for
our people on our terms.' It did not dent Lynch's popularity
when Prime Minister Rishi Sunak argued: 'An increasing
number of [rail] union members want a deal. They are tired
of being foot soldiers in Mick Lynch's class war.'[25]

Grandstanding was an essential part of Lynch's working-
class hero persona. Pulling at emotional heartstrings, Lynch
provided psychological sustenance and satisfaction, even

though much of what he said was both counter-intuitive and counterfactual. For example, take the exclamation that 'The working class is back!' Objectively speaking, the working class never went away, being a 'class in itself' as Marx put it. Subjectively speaking, in 2022 the working class – certainly sections of it – was rekindling its role as an active collective body, or being a 'class for itself' as Marx again put it. Or take 'We refuse to be poor any more.' This was a statement of defiance not of manifest reality, as poverty continued, especially where very few pay deals met or beat the rate of inflation. Lynch was not alone in this. Crow employed the same rhetorical flourishes and the SWP did similarly, publishing a pamphlet entitled *Class Struggle is Back* when class struggle, especially by the ruling class against the working class, never went away.[26] These instances spoke to the left's frequent habit of using 'class' as a cypher for 'working class' no matter the analytical imprecision caused.

In alternative media interviews, which were generally much longer and more hospitable terrain, Lynch was at ease and willing to explain his world view at length, indicating that he was well-read and knowledgeable with a considerable grasp of history to support his arguments (see Chapter 8).

Within the RMT itself, a former NEC member observed:

> Mick picks and can play to his audience. He tailors differing messages and versions of himself. To unknowing union reps, rank-and-file members along with employers, government and media ... he's a noble, pragmatic but principled union leader troubled by an internal ultra-left faction; who as General Secretary is just fighting for his members and the wider working class. To officers, reps and activists who have to work or deal with him close up ... he lets it be known he's the conqueror of any and all left-wing groups in the union, and also any rank-and-file groups in RMT which he hasn't got control of or who may challenge him or the cronies in his orbit.

In various interviews, questions about where these skills originated provided interesting answers. Asked if he had any training, for working with the media or otherwise, for the general secretaryship or previous roles, Lynch said he had never been on a union course and that: 'There's lots of people who could be in my position, doing what I'm doing';[27] 'I don't have a method of dealing with it. I just go to the meetings, answer the questions, make the speeches, and carry on.'[28] Earlier, he stated: 'I bulldoze my way through. I don't know what I'm doing in some ways. I just keep going.'[29] Asked again a few months later, he responded: 'I ... don't know ... [I] just keep getting on with it ... going on the telly ... and it doesn't seem to be any different, and being in a room like this sometimes the room's got six people, sometimes it's got 600 – you've still got to be able to articulate [the] movement's case and our members' needs. I just carry on, but how [I] do it I don't know. I haven't done any training. I'm completely feral.'[30]

But when pressed, Lynch put his communicative capability down to emergence as a union activist in the mid-1980s rather than the cut and thrust of debate around his parents' family dining table.[31] He then added, of himself and other leaders: 'If you want to bring people together, you have to have people that can build those bridges. If you have the ability to articulate cases, you're gonna come forward as a leader if you object to exploitation.'[32]

However, he did suggest reasons behind his effectiveness: 'I think people are fed up with politicians and commentators. They don't have any knowledge of industrial relations or the way working-class people live. I think someone from the outside who has got some ability to articulate a problem destabilizes that equilibrium between lobby journalists and commentators and politicians'[33] and 'plain speaking resonates with people'.[34] Lynch developed this point: 'I think it's that bit of straight-talking and not playing the media game. Using fancy words like 'disingenuous' when what a person is doing is 'lying' ... They are hearing an authentic working-class voice talking about problems that they are seeing in their communities'.[35] This communicative effectiveness was recognised and utilised by RMT Press Officer, John Millington:

> I've always believed that in comm[unication]s, politics and life, you must find a way to your front foot, not be under siege. My assessment was we had some solid public messaging but we needed to deploy our secret weapon to deliver them. Enter stage left, Mick Lynch. I'd seen how unfazed and agile he was in interviews on other matters. So, I thought we must own our decision to strike, create a spectacle and make journalists come to us because we were the story.

> I suggested a rough-and-ready press conference outside our HQ – with Lynch fielding questions from journalists I invited. This way, people got to see an articulate, working-class union leader speak plainly, ducking no questions and clearly setting out the union's position. It was clear he was going to be in demand. So, I invited every major broadcaster to a picket line where he would be for an hour the next day.[36]

Another aspect to his ability, according to Lynch, was:

> Shouting at my brothers in various boozers around West London – that was the training. But the union movement does train you. I do meetings like this in the back of working-men's clubs, railway clubs and pubs up and down the country, and you have to face people who want answers about what's going on. So the best training you can get is from answering fairly rigorous questioning from our members – from going out, standing up and making a ten-minute presentation and then having to take criticism, genuine questions, and sometimes some fairly hostile reactions to what you have done about people's situation. So, no, I've had no training whatsoever. I would completely fail in that kind of training in the first couple of minutes. If people ask me a question I'll

answer it, and if it has got some merit I'll give them a decent answer. But if it's nonsense I'll tell them – that's what I'm used to.'[37]

Nonetheless, he told the *Irish Times*: 'I don't mind doing interviews, I find them quite stimulating ... It's interesting and it's better than not getting any coverage. You don't want to be an obscure union leader in the midst of a massive dispute.'[38] He earlier said the interviews and attention were both 'stimulating' and 'sometimes stressful'.[39]

In an editorial, the *Morning Star* concluded that: '[With his] disarming frankness ... Lynch has rewritten the ... union communications manual by the simple expedient of telling it straight, knowing his facts in detail and presenting them with compelling force and good humour. He also handed down a lesson to communicators of a Marxist disposition to keep it simple, tell it straight and stay on message to the millions of working people whose real-life experiences make them question the way Britain is run and are looking for answers to the questions which this fast-developing crisis of capitalism presents'.[40] An article published two days later added: 'Lynch has thrown a spanner into the works though. He is eminently relatable, and in deploying the judicious use of humour to go along with his impressive grasp of detail, has succeeded in maintaining public support for the kind of strike action that has been long overdue.'[41]

Deprecating demeanour

Lynch has a self-deprecating side to his persona, so his comment that 'I'm at the front of ... trying to take the fight back to the rich in our society' was a relatively rare one.[42] For some, it might have bordered on false modesty, given his attested ability to articulate. Asked: 'Do you want people to know the name, "Mick Lynch" [and] do you want to be a big public figure?', Lynch responded: 'I have some problems personally with that. I don't seek it [but] if I wasn't known to anyone, I wouldn't be doing my job properly. [The profile I have] is not for me. I know that sounds a bit over-humble.'[43] Later, he told the *Irish Independent*: 'having a high profile on social media is one thing, getting a deal in a very tough set of negotiations is an entirely different matter. I would trade any profile for a good deal for our members.'[44] Then, at the Durham Miners' Gala in 2022, one activist reported: 'I said [to him] he was a "working-class hero", but he told me we're all "working-class heroes".'[45] In 2023, he told the *Irish Independent* that the attention paid to him was 'not because of me. I'm not very picture worthy. It's because of what we're standing for, that you can organise and fight back'[46] and the *Irish Examiner*: 'The RMT has always had a bit of a profile. We've always been at the cutting edge and had a leading role in the union movement but it has gone a bit stellar recently. I'm not stellar, but [my profile has] gone into orbit really.'[47] Lynch had insisted, in an earlier article, that: 'I certainly don't want to be some kind of icon. [My] job is to deliver the most effective action and articulate our case',[48] commenting later that: 'I was a fairly obscure union official [though still] ... known in the circles of what I do and in the [rail] industry ... at least it [the publicity] helped us get our message out.'[49] Interviewed on LBC, he remarked: 'People want selfies. I don't relish that. I don't know why the people would want a selfie with me.'[50] And asked about the impact of the media attention on him by BBC *Newscast*, he avoided answering the question, saying only: 'I've got the most boring regulat[ed] life'.[51] The most he would offer when asked 'Does your toughness and steeliness come from your Irish side?' was: 'I am fairly sensitive ... I've got the same sensibilities as everyone else. I'm not a hard nut. But I do like to win the argument, and sometimes it involves a campaign that leads to industrial action.'[52] This was counterbalanced by encouraging RMT young members to get further involved so that 'old geezers like me'[53] and 'old farts like me don't have to go on forever'.[54] But overall, Lynch gave the distinct impression that as *Stiff Little Fingers* sang in 'Nobody's Hero' (1980): 'Don't wanna be nobody's hero/I don't wanna be nobody's star'.

On his new-found public recognition, he continued to demur with the likes of 'I don't want to [have a public] profile',[55] and commented approvingly that: 'My three kids think [my rise to celebrity status is] a bit peculiar like everyone else.'[56] This is not to suggest, in the way of American comedian George Burns, with his dictum of 'Sincerity – if you can fake that, you've got it made', that Lynch was insincere. Indeed, he explained, 'You've got to give a performance but it can't be a performance – you can't put on an act' – 'If you've got something to offer, you get elected.'[57] Only on a couple of occasions did he sound less modest: 'A lot of people are telling me I'm doing good'[58] and 'I'm a more popular person than many of the politicians in this room.'[59] But an hour-long interview alongside Dempsey revealed an assertive, almost arrogant aspect to Lynch, even taking into account his still being in the first flush of media success, before the going got considerably harder as the two national rail disputes ground on.[60] In this interview, Lynch was not only dominant, as would be expected of a general secretary, but also domineering, frequently talking over and interrupting Dempsey and not giving him the space to respond to questions that had been posed to both. During the interview, Lynch joked 'I'm the General Secretary so

I'm right', but there was a sense that this was not entirely a joke in Dempsey's presence. A former NEC member also recalled that in internal RMT meetings Lynch came across as a 'know it all ... always primed and ready to boast ... a person who hates losing an argument and will throw fits, go into a rage [and] storm out of meetings'.

A working-class hero inside and outside

The providence and the provenance of the appellation of 'working-class hero' given to Lynch by those outside the RMT was established earlier (see Chapter 2). As alluded to previously, a union general secretary can sometimes also be perceived to be a working-class hero by his or her own members if the parameters of their own union are transcended, playing a wider role for the union movement as a whole. For example, one branch secretary did keenly consider Lynch a working-class hero because he '[was] not scared to take anyone on in the defence of working people', 'talk[s] with a passion [and] compassion ... when challenging [others] about working-class issues' and is 'more than a spokesman for the union – he is a leader'. Another RMT branch officer took a different perspective: 'Hero status is always reserved for those who make or influence [significant and wider] changes for those they represent over the long term', suggesting that, along with other union leaders, 'being able to impose legislative changes in labour law on an incoming Labour government' would be one appropriate indication. A former NEC member believed that while Lynch was 'briefly a hero for the working class ... [where] he was forced to act in the way he did [because of government intransigence] and it did bring out the best in him', this had to be squared against the two deals he negotiated, which comprised 'wage cuts with strings' (see Chapter 7). While recognising the validity of the components that led Lynch to be labelled a working-class hero, there were also some branch secretaries and activists who were uncomfortable with the appellation for the reason outlined earlier (see p. 52).

Comparisons with Crow and Cash

Some ten years after his passing, the figure of Crow still hung heavily over the RMT – sometimes literally, for his face adorned several RMT banners created after his death. However, some detected a move to downgrade Crow's legacy in the RMT headquarters where Lynch was based.[61] But there was also continued recognition of his importance. Then RMT President, Alex Gordon, who had also previously been RMT President (2010–13) while Crow was General Secretary, told the *Morning Star*: 'In 2002 RMT elected 40-year-old Bob Crow, as our youngest-ever general secretary – a generational shift and a shift of attitude, strategy and tactics.'[62] Yet Crow was seldom called a working-class hero before his death. Of the few examples that exist, the *Sun* called him so in a derogatory way,[63] while the *Guardian* and *Mirror* did so in a complimentary way.[64] After his death on 11 March 2014, most newspapers described him so in a complimentary way – such as the *Daily Record*, *Financial Times*, *Guardian*, *Independent*, *Mirror*, *Times* and *Weekly Worker* – while the *Daily Mail* (but not the *Sun*) did so in a derogatory way. The RMT called Crow a 'radical hero' in a pictorial celebration of his life in 2019. All this highlighted the idiosyncrasy of Lynch being widely lauded as a working-class hero when alive, and that under Crow's leadership the RMT did not engage in any national or nationwide strikes even with the DOO train strikes.[65]

But away from these aspects of appellation, ironically, the *Spectator* was sharpest in observing that '[w]here Crow was defensive, Lynch is deflective', because while Crow often let his anger become visible, at most Lynch showed mild exasperation and irritation but more often bemusement (see pp. 240–41).[66] Indeed, the *Big Issue North* commented that Crow 'could often engage in fiery debate with the press'[67] while the *Guardian* noted that Crow got 'properly angry' when questioned about his socialist beliefs, salary and council housing.[68] Even when Lynch accused a *Sky News* reporter of being what the reporter characterised as a 'government mouthpiece', it was done calmly.[69] All this meant that Lynch was a harder target to hit for the right-wing-dominated media than his predecessor but one. And though Crow described himself as a 'communist/socialist',[70] Lynch insisted: 'I'm not a communist.'[71] This did not prevent the *Daily Mail* trying to argue that Lynch was potentially more militant, and thus more dangerous and persuasive than Crow:

> He looks like Bob Crow. He speaks like Bob Crow. But is it possible that Mick Lynch, the shaven-headed rail union baron who is planning to bring the country to a standstill this week, could be even more militant than the infamous 'Comrade Crow'? In a two-year period shortly before his death in 2014, Crow and his apparatchiks in the RMT staged more than 100 strike ballots. Under the leadership of Mick Lynch ... the RMT has balloted for strike action on 200 occasions. How ironic that some in the industry were quietly relieved when Lynch's election victory was announced; he was seen, at least in RMT terms, as a moderate, a 'centrist'. Even Crow, once described by the *Evening Standard* as the 'Most Hated Man in London' for spearheading guerrilla stoppages on the Tube, didn't manage to orchestrate a national rail strike.[72]

Lynch was able to lead a national strike because the RDG negotiated for the fourteen TOCs, whereas in Crow's time the Association of Train Operating Companies did not carry out this function because bargaining was conducted at franchise level.[73] Moreover, Lynch had the benefit of being able to lead the two national strikes (Network Rail, TOCs) together as the Conservative government was the ultimate employer in both cases and moved on its 'modernisation' agenda in both simultaneously.

Like Crow, Lynch was commonly called a 'firebrand',[74] as he was also capable of making rabble-rousing speeches (see pp. 95, 98–100). This was just one of the reasons, in the context of striking, as to why, since Crow's death in 2014, Lynch has been the most politically and personally targeted union leader in Britain. So, in an echo of the treatment meted out to Crow,[75] and complete with pictures of his commute, the *Evening Standard* branded Lynch a 'hypocrite' on its front page for travelling into his work at RMT headquarters on a DOO train: 'On the day before rail strike over driver-only trains, RMT boss Mick Lynch travels to work ... on driver-only train. It is an image that lays bare the sheer hypocrisy of today's crippling rail strikes. For here is Mick Lynch ... blithely riding to work on one of the very trains that his militant union claims are too dangerous for the public.'[76] Lynch replied to the *Evening Standard*: 'What choice do I have? The company chose to make it DOO many years ago, so I have no choice because that's the train which services my stop. It's like I don't particularly like Sky and Rupert Murdoch, but occasionally I have to watch the football.' *RMT News* then reported: 'Mick commutes in from his West London home on the only available rail service – which happens to be one of the 30 per cent of routes running on DOO. As he told the press: "I don't agree with the privatisation of our water [but] does that mean that as far as [editor] George Osborne and the *Evening Standard* are concerned that I'm not allowed to have a bath?'"[77] The *Evening Standard* returned to the story with the national rail strikes of 2022: 'The hard-left unionist ... was criticised for travelling to work from his home in Watford on a driver-only train, one of the very vehicles his union claimed were too dangerous for the public.'[78]

There were other similarities between Lynch and Crow over and above the passing resemblance based on baldness and not having a driving licence.[79] Like Crow, Lynch was capable of exaggeration in defiance, even though he has said: 'I don't indulge in hype.'[80] For example, Lynch asserted: 'The reason the [Tories] want to bring in more [anti-union] laws is because we're winning'[81]; 'This government, every time they lose an argument they change the law',[82] and 'All the right-wing media, all the commentators, they all hate us. Why do they hate us? Because they're scared of us.'[83] And while Lynch benefitted from Cash's ill health, Crow benefitted by Knapp dying of cancer in 2002 when the period of Knapp's office would have run to 2004.[84] Lynch is also a 'hard-nosed negotiator' like Crow.[85] Lynch has a better command of the English language than Crow, but lacks his swagger.[86]

And yet the comparisons and contrasts with Crow should not obscure the recognition that Lynch was a relatively minor figure under Crow's leadership. Because of this, Crow was not a mentor for Lynch. Rather, Cash was his mentor in terms of how to operate within the union and behind closed doors. Cash was described by Radio 4's *Profile* as having a 'remarkably low profile ... [being] relatively unknown outside the transport industry',[87] with Ian Prosser from the Office of Road and Rail characterising him as being private, modest and humble. Lynch may well have continued to be, in his own words, 'a fairly obscure union official' had it not been for the two national rail disputes.[88] But it was clear that Lynch's public performance capabilities far exceeded those of Cash. Nonetheless, Lynch did follow Cash's approach when Cash said 'we negotiate first, we seek to get deals, but if we can't, we give our members the opportunity to have their say'.[89] By contrast, Crow followed more of a membership mobilisation approach.[90] Indeed, as a seasoned negotiator, Lynch told an RMT activist of the national rail strikes: 'I'm a dealer. I like to do a deal but there's nothing to be done here. I can't be called a sell-out because I've got nothing to sell. It's that bad.' The view of one RMT branch officer chimed with this: 'He is a negotiator first, and that means he will be looking for a settlement and a deal', indicating that what a former CoE member identified (see p. 73) was still the case. Indeed, one former NEC member believed he was 'frantic' to negotiate 'a deal to get the RMT out of the dispute', only acting in the way he did because of government intransigence. And Lynch himself stated: 'My members pay their contributions to our union and employ me on their behalf to get a deal ... you don't get everything in ... negotiations and often you don't get nearly enough';[91] where his approach to a dispute was to see it, in his own words, as a 'problem solving' situation where 'negotiation is a problem [which] you've got to work at'.[92] This stemmed from Lynch's view that 'the job of the trade unions is to negotiate [rather than win] good terms and conditions'.[93] Finally, Lynch's world view was also closer to Cash's than Crow's, for there was no room for revolution as there had been with Crow.

Comparisons with Corbyn

For many years, John McDonnell, Labour MP for Hayes and Harlington, was the standard bearer for the Labour left, twice seeking unsuccessfully to stand for the leadership, in 2007 and 2010. But because he had twice failed to get on the ballot and was also wary of his health, having suffered a heart attack in 2013, McDonnell suggested to Jeremy Corbyn at a meeting of the Socialist Campaign Group of Labour MPs in June 2015 that it was Corbyn's turn to stand, following Ed Miliband's resignation after the Tories' general election victory under Cameron.[94] McDonnell's health was one of the 'accidents of history' helping explain the course of Corbynism. The other was the later regretted decision by the likes of soft-left Labour MP Margaret Beckett to ensure Corbyn gained sufficient nominations to get onto the ballot for the contest, just two minutes before the deadline for receipt of nominations closed. Beckett and others nominated Corbyn so that a full range of views were on offer; she and other Corbyn nominators did not support or vote for him come the election itself. However, what happened afterwards was not an 'accident of history', as Corbyn emerged from his three decades on the back benches as the victorious candidate at the head of a wave of renewed radicalism. For the time being, Blairite 'new' Labour policies were put back in their boxes and 'old Labour' values, as a kind of social democracy, were rebooted. Corbyn heroworshipping took off, even though Corbyn did nothing to encourage it. 'Corbynistas' greeted him with chants of 'Oh, Jeremy Corbyn' to the tune of the *White Stripes'* 2003 single 'Seven Nation Army'.[95]

Part of Corbyn's personal popularity was founded on his simple, honest, no-nonsense approach. He was not arrogant, and projected a modest manner. But it was also founded on his espousing policies that rejected market madness, being based on need and not greed. In the Labour leadership elections in 2015 and 2016, he spoke at countless mass meetings and was welcomed to them as a conquering hero. Even many years after his defenestration as Labour leader, there was still enormous goodwill towards him. Some of this is due to the savaging he took at the hands of the media and right-wing politicians in his own and other parties. But more than anything, it was based on his radical politics being seen as right for the times by many. Both compatible with and in contradiction to the Corbynistas, Corbyn was a leader to whom many looked to fight their battles when they themselves were unable to. It should also be recalled that Corbyn was elected Labour leader late in life, aged 66. Though he was not called a working-class hero and never became prime minister, where he might have effected change, he gave hope to many disgruntled and angry people, representing their radical views and aspirations on the national political stage and providing a rallying point.

It is not hard to draw comparisons between Lynch with Corbyn. Lynch became RMT General Secretary as a result of a similar series of events that can also be described as 'accidents of history'. He was 59 when elected. Had he become General Secretary a decade earlier, he would not have been able to work on the fertile ground on which he found himself. He would have no doubt been long retired. Instead, like Corbyn, Lynch found popularity for his persona and politics because he stood up for and embodied the hopes and aspirations of many at a time when workers were ever more trodden down with the cost-of-living crisis and an increasingly reactionary Tory party. These politics were firmly 'old Labour' social democracy. Inelegant as it is, Lynch is best described as an 'industrial Corbyn' for two reasons. First, with similar social democratic politics, Lynch made his name inside the industrial arena but has clearly stepped outside it into the political arena. Second, after Corbyn's demise as Labour leader, Lynch provided an antidote to fill the vacuum this created. Where Corbyn and Lynch differ is that few called Corbyn a working-class hero, and Corbyn never much stepped into the industrial arena from the political arena. He was seen as somewhat diffident and aloof, and as a supporter of what were perceived by many as minority, fringe interests. Finally, with Lynch's age there was the prospect he may only be a one-term RMT General Secretary. This would mean a span of five years, and though there are entirely different reasons for Corbyn's departure, it would make this comparable to Corbyn's five-year period as Labour leader. All this meant there was much more to the comparison than the *New Statesman*'s observation: 'Lynch's popularity on social media, particularly among younger users, is reminiscent of Jeremy Corbyn's time as Labour leader.'[96]

For the working class but no longer of the working class?

Lynch frequently asserted that he was working-class. On 28 May 2022, he stated: 'I'm working-class, extremely. I live by what I earn.'[97] On 21 June 2022, he told Richard Madeley and Piers Morgan, on *Good Morning Britain* and *Piers Morgan Uncensored* respectively, 'I'm a working-class bloke leading a trade union dispute about jobs, pay and conditions, and service' and 'I'm a working-class leader of a trade union that's in a dispute over jobs, pay and working conditions.' He followed this up with: 'I'm a working-class bloke' to James O'Brien on LBC.[98] Later on, he explained to the *BBC News* online: 'I'm a working-class bloke who's elected by the ordinary men and women of the railway to articulate their case and represent them.'[99] Such a frequent refrain led to reflections on what it was to be working-class in Britain.

The *Spectator*'s opinion, based on salary levels, was that earning slightly above the national average makes a person middle-class: 'If you want to find working-class people, don't bother looking on the railways: it has become a system run by the middle classes for the middle classes' (where 'run by' did not mean managers but workers).[100] Then the *New Statesman*, based on a weighted sample of 1,500 voters in early 2023, found that while 63 per cent believed unions represent the working class, only 37 per cent believed unions are typically led by working-class people, with 36 per cent saying union leaders are typically middle-class.[101] This is the context to considering Lynch's class position.

There is no doubt Lynch was a working-class hero *for* many members of the working class – especially as their values and aspirations were projected onto him – as well as being recognised by members of other social classes as such. Here, 'for' means he articulated and advanced the interests of the working class. But this does not also necessarily mean he was still *of* the working class. 'Of' the working class can have two meanings: first, the aforementioned sense of 'for'; second, coming from or being in the working class. Chapter 3 made clear Lynch was *from* the working class in terms of his family and childhood. This class location carried on in the 1980s, 1990s and 2000s as can be seen from Chapter 4. But having risen up through the ranks to become a highly paid union official with major managerial and organisational responsibilities does radically change the situation, as was the case with Crow.[102] This does not detract from the significance of popular perceptions of Lynch as authentically working-class and that this is a component of being a working-class hero.

Lynch was culturally working-class in some of his tastes and preferences, and emotionally working-class in his psychological attachments. But he was no longer working-class materially, socially or politically even though he stated publicly that the RMT national leadership – most obviously including himself – were 'all working railway employees'[103] and ' We've been on strike for over a year. ... We haven't had a pay rise for four years'.[104] This meant Lynch saw himself subjectively as working-class when objectively he was not. Indeed, like Bob Crow (see p. 166), Lynch often alluded to his management role: 'I won't be able to pay my staff [if the RMT's assets are sequestrated as a result of fines for defying the new anti-strike law]' and under this new anti-union law: 'I have to provide the labour to break my own strike'.[105] It is a phenomenon common to many who have experienced upward social mobility. By virtue of his role as a union general secretary, Lynch had a different social and material position in society from working-class people, and by dint of his all-consuming political beliefs that led him to become a union activist and then union officer. This is not to give succour to the political attacks on him by the likes of the *Daily Express* and *Daily Mail*, using his salary as a stick to beat him with when he argued for his members to be given pay rises. Nor is it to agree with the implications of the Trotskyist thesis of the 'trade union bureaucracy' (see pp. 214) for his conduct as a leader and negotiator.[106] Rather, it is to recognise the complexity to being perceived as a working-class hero. While it is not quite a case of 'nothing is but what is not', as Macbeth said in Shakespeare's play, people make associations by projecting onto individuals certain values and aspirations they wish to see and favour. In doing so, they ignore or downplay other components. It is in the nature of herodom that followers do exactly this.

Any robust definition of 'class' begins from examining which people own and control the means of production, distribution and exchange (PDE) and benefit accordingly. They are, as Lynch often pointed out, the ruling class. Workers are those who do not own and control, or benefit from, these means. They are thus bound to sell their labour, gaining less than its true value because they are exploited, with this exploitation providing the basis for profit. Again, as Lynch pointed out, they are then the working class. But just as importantly, workers are also those who do not have control over other workers, and do not direct their labour as managers do (especially over hiring and firing, discipline, performance appraisal, etc.). Union leaders are thus neither capitalists nor workers. However, what this does not appreciate is that as capitalism developed, capitalists themselves could no longer directly manage their operations. And, as the state developed and expanded through the likes of a welfare state, public education system and the civil service, a new group of senior administrators and professionals was created. Together they form the professional-managerial class, located in between the working and ruling classes. What differentiates them from the ruling class is that they do not own the PDE. But they are invested in those that do because they are well paid for their labour, which allows them to live a comfortable middle-class lifestyle. In other words, they are insulated from the worst workings of the market by dint of their wages, conditions and job security. What distinguishes them from the working class is that they, unlike workers, control the labour of others while also having autonomy at work from being controlled by others. This means they are powerful people, if still somewhat subservient to higher masters. And when times get hard they have more resources to fall back on, so it is not quite the case that they are 'never more than a month away from penury and destitution', as is often said of the members of the working class when they lose their jobs. Lynch's position may be seen to have some similarities with the professional-managerial class. Indeed, he stated: 'I'm now a professional trade unionist.'[107]

Along with the NEC, Lynch was responsible for leading and running the RMT between its annual conferences (see pp. 80–81). The RMT had an annual income and expenditure of tens of millions of pounds as well as investments and assets of tens of millions of pounds, and employed around a hundred staff in its thirteen offices. In conventional terms, Lynch's salary was commensurate with his role and responsibilities. In times of industrial disputes, the pressure of the job and the working hours dramatically increased. Like his predecessor, Crow, Lynch did not practise the policy of basing his salary on the average worker's wage of those he represented, or on the number of RMT members, given that other unions with much larger memberships pay their general secretaries, in both absolute and relative terms, much less. All this remains the case despite the reduction in salary of the RMT General Secretary proposed by Lynch (see p. 91).

While Lynch is a devout football fan, which is still a mass working-class pastime and pursuit, he is also well read and an avid film buff, marking him out as different from the average working-class person. This and his aforementioned social, material and political positions meant he 'doth protest too much' (as Shakespeare wrote in *Hamlet*) when he batted back the likes of Piers Morgan and Richard Madeley with 'I'm [just] a working-class bloke leading a trade union dispute.' Many union leaders overly romanticise their position as leaders of the working class in order to portray themselves as quintessentially still of the working class. This inflection speaks to a narrative of desiring authenticity and the necessary political capital to amass support for their left-wing political projects even though it stretches the point a bit too far. Lynch was no different to Crow in this.

But this workerist streak also speaks to another perspective: that working-class people are needed to represent the working class (see also pp. 172–73). At one level, this is eminently sensible. Notwithstanding the likes of Tony Benn, who relinquished his position as Viscount Stansgate, and the pioneers of socialism like Marx, Engels, Lenin and Trotsky coming from a mixture of middle-class and wealthy families, those of the ruling class cannot be relied on to do so. But at another level, it is not eminently sensible. There have been many examples of radical, left-wing Labour MPs from the working class being seduced by Westminster's trappings and, as the saying goes, 'forgetting where they came from'. They stretch from the 'Red Clydeside' MPs of the early 1920s to Neil Kinnock in the 1980s and 1990s. But they also include union leaders, albeit they inhabit a different environment. Some examples of those who were not seen to represent the class they came from are Frank Chapple (EEPTU), Eric Hammond (EEPTU), Neil Greatrex (Union of Democratic Mineworkers (UDM)), and Gavin Laird (AEEU). Working-class-ness is at best seen as being necessary but very far from sufficient to guarantee robust representation of working-class interests. The sufficient component is the commitment to working-class interests as a result of a political understanding that cannot be undone or undermined by a preference for personal aggrandisement.

Even though Lynch is liberal and progressive in his views on social issues of lifestyle and sexuality, there were limitations, as he was aware, to his appeal as a working-class hero because of his age, race and gender. For example, he emphasised: 'I am white working-class.'[108] And, despite having recently elected for the first time a woman president and a few women NEC members, the RMT was still very much a 'blokey' organisation. All its national officers and regional organisers in 2022 and 2023 bar one (Kathy Mazur) were middle-aged men. They were a good and accurate representation of the union's membership, but for Lynch as a figure with an audience well beyond the ranks of the RMT this was a limitation for some.

Conclusion

This chapter has delved more deeply into the phenomenon of Lynch as a working-class hero in terms of the skills and traits that led to this perception of him being formed. Prime amongst these were not just his communicative capabilities but also the content of what he conveyed. Recalling one of the criteria laid out in Chapter 2, this chapter also considered the precise nature of the phenomenon of Lynch as a working-class hero where the subjective situation – being seen as *for* the working class – trumped the objective one – of not being *of* the working class – thereby giving substance to the importance of the process of public perception. Though Lynch was deemed by many to be 'on the side of the Angels', the discussion here about his subjective and objective class position was not one of 'How many Angels can dance on the head of a pin?' because sociological studies are compelled to scratch beneath the surface of such situations. The practical import is that despite rising out of his class, Lynch maintained his psychological attachment to it. The context of becoming a working-class hero was also explored and illuminated by way of comparisons with Cash, Corbyn and Crow.

7

Power and participation

This chapter analyses the two national rail disputes and the undercurrents running beneath them concerning union power as well as participation by the union membership. It starts by recounting the unfolding of the disputes. From here, it then looks at the strike strategy, the nature of the strikes and the bearing of public opinion on them, the regulation of industrial action and industrial relations, and extra-workplace campaigning. Finally, it considers the issue of internal union democracy and membership participation. The problematic of turning 'power to' into 'power over' is the thread that runs through all of these.

Striking times

The first lawful ballot mandates were gained on 24 May 2022, with RMT members in Network Rail and thirteen TOCs voting, on average, by 89 per cent to strike, on a 71 per cent turnout. Only RMT members on Govia Thameslink Railway voted against striking but for IASOS, and later they did vote to strike in the reballot in November 2022. The issues were pay, jobs and conditions in both disputes, with Lynch sometimes explaining that 'pay is not our priority – actually it is at the bottom of our agenda [after] jobs and conditions'[1] because 'without jobs there can be no pay rises'.[2] In terms of pay, the RMT sought a 7–8 per cent pay rise for the year of 1 April 2022 to 31 March 2023.[3] In line with government pay policy, both sets of employers initially offered 2 per cent with an additional 1 per cent linked to productivity improvements through job losses. With formally two different disputes, negotiations took place separately with Network Rail on the one hand, and TOCs through the RDG on the other, but for most of the time the strikes in both were synchronised with each other. These ballots were preceded by RMT strike action on the likes of TransPennine Express and CrossCountry trains over DOO in 2021–22.

The campaign of strikes began in late June 2022 with serious intent. The choice of three strike days (21, 23, 25 June) across five days generated a level of disruption greater than a three-day strike alone would cause. However, despite no movement in either set of negotiations, the next strikes were not until just over a month later and only for one day, 27 July. Lynch explained the choice of date was to avoid action during the Commonwealth Games in Birmingham between 28 July and 8 August.[4] Again, with no movement from the employers, the next strikes were over a month later, being two one-day strikes (18, 20 August). Further one-day strikes were scheduled for 15 and 17 September but were cancelled after the death of Queen Elizabeth II. The next strikes were one-day strikes at the weekend in early October (1, 8 October). The 1 October strike was the first action taken when ASLEF TOC members were also striking. After this, the next strikes were planned to be nearly a month later. These were on 3, 5 and 7 November but then became rescheduled for 5, 7 and 9 November (as a result of wishing to avoid preventing Royal British Legion members travelling to London for its Poppy Day events) where only RMT TOC members would strike on 5 November but RMT Network Rail members would strike on all three days. These strikes were called off on 4 November as a result of the RMT entering, in its words, into 'intensive negotiations'. The next strikes on both Network Rail and TOCs were 13, 14, 16 and 17 December and 3, 4, 6 and 7 January 2023, representing a re-escalation of action. A small number of RMT train driver members struck on 1 and 3 February 2023 when ASLEF TOC members were also striking. The rejection of the revised offers from Network Rail and TOCs, both on 10 February 2023 (after extensive membership consultations at branch and regional levels), did not lead the RMT to immediately give notice of further strikes, this not being until 16 February 2023. Then it announced that members in Network Rail and TOCs would strike on 16 March, followed by TOC members also striking on 18 March, 30 March and 1 April. Meantime, Network Rail members would conduct an overtime ban for six weeks in maintenance and operations functions. The reason given for not striking on Budget Day, 15 March 2023, was to allow NEU members to travel to London for their mass strike demonstration, with Lynch saying in an RMT communication to members: 'We will run the national railway on 15 March to facilitate this mobilisation of our fellow striking workers and carry out our own strike action the following day. This will be a powerful message of workers' solidarity.'[5]

However, all action scheduled on Network Rail was suspended by the NEC on 7 March 2023 after the union received a revised offer. Lynch called it 'a new and improved offer',[6] compared to characterising previous ones as 'dreadful' and 'substandard'.[7] The pay offer of 5 per cent backdated to

January 2022 and 4 per cent from January 2023 was revised slightly upwards.[8] It was weighted in favour of the lower paid so that the offer, the RMT argued, equated to a 14.4 per cent increase for these workers (9.2 per cent for the highest paid) along with an additional 1.1 per cent on basic earnings and increased backpay amounting to 15.2 per cent and 10.3 per cent respectively due to moving forward a settlement date.[9] The offer was not conditional on accepting the modernising maintenance agenda, which the RMT opposed but which was already being imposed from Christmas 2022 onwards, as Lynch told LBC.[10] Finally, the offer included a 75 per cent discount for leisure travel and a pledge of no compulsory redundancies until January 2025. The *Guardian* assessed the deal as 'barely catch[ing] the coat tails of inflation … look[ing] little different from the one its NEC rejected last month, or another that failed to win a vote before Christmas … [T]he valuable perk of hugely discounted rail travel is one most … already enjoy. And with ticket offices facing wholesale closure, a promise of no compulsory redundancies until 2025 looks like just a short stay of execution.'[11]

Unlike with a previous offer – in December 2022 – which was balloted on and carried a 'reject' recommendation, this offer carried no recommendation in the ballot that ran from 9–20 March 2023. Membership meetings were not organised by the national union, as before, to discuss the offer. The offer was accepted by the 20,700 members with a 76 per cent 'yes' vote on an 86 per cent turnout. Nowhere did the RMT point out in its press releases (8, 20 March 2023) that the deal was for two years, making the headline figures look rather less compelling than would otherwise have been the case. Indeed, the RMT stated that '[the] RMT was told that Network Rail workers would only get two per cent to three per cent' without mentioning this was for a one-year offer.[12]

Yet, what the *Guardian* did not point out was that the deal was effectively a three-year deal as the last pay increase had been in 2020 because of a pay freeze in 2021. Moreover, in 2022 Lynch stated that many striking members had not had a pay rise for three years,[13] and in late January 2023 he said of the same basic deal:

> We've got a new offer this week, which is as bad as it could be. It's 5 per cent plus 4 per cent over two years, which is 9 per cent – during that period the inflation rate would have been 22 per cent, 23 per cent, so you don't have to be clever to work out that's less than half. But for that we've got to give up everything that we've negotiated, virtually all of our conditions are on the table to be butchered and many of our members say they'd rather not have a pay deal than give up those conditions.[14]

Consequently, even taking the most generous figures of 15.2 per cent and 10.3 per cent, the average yearly increase (albeit not compounded) was 5 per cent and 3.4 per cent respectively. In the BBC two-part documentary, Lynch offered a more balanced assessment: 'It's not a great deal ... They've made a couple of improvements but they're still seeking to bring in changes [the members] ... don't like ... We've taken the worst aspects of the company's proposals off the table ... We've made some advances but we're not pretending this is an overwhelming victory.'[15] Oblivious to the deal being for two years, the *Morning Star* entitled its coverage: 'RMT members accept inflation-busting deal', pronouncing that it 'include[d] an inflation-busting wage boost for the lowest paid'.[16] *Socialist Appeal* was equally oblivious.[17] Others were more balanced in their assessments.[18] And Network Rail's chief executive characterised the settlement as a 'sub-inflation deal',[19] while one of its executives believed: 'The offer was essentially the same one in the summer [of 2022] to the one settled on', adding: 'I think I heard from Eddie [Dempsey] and Mick [Lynch] an acknowledgement that it was time to move on'.[20]

The 16 and 18 March TOC strikes went ahead, but some 40–50 per cent of trains still ran.[21] Until then, as Network Rail signallers had shown, they were capable by themselves of effectively shutting down the railway system so that only 20 per cent of trains ran,[22] masking RMT's weakness amongst TOCs. In that context of less disruptive power, the RMT's susceptibility to accepting a similar deal was believed to have increased.[23] Indeed, just a few days after the Network Rail deal was accepted, the scheduled TOC strikes for 30 March and 1 April were called off after the RDG tabled a further offer. This was based around a 9 per cent pay increase over two years, weighted towards the lower paid, but with the second-year increase of 4 per cent dependent on productivity savings, negotiated on a company-by-company basis, along with a no compulsory redundancy pledge until only 31 December 2024. This same basic offer was also earlier dismissed as 'dreadful' by Lynch. During a period of internal RMT consultation on the offer, according to the RMT, the RDG then imposed a new condition in the offer, namely that the 5 per cent pay rise for the first year required the RMT to repudiate any industrial action mandate it had. Essentially, this was to ask for a 'no-strike' pledge. The RMT rejected this, undertaking another one-day strike on 13 May 2023. But all was not quite what it seemed.

The RMT was given the new RDG offer on 13 April 2023, circulating it to members the same day. Found in the main text, on the first page of the eleven-page document and not tucked away in any footnotes, one of the conditions for accepting the offer was that '… no further industrial action or legal challenges associated with this current dispute both at an industry and company level will be pursued by the RMT'.[24] A few days later, Lynch told an RMT grades conference: 'We can get the 5% then we can still go into dispute after year one. [RDG chair] Steve Montgomery is concerned we've noticed the weak wording in the proposal that will allow us to do this'.[25] But within the space of a few weeks, Lynch was stating in videos addresses to members on 26 April and 5 May 2023, respectively, that 'we would have to terminate our dispute, end all industrial action and terminate our industrial action mandate' and that what the RDG was 'requiring us to do was disarm ourselves and go into negotiations where we would have had to declare that the dispute had ceased and it was terminated and that we would have to go back to those negotiations without any leverage of having a ballot mandate. We will never do that'. Lynch made no mention of the 'no-strike' clause in his video address to members on 21 April 2023. Announcing a one-day strike on 27 April for 13 May 2023, Lynch accused the RDG of 'reneg[ing] on their original proposals and torpedo[ing] these negotiations'[26] with the suddenly discovered 'no-strike' stipulation. What then explains this *volte face*?

The distribution and then discussion of the document to RMT members cohered into a restlessness among many members against the progress of the dispute and the latest terms offered. This began to come together in the form of the 'Change Course Campaign' grouping. Recognising this, Lynch was forced to change tack and used the seeming discovery of the text on ending the industrial action as the pretext to do so given his earlier position of favouring the deal, that is, entering the specified procedure set out for settling the dispute. This was why the RDG reported it was 'blindsided'[27] by the RMT's final verdict on the offer. Indeed, the *Guardian* reported the RMT accused the RDG of '"reneging" on its proposals. The RDG said it was mystified. ... According to Mick Lynch ... a conversation clarified terms of the deal that would have stripped the union of its immediate mandate to strike while still negotiating towards a second year. That is deemed unacceptable – although rail firms question why the RMT failed to notice the wording laid out on page 1 of the offer immediately.'[28] The context of Lynch's video statements was not only the membership revolt but his pleas to members to renew the strike and industrial action mandate in case it was needed. The reballot to gain another six months' mandate for strikes and IASOS ran between 6 April and 4 May 2023. The reballot result of the RMT's 20,890 TOCs saw 91 per cent on a 69 per cent turnout vote for strikes and IASOS. The 'mystery' of the suddenly found no-strike requirement is further deepened by it also being found in the RDG offer of 19 January 2023, suggesting it had a longer genesis. Lynch was the key RMT officer negotiating this offer and the 13 April 2023 one, even if that meant that he was not fully honour-bound by the process which he was involved in and which produced the new offers. The 19 January 2023 offer consisted of sixteen pages and thrice stated the RMT would be required to cease any future industrial action over the issues at hand. In the RMT's summary of the 19 January 2023 offer, no mention was made of the no-strike requirement. Neither the *Guardian*, nor *Socialist Worker* or *Off The Rails* picked up on this component.

As before and with no sign of any movement from the RDG, the next strike after the 13 May one[29] was a single day strike on 2 June 2023.[30] Again, some 40–50 per cent of trains still ran. On the picket line at Euston station on 2 June, Lynch argued: 'We've pushed the [RDG] back on all the stuff they wanted to do: they wanted to make thousands of our people redundant; they wanted to shut every booking office in Britain, restructure our engineering workers, cut the catering service. They haven't been able to implement any of their plans ... Other people seem to have been inspired to fight back and take action in their own industries, so it has been a success and it's put trade unions back on the map in Britain.'[31] Looking back on the April document debacle, the *Observer* opined the impasse resulted from either 'duplicitous legalese in the written detail (as the union maintains) or because Lynch could not persuade a hardline union executive (as the train companies maintain)',[32] while the RDG accused the RMT – effectively Lynch – of 'negotiating in bad faith'.[33] Meantime, Lynch told *Tribune*: '[The RDG] phoned us up and said, "You need to come and see us because what you're telling your people is not what we're gonna do." They told us that we have to declare that our dispute is over to get this down payment. We said, "That's not our understanding," and I think that they suddenly realised what they had let themselves in for.'[34] On 22 June 2023, the RMT gave notice of strikes on 20, 22 and 29 July. All three went ahead. Prior to these strikes, it was estimated the average loss of wages as a result of striking amounted to, on average, £2,000.[35] Then on 11 August 2023, as a result of no revised or improved offer from the RDG and the continuation of no formal contact with the Westminster government, the RMT gave notice of two one-day Saturday strikes on 26 August and 2 September. Again, both strikes went ahead. On the day of the 26 August strike, the RMT wrote to the RDG with its proposals for ending the dispute. According to the RMT, the RDG did not even acknowledge receipt of the letter, saying instead the RDG briefed the media that it had rejected the RMT proposals without telling the RMT of this.[36] By now, twenty-five days of strike action had been taken on the TOCs (compared to the sixteen on Network Rail). With each further TOC strike, the 'soft' power media impact appeared to grow slighter. Through an RMT-led campaign some 680,000 submissions were made to the consultation against the closure of all ticket offices.[37]

All TOCs were in private ownership other than those in Scotland and Wales, where the Scottish and Welsh governments had taken the franchises over in 2022 and 2021 respectively.[38] At ScotRail in late 2022, two days of strike action led to a one-year pay deal with rises of between 7 and 9 per cent backdated to April 2022, an extension of the no-compulsory redundancy guarantee for six years and a series of payments to enhance wages on a yearly basis. In 2023, the RMT accepted an offer of a 5 per cent basic pay rise (with the lowest paid receiving up to 8 per cent) from Scotrail after negotiations which involved no industrial action.[39] Lynch commented this was a 'modest pay deal'.[40] In Wales in 2022, a one-year pay rise of between 6.6 and 9.5 per cent was won without striking. At Merseyrail, the influence of the regional (metro) mayor where the Department for Transport had no direct role to play was attributed by the RMT as the key reason why a 7 per cent pay increase for 2022 was agreed without any industrial action.[41]

Strike strategy

This extended overall course of events confounded what Lynch had hoped for, and ultimately predicted: 'We want to get in, take action, negotiate, get a deal, and get out with a clean break. We'd much rather do that than get involved in a long attritional war because you're going to get less of a deal at the end of a long dispute, frankly … So, we've got to be very nimble in our tactics. I'm not going to turn around and say, "We're out for six months without a break." I don't think the members are ready for it. So, we'll be smart in what we do.'[42] He added: 'we want to get a solution and get out of this dispute.'[43] By the turn of 2023, he admitted some members were experiencing fatigue and war-weariness: 'It's tough and they're taking some blows. They lose all their wages ... so this is a big sacrifice.'[44] Indeed, the RMT's strike strategy was predicated on limited action. Before the strikes, Lynch vowed: 'We've got a strong mandate but we'll use that responsibly'[45] and later told LBC: 'We've not been that forceful in this dispute ... we have been spreading it out to try and allow for ... our members to get some respite',[46] often saying on picket lines: 'It's a marathon, not a sprint.' For example, on *Good Morning Britain*, Lynch stated: 'We told [RMT members] it wasn't going to be a sprint, it was going to be a more long-term issue'[47] and in a Cardiff speech, 'We did a lot of broadcasts way back in the spring of last year saying this is a marathon not a sprint [and] we will not get out of this with a clean result.'[48] This was followed by setting out the strike dates prior to Christmas and New Year 2022–23: 'We've tried to miss out the services that the public will use.'[49] In effect, there were long periods of 'neither war nor peace',[50] even when no negotiations or reballoting were taking place. The RMT often had no improved offers, or rejected deals (including using reballoting as a de facto referendum to do so) but no new action was called. Just as importantly, and as lead negotiator Lynch made it clear: 'We realise that there's going to be a compromise at some stage.'[51]

Recalling that the first RMT strikes were held in late June 2022, striking at the end of the Boris Johnson Tory government (until 5 September 2022) and then during the Liz

Truss Tory government (6 September to 25 October 2022) was not the most opportune time because neither government was in much of a position to act in a satisfactory way. Division and implosion would normally signal abject weakness but in this situation, instead, it meant neither government was capable of negotiating a surrender – even if it wanted to. The Johnson government was not willing to act as it had not only gone AWOL since 5 July 2022 when Johnson announced his resignation, but was under pressure not to do anything which might tie the hands of the incoming prime minister. It was also preoccupied with factional infighting before 5 July 2022. This allowed Transport Secretary, Grant Shapps, to pursue his approach of stonewalling and 'at distance' interference in the two disputes without ever coming under much scrutiny from his superiors. The incoming Truss government would not act until it was established after 5 September and was concerned with wider issues such as the energy price crisis. After the disastrous Budget of 23 September 2022, the Truss government rapidly collapsed. In the period of the national rail disputes, there were three Secretaries of State for Transport (Shapps, Anne-Marie Trevelyan and Mark Harper) and three Ministers for Transport (Wendy Morton, Kevin Foster and Huw Merriman). Moreover, the first other big strike – by CWU's Royal Mail members – was not until late August 2022. This choice of timing has to be held alongside other factors (see, for example, p. 24) in explaining why the RMT strikes were ineffective if a quick and substantial victory was sought. Lynch recognised some of the force of this situation when he commented: 'We've got the rally of the right in the Conservative party with the[ir] leadership ... election ... which is driving that party to the right, and it will be very difficult to get a settlement this side of their selection of their leader and it may be even more difficult after they've done that.'[52]

The strategy and tactics deployed in 2022–23 broadly replicated those of previous disputes, but the key differences were the stop–start nature of the action over a much longer period of time and that, instead of some two-day strikes as in 1994, around half of the one-day strikes (in the case of both Network Rail and TOCs) were situated a day apart in order to maximise disruption, bringing more interruption to services than a simple two-day strike was likely to deliver for the same amount of sacrificed wages. This is because it takes up to half a day the following day to get the rolling stock back into the required locations. But again, this proved to be insufficient to gain the union's bargaining demands. It mattered not that the TOCs were effectively contractually indemnified against strike losses (see pp. 24, 141, 205, 208), as this was known in advance. Indeed, it merely made a stronger case for more concerted strike action and the RMT helping to organise a more generalised fightback against the government. The reason for taking these relatively limited forms of industrial action was that RMT union leaders believed members would be unwilling to take a big and quick 'hit' to their incomes given that there was no union strike pay – the issue of the unnecessary absence of strike pay is dealt with later (see pp. 207, 208, 257). The outcome of this was that no matter how well Lynch performed in advancing his members' media case, this was not enough to make up for the lack of sufficient industrial leverage. While the RMT's strikes were sufficient to gain an increase in the initial pay offer from Network Rail and TOCs from 2–3 per cent for 2022 to 9 per cent over two years (when the demand was for 7–8 per cent for 2022), they went no further, and several other components need to be factored in. Inflation rose above 10 per cent after the 7 per cent demand was made, and in both Network Rail and the TOCs the 9 per cent offer was to be self-financing through productivity savings (via job losses and changed working practices). These factors are all the more emphasised because the RMT ran the strikes in the two disputes together in the main, so RMT's relative weakness in TOCs was not revealed until March 2023, but neither did it have any obvious benefit.

School of hard knocks: 'power to' ≠ 'power over'

In some small parts of the private sector, using its leverage approach (see pp. 37, 135, 141), Unite showed it had identified one mechanism by which to translate 'power to' disrupt into 'power over' bargaining opponents (see Inset 3). And it may be thought that even some other workers in the public sector, where operations are time-sensitive and the consequences of disruption immediate and significant (such as in the fire and rescue service, NHS (doctors, nurses, ambulances) and border security), also have the ability to translate 'power to' into 'power over'. Yet that has not proven to be so in 2022–23. RMT rail strikes, certainly amongst signallers, have shown the power *to* close down most of the rail network. But that does not mean the RMT members' strikes have generated sufficient power *over* its bargaining opponents to win its bargaining demands.[53] This stresses that power should, necessarily and ultimately, be conceived as the ability of one party to inflict on another an outcome that harms and contradicts the other's interests and ideology while advancing and supporting its own. And power cannot be shown to manifestly exist until this has been achieved. How is this to be explained? There are several components.

Inset 3: Unite's leverage strategy

Under Sharon Graham's leadership, before and after being elected General Secretary in August 2021, Unite pioneered the 'leverage' campaign in Britain. From August 2021, as part of her pledge of 'back to the workplace', the number of leverage campaigns vastly increased compared to the period when Graham led the union's Organising and Leverage Department in the decade before.[a] The success rate of the post-2021 leverage campaigning was relatively high. To some extent this is explained by the ability to identify the weak points in employers' operations and apply pressure on them – be they investors and shareholders being susceptible to the financial impact of reputational and other damage, use of just-in-time production systems, or upstream buyers and downstream suppliers. But it is also explained by the combined effect of three other factors. First, the location of these employers in the private sector meant that, ultimately, they are susceptible to disruption to their profit-seeking operations. Second, the employers' operations are vulnerable to disruption which has an immediate and considerable impact. And third, Unite members, unlike members of nearly all other unions, can claim strike pay, set in 2022 at £70 per day. Even though this does not equate to full recompense for lost wages, it has been critical to the willingness to strike and to do so extensively if need be. Consequently, and taking together the impact of all these factors, both the quickest and most impressive victories on pay – and with least cost to members themselves[b] – were found in the likes of transport (air, road) and refuse collection.

By contrast, with public sector employers the ability to apply pressure on operations is more difficult, as Unite has found in the cases of Coventry City Council, University of Dundee, ambulance workers, Highlands and Islands airports and the Financial Conduct Authority among others since 2022.[c] This is all the more true where a government wishes to make a fist of 'standing up' to the unions. Moreover, other unions at best have hardship funds which are means-tested or strike funds which are inadequate in relation to the size of their memberships. By contrast, created from funds centrally as well as locally and topped up monthly, Unite's strike dispute fund began in 2012 with £25m, and by 2016 amounted to between £35m and £45m in 2021. By 2022, it still amounted to some £35m. By comparison, most unions have either created – or solicited donations to – hardship or strike funds in the few months leading up to striking, showing a lack of serious strategic planning.

a See L. McCluskey, *Always Red* (London: OR Books, 2021).
b It should be remembered that 'least cost' does not mean 'no cost' as wages have still been lost. Consequently, in cost–benefit analyses of the dispute settlements, wage rises well above the rate of inflation would be needed to leave the strikers better in off in real terms after the deduction of loss of wages, pension contributions and the like.
c See also G. Gall, 'Sharon Graham's strategy shows unions can win without the Labour Party', *Novara Media*, 29 August 2023.

First, the pandemic period of enforced public regulation had a deleterious impact on the RMT's disruptive power, and thus its bargaining power. The force of this development stands even though passenger numbers during the course of the RMT's 2022–23 national strikes fairly quickly returned to near their pre-pandemic levels. So, as people had become accustomed to the adjustments in working arrangements (via digital technologies like Zoom and Microsoft Teams to facilitate homeworking) this meant disruption to the flow of work from strikes, due to not being able to get to one's workplace, was now much less than it had been before. Put simply, for white-collar workers and professionals, working from home is now technologically much easier, more conventional and more manageable (especially by managers). Moreover, after the lifting of the pandemic restrictions in the spring of 2022, many white-collar workers did not return to full-time office working, given their demands for flexible working. This gives some basis to understanding the phenomenon that in January and March 2023, YouGov polling found that only 39 per cent and 32 per cent respectively said rail strikes were personally 'very disruptive' or 'fairly disruptive', while 56 per cent and 63 per cent found the rail strikes were personally 'not very disruptive' or 'not disruptive at all'. Then the increased public subsidy for the railways during the pandemic, amounting to over £10bn, had the effect of increasing the government's determination to gain so-called 'efficiency savings' and implement a 'modernisation' programme, both meaning fewer workers would do more work for less money in real wages. This has added to the existing trajectory set out by the McNulty and Williams reports (see p. 51).

Aside from the pandemic effects, there are two other components to consider. One is that since 2010 there has been an increase of around a third in the tonnage of goods and materials moved by rail freight, so that by 2022 nearly 75m tonnes were moved. However, this is still a small fraction of the tonnage moved by road, which has been in excess of a billion tonnes for over a decade. Figures from Eurostat indicate, for example, that in 2020 road freight accounted for 77 per cent of the total inland freight transport, followed by rail (17 per cent) and inland waterways (6 per cent). The implication for the RMT's bargaining leverage was grave. Contrary to the scare stories in the media in June 2022 about supermarket shortages, RMT's Network Rail strikes had little impact on moving food and non-food goods and materials, so that very little leverage was created here. That kind of leverage could only be created if rail freight accounted for the absolute and relative tonnage that is moved by road.

Another is that the rail minister, Huw Merriman, told the House of Commons Transport Select Committee the strikes had 'cost' the rail industry £25m a day on a weekday and £15m a day at the weekend in 'lost' revenue, and cited a study saying the 'cost' of strikes in terms of 'lost' income and revenue to the wider economy from June to December 2022 was £700m.[54] Asked at the Committee about whether the cost 'of over a billion so far ... would easily be enough money to have solved this dispute months ago', Merriman responded: 'If you look at it ... [like] that ... then absolutely, it's actually ended up costing more than would have been the case if it was just settled.'[55] Given the level of public subsidy to the rail industry and the disruption to profit-seeking businesses, this was as good an indication as any of the lengths the Conservative governments were prepared to go to in their bid to bludgeon the RMT into submission as part of the attempt in 2022 to escape the party's electoral death spiral (see below). There was political capital to be won by standing up to the RMT and political capital to be lost by not doing so. For the Tories, all this was very much a price worth paying in trying to resuscitate their electoral fortunes. Indeed, the Tories suffered no individual or collective financial loss as the money that was 'lost' or expended was not theirs. In this sense, it was a case of 'loss without limit' in their use of public resources. Lynch recognised the stratagem by identifying that the Tory government in the dispute had an 'ideological position';[56] 'They think the RMT is the biggest enemy they've got and ... they want to knock us back like they've knocked the miners back';[57] and it was pursuing an 'ideological approach'.[58]

Moreover, the traditional Thatcherite tactic of 'divide and conquer' by taking on one group of unionised workers at a time and setting one group against another – both to increase the chances of victory – had been dispensed with by these Conservative governments. With the Tories in an electoral death spiral, a desperate attempt was made to salvage their electoral fortunes following the likes of the 'Partygate' scandals of Boris Johnson and the disaster of Liz Truss's premiership. This has taken the form of seeking to engage in an almost all-out battle with the unions to create a bogeyman with which to try both to attack and undermine Labour's growing ascendance in the polls and win voters back to the Tory fold in the run-up to the next general election, scheduled for no later than 28 January 2025. But compared to the 1980s, the Tories were battling against a smaller and weaker union movement. For unions, the main element of political strikes is to try to show that the incumbent party of government is unable to govern effectively and is not in control, by highlighting it to be incompetent and weak, forcing divisions to emerge. The situation from mid-2022 onwards showed the Conservatives were willing to stand intransigently against any and all public sector workers, including nurses (for whom there is the most significant public support), aiming to set the public against strikers and their unions.[59] The strategy was to try to variously recreate a combined bogeyman, 'Public Enemy No 1' or the 'Enemy within', that it could then be seen to successfully slay.

Central to this project were the RMT, its members and General Secretary, because they could be perceived as more militant[60] and less deserving of pay rises than their counterparts elsewhere. Indeed, Lynch acknowledged that the RMT was being made an 'enemy within' when he said the Conservatives '[have] got us in their cross hairs'[61], want to 'make the RMT an enemy ... The RMT is an immediate target'[62], have 'spent the last year squandering billions of pounds on a futile war against the rail unions',[63] 'They seem to pick out the RMT as a special category where they can't negotiate on a reasonable basis',[64] and '[The new strike law] ... has been specifically designed with RMT in mind.'[65] He also acknowledged that he was being made a scapegoat: 'I'm public enemy No 1'.[66] And, after the end of the Network Rail dispute, its chief executive commented that 'the shareholder, the government, was prepared to tolerate more pain than in the previous 14 years [in terms of disruption and lost revenue].'[67] This indicated the Conservatives wished to keep the 'bogeyman' scenario going for as long as possible. One obvious instance was the insertion by the Department for Transport of DOO into TOCs' proposals in the run-up to Christmas 2022. This was against the wishes of the TOCs, but achieved its intention of torpedoing a possible deal. All this meant the RMT would have to be increasingly innovative in its strategy and tactics.

Political strikes and the pressure of public opinion

Listening to many Tory pundits and politicians made it clear they hoped a substantial and growing section of hostile public opinion would undermine RMT members' determination to continue striking. By contrast, the RMT hoped public support would sustain their members' determination to continue.

But as previously noted, with strike cancellations and conscious choice of strike dates, the RMT was also concerned about the impact of hostile public opinion. So public opinion was a contested terrain, but what was its actual significance in explaining the process and outcomes of the strikes? Was it a form of 'soft power' that could complement 'hard power' to produce 'smart power'? And, what was Lynch's role in this?

Public sector strikes are more political strikes than they are economic strikes. Where the employer is a public sector body,[68] the rationale is still to cause disruption – in this case to the provision of services – so that the strikers will hold more sway over the party of government (local, regional, national) of the day – being, essentially, the ultimate employer – to gain their bargaining demands. This rationale of causing disruption to the provision of services is intended to create the perception that it is the party of government that is unable to provide the expected services, and not being able to do so courts unpopularity. The rider to this is that any consequent unpopularity can be dispelled by acceding to the strikers' demands in order to resume normal service, especially in the run-up to elections or during bouts of its existing unpopularity. Some services are more time-sensitive than others and have a disproportionate impact (such as refuse collection compared to libraries). And even though rail strikes create wider economic disruption, two idiosyncratic features – TOCs being indemnified from strike losses[69] and the Westminster government being the final arbiter in negotiations between the RMT and both stated-owned Network Rail and the vast majority of the heavily stated-subsidised TOCs – mean that public opinion as part of a political battle may be thought to be critical, as some initially believed.[70] The rail strikes thus take on a more political than economic character and are more akin to public sector strikes. However, this rationale of the role that public opinion can play in such strike situations is based on several questionable assumptions.

The first of these is that such public opinion matters to governing parties when set against public opinion on other issues of the day, whether domestic – like the state of the economy and public services and the party of government's culpability in accounting for these – or international, such as foreign wars and the governing party's response. In other words, public opinion may see there are more pressing issues and criteria by which to judge the governing party. However, where public opinion on strikes may have some influence on the governing party is where it aligns with existing public opinion on other issues and is seen as part and parcel of an overall picture, and where the governing party's existing unpopularity experiences a tipping point due to strikes. The second is that public opinion is seldom collectivised and mobilised into a tangible and manifest force that can then apply leverage on the governing party. The most obvious way is through mass demonstrations of millions on the streets of a country's capital that are seen in France, Greece, Italy and Spain, sometimes with rioting, but not in Britain. The third is that from 2022 onwards, the Tories have actively sought confrontation with unions in order to be seen to 'hang tough' in their efforts to resuscitate their flagging electoral fortunes (see p. 138). The Tories are not wholly insensitive to public opinion but sought to remould it, not bow down to its existing state. Fourth, the ideology and material interests of the Conservatives and the capitalist ruling class which they most ably represent are best served by the continued implementation of the politics of greed and austerity, so that public opinion is not necessarily seen as an influential factor in pursuing this. And, lastly, Labour's unwillingness under Starmer's leadership to make a political 'hot potato' out of the strikes means the expected kind of attempt by the opposition to skewer the Conservatives did not happen. This resulted from a reluctance to back the strikes, especially in the context of projecting an image as the party representing the 'national interest', and not wishing to risk denting Labour's poll lead (see pp. 180–81).

That said, having significant public support does normally at least have the effect of either buoying up workers' determination to strike or helping to prevent their determination to continue with striking being undermined. There are many ways in which the mood of public opinion on strikes can be judged, from drivers honking their horns as they pass picket lines, formal messages of support and social media posts (and associated likes and comments). Though no less apparent for it, these instances are self-selected and not representative of wider populations. On this basis, it is therefore worth examining polling evidence on public support, especially where there is time series data. Because polling seeks to be representative and typically asks a series of questions so that comparisons can be made between different groups, it is more likely to be seen as authoritative and legitimate, and thus reported on by mainstream media. Potentially, this makes it more widely known of and taken into account. Typically, between 1,000 and 2,000 people are questioned per poll, with the results weighted by demographic, geographical and other characteristics so that, while not necessarily random, the polls do give a reasonably reliable snapshot of the public mood at any one point.

YouGov polling in December 2022 and January 2023 indicated that only NHS workers, ambulance staff and firefighters had majority support ('strongly support'/'somewhat support') for their strike action, while for rail workers it was 43 per cent (with 49 per cent opposing: 'somewhat oppose'/'strongly oppose') and 40 per cent (with 52 per cent opposing) respectively. In March 2023, the figures were 38 per cent supporting (with 53 per cent opposing). In three polls from early June to early July 2023, levels of support and opposition remained static with 41 per cent supporting and 52 per cent opposing. Earlier YouGov polling indicated similar ratios for rail workers: 41 per cent supporting and 47 per cent opposing in November 2022, 45 per cent supporting and 42 per cent opposing in October 2022, 41 per cent supporting and 41 per cent opposing in August 2022, 41 per cent supporting and 45 per cent opposing in late June 2022, and 37 per cent supporting and 45 per cent opposing earlier in June 2022.[71] Polling from Ipsos exhibited a broadly similar overall pattern. In June 2022, 35 per cent were in support ('tend to support'/'strongly support') while 35 per cent were in opposition ('tend to oppose'/'strongly oppose'). In September 2022, the figures were 43 per cent supporting and 31 per cent opposing, but then changed in December 2022 to 30 per cent supporting and 36 per cent opposing. Into 2023, the figures were 34 per cent supporting and 28 per cent opposing (early January), 35 per cent supporting with 39 per cent opposing (late January), 39 per cent supporting and 37 per cent opposing (February), 32 per cent supporting and 45 per cent opposing (early March), 35 per cent supporting and 40 per cent opposing (late March), 34 per cent supporting and 41 per cent opposing (April 2023) and 36 per cent supporting and 37 per cent opposing (June 2023). However, polling from Savanta, albeit over a shorter period, suggested higher levels of support: 58 per cent in support and 33 per cent opposing in July 2022, then in November 2022, 50 per cent in support with 29 per cent opposing, and in two polls in December 2022 the split was 47 per cent (support) to 34 per cent (oppose) and 45 per cent (support) to

35 per cent (oppose). Taken overall, where the YouGov and Ipsos polls are more robust longitudinally, this suggested that while there was some stability in the overall levels of support, it had fallen back after rising at first. In January 2023 Lynch recognised this, saying: 'We've taken a little bit of a dent in public opinion.'[72]

But returning to the issue of what bearing public opinion has, the comments of one RMT rep were apposite: 'In order to understand whether public support matters, we have to understand the strategy that we're following. Has public support done anything for that so far? Has Network Rail felt pushed back? Does this mean we are just going to keep doing one-day strikes, and having people waving at us on the picket line, and losing? Or are we going to ramp up, which is going to involve people starting to hate us?'[73] Such questions shone a searching light on other comments made during what seemed like the first flushes of success by the likes of Alex Gordon, RMT President: '[We've] never seen anything like [this] ... We're quite used to being unpopular because, when we take strike action, it affects people's daily lives. We've got the public on our side, as there's a growing tide of anger in this country.'[74] Indeed, Crow often used the Millwall Football Club slogan of 'No one likes us, we don't care'[75] to highlight that it was RMT members' potential power that was critical to gaining bargaining outcomes, not public opinion. And, Lynch argued: 'We don't need [Keir Starmer] particularly ... we will win or lose our dispute or get a score draw whichever way it goes on the merits of our industrial action and not much else.'[76] Although the Labour Party's role is a separate issue (see pp. 180–81), the point still holds that significant public support does normally at least either buoy up strikers' determination to strike or help avoid undermining their determination to continue with lengthy strike action.

Injunctions and the regulation of strikes

For workers in Britain, unlike in many other Western economies, there is no fundamental, positive right to strike. Workers have the right not to be sacked for up to twelve weeks during a strike but are still in breach of their employment contract by striking. Dating from the Trades Disputes Act 1906, instead, unions have immunity from prosecution for loss of business caused by strikes and industrial action where there is a 'trade dispute' over terms and conditions of employment. This is termed a 'legal privilege'. Unlike previously,[77] the RMT did not suffer a spate of applications for court injunctions – or threats to apply for them – at the hands of employers during the two national rail disputes. Employers can apply for injunctions to prevent a strike or other forms of industrial action from going ahead or to stop action that is already taking place if they can convince the judge-led court that a breach of the law on strikes and industrial action has taken place due to the union's actions, whether through negligence or otherwise. Often this does not have to constitute a breach that would have a serious and significant material impact on the employer's operations. The potential grounds are many and varied, ranging from errors in the notice of a ballot for industrial action, to the notice of the result of the ballot, to the notice of the strike itself. Failure to abide by the court judgement opens the union up to contempt of court proceedings and possible fines and claims for damages. From 2005 onwards, thirteen applications for injunctions and ten threats to apply for injunctions were made against the RMT, most from Network Rail or TOCs.[78]

From the 'hot strike summer' of 2022 onwards, very few unions experienced applications for, or threats of, injunctions from employers. On a proportionate basis, using data from 2005 onwards, there were far fewer than might have been expected given the increase in the number of ballots for industrial action undertaken and then the increase in the number of strikes. This is especially true for the RMT, given that its strikes affect transport and have an immediate and large-scale disruptive impact. The reason the RMT did not suffer injunctions in the national rail disputes was that employers and the government feared exacerbating an already fraught situation for no obvious gain and much potential loss. In particular, the Trade Union Act 2016 has paradoxically given strikes a greatly enhanced legitimacy, for their ballots have thus surpassed the raised thresholds for lawful mandates. In the case of the RMT's ballots, there was a double threshold for transport strikes, meaning not just that they had to attain a majority (50 per cent +1) of turnout, but also that the majority voting for action must constitute at least 40 per cent of all those entitled to vote (such that non-voters are effectively counted as 'no' votes).

The overall result of the first ballots for Network Rail and the fourteen TOCs[79] was 89 per cent for striking on a 71 per cent turnout, meaning the 40 per cent threshold was surpassed, with 63 per cent attained. The Network Rail ballot result was a 92 per cent vote for striking (and 96 per cent voting for IASOS) on a 73 per cent turnout, meaning the 40 per cent threshold was surpassed, with 67 per cent attained. As stipulated by the Trade Union Act 2016, the lawful mandates for taking action (strike or IASOS) only last for six months. Come the results of the reballot, announced on 16 November 2022, the overall result across Network Rail and the fourteen TOCs was, on a 70 per cent turnout, a 92 per cent vote for striking, meaning the 40 per cent threshold was surpassed, with 64 per cent attained. The Network

Rail ballot result, on a 70 per cent turnout, was a 91 per cent vote for striking (and 94 per cent voting for IASOS),[80] meaning the 40 per cent threshold was surpassed, with 64 per cent attained. After taking eight days of strikes and with meagre progress in negotiation, these reballot results were 'strikingly' good, indicating a determination to continue with the dispute to win the union's bargaining objectives.[81]

On this basis, the employers and government showed no willingness to use any arcane or obscure part of the laws governing strikes in order to try to challenge and invalidate any or all of the RMT's strike mandates via the route of injunctive relief. To do so would have looked malicious and mendacious, possibly backfiring by undermining the position of the employers and government. It may have made Lynch and the RMT even bigger 'heroes' to the wider public than they already were. By contrast, Royal Mail threatened the CWU with an injunction over its planned strike in February 2023, and the CWU then stood down the action. The difference here was that Royal Mail was unlikely to suffer any similar public and political backlash given that it is a private company which is not subsidised by the government (see pp. 34–35).[82]

But instead of pursuing injunctive relief, the Conservatives opted to legislate for minimum service level provision during the strikes. This meant employers would be able to determine how many staff and which staff were needed to run a minimum level of service. Failure of those selected to work could lead to dismissal, and failure of the union to cooperate could lead to contempt of court proceedings and hefty fines. Lynch likened the Bill's effect to 'conscription' and 'a suppression of our human rights'.[83] The intention to introduce a minimum service level provision was a long-standing Tory manifesto commitment from the 2019 general election (and the Queen's Speech shortly afterwards) and even before, in the wake of the long-drawn-out strikes on TOCs in southern England during the late 2010s (see pp. 24–25). At first, the Truss Tory government introduced into Parliament a Bill to impose a minimum service requirement during strikes and industrial action just in transport services (on 19 October 2022). This Bill was shelved as a result of the debacle of her premiership, but its offspring was introduced by the Sunak Tory government on 10 January 2023, with the extension of the minimum service requirement to also include health, education services, fire and rescue, border security and nuclear decommissioning. Along with transport services, these were exactly the same sectors that were already subject to the second (40 per cent) threshold of the Trade Union Act 2016. This indicated that, on the one hand, the Trade Union Act 2016 was not having the desired effect that the Tories sought and, on the other hand, introducing a Bill into Parliament where they had an inbuilt majority to get it passed was a more certain and desired outcome than applying for injunctions (which are not always granted[84]). Moreover, the Strikes (Minimum Service Levels) Bill 2023 was part of the attempt to resuscitate the electoral fortunes of the Conservative party by fighting the so-called union 'bogeyman' (see pp. 139–40), and was rushed through at an unseemly pace with parliamentary objections and criticisms casually swept aside.[85] The Bill became law on 20 July 2023, after the settlement of Network Rail – but not the TOCs – national rail dispute. After a period of consultation, ending on 6 October 2023, on a code of practice for issuing 'work notices', employers were able, if they so wished, to coerce workers into breaking their own strike. As the TOCs dispute dragged on, it became increasingly likely the RMT's strikes would be subject to work orders, further undermining the strikes' disruptive power. Although most unions adopted defiant poses towards the Bill, including the RMT and Lynch,[86] it was only FBU leader, Matt Wrack, who attempted to act strategically by putting 'meat on the bones' of this rhetoric of defiance.[87]

Collective bargaining and collective begging

A central problem for unions and industrial relations in Britain, which was easily exposed from the 'hot strike summer' onwards, was that there are almost no means of resolving industrial disputes which do not involve either industrial action by workers or their reluctant resignation to their fate. And there are few mechanisms by which to avoid industrial disputes in the first place. Over pay, for example, there is no sliding scale of wages or indexation of wages. The former is constituted by increasing the wages as prices rise in order to maintain the workers' purchasing power even if there is inflation.[88] Not entirely dissimilar, the latter involves linking wages to an index representing the cost of living, so that wages are automatically adjusted up or down as the index rises or falls.[89] Once there is a dispute, the purchase of conciliation, mediation and arbitration is extremely limited. That is why Lynch told the *Guardian*: 'The Bishop of Durham was on a panel [at the launch of EiE!] with me last week, saying: "I identify with the issues, but I don't think strike action is the answer." But what is the answer? Do we pray, or play tiddlywinks, or have a sponsored silence? What is there for working people to do if they're not organised? ... You don't think strikes are the answer? What is?'[90] Earlier, he argued: 'If you're not bargaining, you're begging. The British working-classes should not have to beg' and 'What else are we to do? Are we to plead? Are we to beg? ... I don't want any working-class people in this country to have to beg their employers for a decent living.'[91]

The purchase of conciliation, mediation and arbitration is extremely limited because, as with the main characteristic of industrial relations in Britain (except for the regulation of unions and industrial action), collective employment relations are largely subject to voluntarism or collective laissez-faire. This means employers are pretty much given a free hand to act as they wish, because the regulation of their behaviour is very limited. Thus, conciliation, mediation and arbitration are all voluntary. A union cannot compel an employer to enter conciliation, mediation or arbitration and any outcomes of these processes are not binding. Arbitration is the most salient of the three for ending industrial disputes because it is the process by which an independent and impartial third party – an arbitrator – makes a decision to resolve the dispute, and which the two parties (union and employer) are only morally obliged to accept.[92] It is different from conciliation and mediation, where an independent and impartial third party – a conciliator or mediator – tries to resolve the dispute through dialogue. Arbitration is well practised in many European Union member states although it is only mandatory in a few, like the Czech Republic, Denmark, Portugal and Spain. In Britain, arbitration is little used and is entirely voluntary save for the case of police officers represented by the Police Federation. On the railways, the Rail Staff National Tribunal was abolished in 1992 in the run-up to privatisation.[93] It played a role in ending the 1989 strike by awarding an increased pay offer to NUR members.[94] Arbitration is still available in the fire and rescue service, but is entirely voluntary and seldom used. This is all despite the state-funded bodies, the Advisory,

Conciliation and Arbitration Service (ACAS) and Central Arbitration Committee, being in existence since 1976 and with their predecessors existing since 1896. Only during the world wars was arbitration compulsory. So, in the ten years between 2012 and 2021, according to ACAS annual reports, just 179 requests were made to ACAS for arbitration, and of these only 125 took place as both parties needed to agree to enter arbitration freely and willingly.

For unions, the most vexed issue still remains whether arbitration is binding or not. Without being binding, arbitration is unlikely to lead to the conclusion of a dispute. But if it is binding, it is less likely to be used by either side as it potentially ties both parties into an unknown and risky outcome. This is a Catch-22 situation. So, even though unions desire ways in which to compel employers to meet their demands, especially in times of their enhanced weakness, by and large they remain highly suspicious of any nominally independent system that would in any way bind them through arbitration into a particular pay award or dispute resolution. The preferred method remains resolution by negotiation, with possible conciliation and mediation, where union members have the final say on any proposed settlement through the union's democratic processes. Yet this means the freedom to have this choice to decide potentially comes at the price of a poorer agreement where unions cannot turn 'power to' disrupt their bargaining opponents' operations into 'power over' their bargaining opponents to obtain their own demands.

Enough is enough!

If the RMT could not win its bargaining demands on its own, was there the prospect that other workers might assist? Without making the successful Saltley Gate (1972) or unsuccessful Wapping (1986–87) mass pickets the essential condition of solidarity from one group of workers to another, like nostalgia, solidarity today is unfortunately not what it used to be. As a value, solidarity has become more and more entwined with sympathy and empathy, and its actions more and more associated with social media messages of support, rather than physical activity like secondary action such as picketing or walkouts. Some of this is attributable to the legal restrictions imposed by Conservative governments from 1979 to 1997 (and which were not repealed by the Labour governments of 1997 to 2010). However, some of this deleterious change was also attributable to the decline in the presence and influence of unions, changes in their internal organisational cultures, and the loss of much class consciousness and confidence amongst workers. Though there has never been a tradition of such solidarity unofficial action – or any unofficial action undertaken since the late 1980s – in the RMT,[95] even in the union which sustained the strongest tradition of this type of action of any union, namely the CWU,[96] it has declined dramatically since the early 2000s. So, outside of the industrial arena, was there a way to win in the political arena? The issue of Labour has been touched on and will be examined more closely in Chapter 8 – as will a general strike. For the time being, the initiative to launch EiE! is considered here.

Lynch was an advocate of wider social campaigning so that union struggles based around strikes did not become isolated from wider working-class forces. He argued unions needed to broaden out their vistas and activities to include social and environmental justice movements,[97] especially because he believed that 'in order to achieve [reforms] we need people on the streets and we need mass protests ... we can make any government do that if we get enough people out'.[98] The form that this took was the initiative to launch EiE! Lynch's conception of it gave a flavour of his thinking on the matter:

> Enough is Enough! is a social movement ... a platform ... not a political party ... it won't stand in the elections ... it will plant our flag and our values in working-class communities all over this country ... then it's up to all those people that are interested to make those changes in their communities and find ways to politically organise ... [Enough is Enough! will be] a wave of campaigning and a wave of ideas, and getting people out there, not just sitting at home moaning. It's no good being alienated and pissed off – you've got to find a way to organise and effect change, so that's what that's going to be about. But it can't be mired in the traditional left-wing stuff. Yeah and it's got to be available for everybody ... [not] let's have a break away from enough is enough [as] it's not quite enough.[99]

Established by the CWU and supported by the RMT, as a result of Labour's ineffectual stance under Starmer, EiE! experienced a similar fate to the campaigns that went before it, like the People's Charter, Coalition of Resistance, People's Assembly and the likes of the TUC's various 'March for the alternative', 'A future that works', 'Britain needs a pay rise' and 'We demand better' initiatives. So not only was EiE! not a social movement but rather a campaign of sorts, it was also one created from the top and was never more than embryonic. This helps explain why EiE! was not capable of delivering any effective, even limited, leverage in a way that grass-roots social movements like Ya Basta! ('Enough is enough!') and Tute Bianche ('White Overalls') in Italy in the mid-1990s, the Indignados ('The Outraged') in Spain in 2010s and the Gilets Jaunes ('Yellow Vests') in France between 2018 and 2019 were. EiE! did not have the social weight of these social movements, testifying to the different origins and dynamics involved. Consequently, it organised local and national protests, rallies and meetings but not much more. This was despite Lynch wishing it would teach workers in their communities how to organise so that they could be empowered – or empower themselves – in these communities. For example, Lynch told a fringe meeting at the rescheduled 2022 TUC in Brighton that he wanted it to 'coach and mentor people to bring back working-class democracy'.[100]

This kind of top-down approach may have worked well for the likes of the Stop the War movement in the early 2000s,[101] given that it did not try to stop – through direct action – the organisation of war by disrupting the manufacture of weapons and associated supply lines and logistics.[102] Rather, it sought to put millions on the streets in order to influence, via mobilised public opinion, the Tony Blair-led 'new' Labour Westminster government. In this it was ultimately unsuccessful in stopping that war. EiE! and others like the TUC were not able to mobilise on anything like the same scale. And yet the model EiE! wished to emulate was the anti-poll tax movement of the late 1980s and early 1990s. It was much more than just protesting against the poll tax, but also organising direct action to disrupt the registration for, and then payment of, the poll tax in people's local communities.[103] The success of the anti-poll tax campaign hinged not just on the cost of the poll tax being quantifiable to individuals, where rich and poor paid the same in each local authority, but that the campaigns established ways to exercise local leverage based on payment being made from citizen to government and not vice versa. In other words, the poll tax required citizens' cooperation. While EiE! had the advantage of rising prices and falling incomes being quantifiable for many, it did not put forward a way by which these could be acted on through local direct action.

Lynchian notions of democracy and leadership

The rather top-down nature of EiE! may be seen to be a counterpart to Lynch's views on union democracy. In a Bennite way (see p. 10), he articulated a limited notion of indirect, representative democracy, testifying to the internal tensions before he was elected General Secretary. He emphasised the election of union officials above all else.[104] Thus:

> I do think our union is unique, I was working as an electrician this time last year. I don't think there is another union in this country who would elect someone directly from the shop floor into a leadership position such as this.[105]

> All our officers have to be from the rank and file. You have to have done your time on the tools. You can't go off and do a degree in politics and be an officer in the RMT. You have to get a job on the railway, work your way through, and get elected by your peers.[106]

> I can be got rid of by my members.[107]

> All of our officials are elected and the best thing about it is we can be chucked out. Not many unions do that and officers do lose their job in our union because they get voted out ... we are elected tribunes of the people, without being pompous.[108]

So, electing officers was for Lynch the mainstay, somewhat strangely leading him to then conclude: 'It sounds a bit pompous, but the members are sovereign in this union. They tell us what to do',[109] and 'I've got to do whatever the members tell us.'[110] Intriguingly, when Lynch recounted that there was a 'robust' internal RMT culture, his emphasis suggested he saw his role not so much as first among equals but as the actual leader, saying in an after-the-fact manner: 'I have to justify myself to the NEC' as opposed to taking his instructions from the NEC; 'My job is to run the union properly, make sure it survives and is visible';[111] 'My job is to get results for our people';[112] and of members' meetings: 'Members ... want to know that we are getting deals ... they want to know what is going on in their union'[113] and '[they want to know] ... what you have done about [their] situation'.[114] By contrast, the competing concept of democracy was one where members, albeit active members, through their branches and regions and then AGM, direct the NEC as the leading permanent body of the union (see p. 81). Here, officers would be subservient. Lynch's conception was more of a managerial and professional one,[115] with elected officers playing the primary role. Only once did Lynch allude to another democratic dynamic: 'The members ... boot ... us sometimes where we don't want to go and we're going: "Are you sure you want to do that?" and they're saying "Yes, we do." We don't have to drag our members into disputes our members are kicking us into.'[116]

The overall import here is that members' direction and control of the conduct of the national rail disputes was not much in evidence. Grass-roots activists believed most NEC members were not sufficiently in touch with their branches to take their temperature. Consultation was not synonymous with control, and strikes were scheduled and cancelled without consultation. Such control was difficult without independent horizontal organisation amongst activists and branch officials across Network Rail and TOCs. Belatedly, there was only limited evidence of this emerging in April 2023, often around the 'Change Course Campaign'. On the other hand, the national full-time officers and lay officials in the RMT, especially embodied in the position of the general secretary, did lead from the top and front as such leadership obliges. Undoubtedly, they provided leadership. But questions then arose about the nature and efficacy of that leadership, specifically how well it then interpreted and reflected the majority membership's views, how it chose to act on them and how effective the strike strategy was in gaining the union's bargaining demands.

Returning to the issue of Lynch's leadership role and the six functions of leadership, one lesser-known side to Lynch was that he saw himself as more skilled in the art of negotiation than in mobilising members (see also p. 73). This may be thought of as putting him at odds with the more militant tendency on the NEC – or at least some of its members – in as much as collective bargaining outcomes are then seen to be more dependent on negotiations than membership mobilisation. The evidence for what the balance between the two was during 2022 is not clear, but come 2023, and with strike fatigue setting in, Lynch told one of the other rail union general secretaries at the House of Commons' Transport Select Committee on 11 January 2023: 'There aren't going to be any more [RMT] strikes.' He was overruled by the NEC, who kept to a series of scheduled strikes and then set a series of new strike dates. But as the final offer from Network Rail was not substantially different from those that had been previously rejected – but did show slight improvements through negotiation – it would be reasonable to assume that Lynch did then win out against recalcitrant NEC members. So, as with Crow, even a forceful character as general secretary did not exercise unilateral influence. One of the other features of leadership is alliance or coalition building, both internally and externally. Internally, Lynch helped establish a large degree of 'political congruence'[117] where alignment occurred between the values, aspirations, expectations and desired outcomes of leaders, activists and members (though this was not part of a strategic, transformative organisational process (see pp. 209–13)). Externally, the strongest evidence came from EiE!, but this lacked alignment with the majority of other unions.

In terms of the RMT's democratic processes and culture, especially with regard to the AGM where activists and branch officials have the potential to make their mark on union policy and its implementation, RMT general secretaries can face a range of scenarios in terms of their ability to determine policy and implementation. Crow's ascendancy to the general secretaryship resulted from the formation of an insurgent grouping in which he was the dominant character.[118] This grouping then came to dominate the union's other leading positions, and Crow's force of personality, along with attending his own branch's meetings to allow him to successfully put forward motions to the AGM, were the kind of *modus operandi* by which Crow, to a large extent, personally dominated the union. Crow excelled in all six of the functions of leadership. And there is some similarity when it comes to Lynch in terms of his ascendancy, although this was more contested compared to that which Crow faced. In office, Lynch has constructed a working alliance with those around the RMT Broad Left, which has benefitted from the impact of an external unifying force – namely, the Conservative government via Network Rail and the TOCs. Lynch clearly excelled in media interviews, was forceful at public speaking to mass audiences, maintained the legacy established by Crow in terms of his critique of employers and government and political defiance of them, and previously negotiated satisfactory deals as an employed officer. Where he has come up short in negotiating is not a result of personal deficiencies but the nature of the political economy of the two rail strikes. Here, it is not as though he has been unable or unwilling to play his part in mobilising members in collective action – as Crow did before him – but that there have been limits to the force of the strategy the union has adopted and deployed. Lynch has not been publicly identified as being critical of that strategy, by either saying it has been too moderate or too radical, for in front of a hostile media he has always defaulted to the concept of a collective leadership in the union, comprising not just the senior officers and not just the NEC. Finally, in terms of the functions of leadership and in regard to strategic planning, it might have been expected that as a senior national official and then General Secretary, and knowing the battle over 'efficiency savings' and 'modernisation' was a long time coming, Lynch would have made moves to win support to establish a strike fund to sustain prolonged strike action (see also p. 257). Here, a former NEC member noted: 'If [Lynch] had ever meant to be part of launching a working-class movement, he would've had to this time address his members' reluctance to take prolonged strike action.'

Conclusion

This chapter examined the RMT's strike strategy in the two national rail disputes of 2022–23. Contrary to what many might have expected, the RMT found itself 'between a rock and a hard place', even with Lynch's leadership. Successfully meeting the challenge of turning 'power to' into 'power over' remained somewhat elusive. A more participative internal union process may have helped resolve this, for leading one's followers is not all. Sometimes, followers need far more to be leaders – or at least far more ordinary involved 'heroes' and 'heroines'. This is especially so in regard to the repertoire of available actions (see the Conclusion to this book) and the tensions between more disruptive actions and members' strike sacrifices on pay. Arguably, Lynch revealed himself to have authoritarian and autocratic aspects to his leadership (see also Chapter 6 and the Conclusion). The next chapter considers Lynch's world view, where he espoused a political philosophy where national leaders and not – contrary to what might be expected – grass-roots members play the largest role, corresponding to how he saw his role as RMT General Secretary.

8

Social democracy and socialism: reform and revolution

Media interest in Mick Lynch during the rail strikes allowed him ample opportunity to articulate his wider world view to a mass audience. This chapter looks at its components and how they related to the strikes, wider political change and the notion of a working-class hero, especially concerning Labour and a general strike. This begins with looking at his analysis of capitalism. As will become clear, Lynch was a radical reformer of a reformist, social democratic – and not revolutionary socialist – bent.

Social class and social conflict

Lynch had a class-based analysis of Britain as a capitalist society. Rather than using only non-class-specific terms such as 'workers' and 'working people' or class-inflected but rather more populist terms such as 'them and us', 'rich and poor', 'have and have-nots', '1 per cent and 99 per cent' or 'the many and the few', Lynch frequently and deliberately used the terms 'working class' and 'ruling class' (albeit the latter somewhat less). On occasions he referred to a 'class war' between the two. He did this to describe workers as a class, and the owning and governing rich and powerful elite as another class.[1] In one example, at the TUC's 'We Demand Better' rally on 18 June 2022, he accused the Conservative government of 'seeking to butcher the working class', where RMT members were locked in 'a class struggle'. The next day, on *Sky News'* 'Sophy Ridge on Sunday' programme, Lynch was asked whether the strikes amounted to 'class war'. He responded: 'There's a class aspect to everything in the economy. There are lower paid people and there are wealthy people in this society and what's wrong in this society is that there is an imbalance between the people that do the work to keep this country going, who create the wealth of our civilisation and don't get a fair share of that wealth because it's going to people who are vastly wealthy.'[2] Another example of his use of the term 'working-class' is illustrated by one of his contributions to the (rescheduled) 2022 TUC congress: 'We are the organised working-class. And we must lead the entire working-class ... We need a mass mobilisation of the working-class.'[3] It was then easy for the *Guardian* to note that: 'Lynch has a subversive conception of class, whereby those without wealth or power can pursue their interests through collective action.'[4]

Lynch also identified the processes leading to this social stratification and that the relationship between these two named classes was more often than not a zero-sum game. In other words, what one class won, the other lost and vice versa. Indeed, he commented that his perspective 'is based on a class analysis', saying in a somewhat self-deprecating style: 'Some people might say this is a Marxist analysis. It is not. It's a simple analysis'[5]; 'It may be Marxist, it may be something else, it may even be off a building site'[6] and 'Class conflict is every day. You don't have to be a Marxist to know you're experiencing it. If they're cutting your pay, taking your job, cutting your pension, your holidays, taking your sick pay in order to make more profit, you are in a class situation, whether you like it or not.'[7] Despite all this, he then stated: 'Maybe I'm some kind of Marxist but I'm not in any Marxist organisation.'[8]

Though it may seem self-evident, it is worth drawing out the implications of a class-based analysis. Consequently, Lynch did not advocate a form of sectional subclass analysis. Typically, these can take the form of industry or sector or even workplace or factory. Thus, he did not see rail workers as a case apart from other workers, as some of his very early predecessors did on the railways in terms of being an 'aristocracy of labour', where those of a skilled trade set themselves apart from the causes of unskilled or semi-skilled workers. Moreover, the values underlying his class-based analysis were more than just oppositional, for he advocated an alternative. Indeed, he commented: 'You've got to work out what you're for, as well as what you're against.'[9] Moreover, though these included the liberal notions of 'fairness', 'equality' and 'meritocracy' for all, regardless of class, the values were based on more than just these. Here, Lynch argued: 'The industrial, class politics side of it has to come back. If you don't do it, you're just a lobby group. And being a lobby group is just asking people to do things because you think they're right or moral.'[10]

Lynch's language and vocabulary were vital components to his making as a working-class hero. But having a class-based analysis of capitalism did not make Lynch a Marxist or revolutionary socialist. This may seem an odd state of affairs because it seems – outside academia – that presently pretty much only Marxists and revolutionary socialists now talk of class in a consistent, constant way. However, it only served to highlight the evisceration of social democracy as an ideology and political practice since the mid-1970s. Since then, Labour – like other European formerly social democratic parties – had ceded so much ground to neo-liberalism that it was no longer social democratic but rather liberal democratic. Other than Corbyn's interregnum of 2015–20, Labour spurned the central – indeed, quintessential – tenet of social democracy, namely using the state to intervene in the processes and outcomes of the market to ameliorate the consequences of 'free market' capitalism so that inequalities in wealth and power are significantly lessened. Social democracy used to be a vibrant 'third way' between free market capitalism (which is now better categorised as neoliberalism) and communism (sometimes referred to as 'state socialism').

The socialist scholar Hal Draper some time ago summarised the two long-standing approaches to socialism, posited as socialism 'from above' and 'from below'.[11] The former, also known as democratic socialism or social democracy, refers to a political philosophy where collectivised property is administered by an elite on behalf of, and for, the benefit of others, mainly workers. The latter conceives common ownership of property as administered by workers themselves and for their own benefit. The former approximates to reformism and the latter to revolutionism. However, revolutionists favour reforms not as ends in themselves – as reformists do – but only to generate revolutionary capacity, namely consciousness and collective action. Consequently, there is room for some ambiguity in delineating the two approaches in practice.

When examining a particular dimension of what type of class analysis Lynch espoused, some parallels with Crow are obvious. Though Crow believed there were just two social classes,[12] he defined a rich person as 'anyone earning more than £100,000',[13] while Lynch has stated:

> My view is traditional. If you don't own the means of production and are dependent on an income that you work for, you are working-class. You may be fairly affluent, you may be on £100,000 a year with a million-pound mortgage. But if you lose your £100,000 job, you're in exactly the same position as somebody with a £200,000 mortgage and a £20,000 salary. You become working-class very quickly … lots of working-class people become barristers or lecturers or teachers – and more power to their elbow, that's exactly what we need. But they are still working-class.[14]

And though Crow declared he was working-class, he also stated: 'I would be upset if 90 per cent of RMT staff didn't say I'm the best employer they have worked for',[15] and played a large role in appointing staff and directing an organisation of considerable human and financial resources. In Lynch's class-based analysis, there was no room for the professional-managerial class and the likes of union officers (see Chapter 6). Here, Lynch did not take account of the resources that high-earning individuals built up and through which they could insulate themselves from the ravages of the market and the deleterious diktats of government policy, unlike members of the working class (see also p. 13).

Militant revolutionary or pragmatic reformist?

Much of the right-wing media sought to paint Lynch as a dangerous militant Marxist revolutionary, making good on the RMT's rule book aim (Object 4b) of 'the supersession of the capitalist system by a socialistic order of society'. He is not. Instead, he is a pragmatic and social democratic reformist. Lynch defined his socialism as being where 'the fundamental of socialism [is] the abolition of poverty',[16] as opposed to socialism quintessentially comprising the self-emancipation of the working class, the abolition of capitalism and the remaking of society by the working class in its own image and for its own benefit. Later on, when defining socialism as 'the elimination of poverty', he argued this would be achieved 'through pragmatic reforms to our system' rather than via an 'ideology-based party'.[17] Lynch was not ignorant of the issue of self-emancipation, for at a London and Anglia region event in early 2019 for organising subcontracted caterers and cleaners, he argued that the 'emancipation of sub-contracted workers must be the act of the workers themselves using the structures and resources of the whole union',[18] and then advocated at the 2019 AGM that these workers occupy the offices of the clients that subcontract such work, such as Virgin, Siemens and Hitachi.[19] At a TUC rally on 2 November 2022, he also declared: 'Our emancipation is in our hands! Our emancipation is in our organisation! So, let's commit ourselves to struggle!'

The abolition of poverty was to be achieved not through direct workers' control[20] based on workers' councils like soviets, but primarily through the indirect representation of parliamentary democracy guiding state action and using the 'tax and spend' method above all else. This was the sense of what Lynch meant when he declared at the RMT 2018 AGM: 'If you don't have democratic control of the creation of wealth, the creation of money, you will not achieve a socialist system of society [where the] democratic control of the economy [was] what we've been aiming for since the start of trade unions.'[21] After being elected General Secretary, he insisted: 'I am not a centrist. In my community, I am regarded as a radical and a leftist, but of course these things are relative. What I am, though, is in the mainstream of where our members are.'[22]

The interest in Lynch from May 2022 onwards allowed him to articulate his views at much greater length:

I am a socialist [with] a set of principles based on traditional Labour values. I am left-wing but I am not affiliated to any group. I don't take orders from [any] particular group ... I want a fairer and more equal society.[23]

For me socialism is not ideological, it's organic ... [and] practical whether that be through the unions, Labour Party or cooperatives ... I'm not a Leninist, Trotskyist, Stalinist or anarchist ... I am a reformist ... I don't particularly want a revolution that destroys the important structures of our community [and society]. I believe in labour movement values ... [to] organise and educate [people] and move them on through continual reform ... I believe we do need the state. I don't want to tear it down. I want to change it ... [capitalism can be made better] though regulation ... progressive taxation is the greatest equaliser ... tax is a good progressive thing.[24]

I'm more pragmatic. I'm a reformist and I'm not a revolutionary ... I am an assertive democratic socialist reformist ... the Labour Party has gone so far away from that idea, the concept of assertive constant reform and improvement, that they can't understand it that a reformist democratic socialist may use the strike weapon and the strike strategy and industrial disputes to get to a position where we change society.[25]

Progressive tax ... is the best form of equality you'll get.[26]

I'm a pragmatist. I'm from a socialist background. The sort of things I want are traditional labour values. I'd like to see a decent Labour government that builds houses and has public ownership. I'm not a communist. I'm not even affiliated to an ideology ... I'm not a member of the Labour Party or any other political party and I'm not joining one.[27]

So, Lynch's conception of socialism was not entirely statist as many social democratic conceptions are, for it involved – as both means and ends – cooperatives, unions, Labour, tenants' organisations and community organisations where the emphasis was on self-reliance. Indeed, he argued:

> It's something we've got to rebuild that we do it for ourselves and make alternative models and we've got to do things like go back to the concept of public ownership itself – the community owning assets and industries and the distribution of the goods that they produce and the energy that's produced ... things like that [are] good in and of itself, not just as an alternative to capitalism, but is a better model for people to exist within ... the original socialist Labour socialism ... [is] that [resources] ... stay in the community and when you've used it and finished and died you pass it over, you pass it back to the community, back to the council under democratic control and they give it to another worker.[28]

Nonetheless, and often describing his politics as 'old Labour',[29] he earlier explained he was 'straightforward old Labour' which meant supporting 'tax and spend legislation ... to redistribute the wealth in the economy'[30] and that 'tax is the means by which you create equality'.[31] Lynch then frequently put forward the likes of: 'You don't have to be a social scientist to go to Scandinavia, the Netherlands or Germany and say "this country looks a bit less shitty than our one"'[32] and 'The Swedish, German, European model, social democratic model if you want to call it that – I think that's a really good thing.'[33] What Lynch admired here was the more equitable regulation of the relationship between capital and labour by the state under capitalism. Lynch logically then also extolled the post-war social democratic settlement in Britain and the figures of Nye Bevin, Clement Attlee and Harold Wilson, saying:

> I'm nostalgic for the power and control and values we had [back then] and for the balance we created.[34]

I think Harold Wilson was a bit of a hero, looking back.[35]

Wilson was a progressive prime minister. He wasn't from the ultra-left, but he brought in legislation about sex discrimination, race discrimination, and health and safety at work, that is still on the statute book today. Attlee's greatest achievements – on education, the welfare state ... [etc.] – are still there and have never been removed – though they've been attacked and chipped away at. Neither of these men was left-wing, but the party was left-wing, the activists were left-wing, the unions were militant and the people were demanding change.[36]

Our forebears delivered a fundamental change in favour of working people, a fundamental redistribution of wealth, and not just money, but the material wealth of our society, including knowledge and civilisation itself via education and health care.[37]

If Harold Wilson could [talk in class terms], if Jim Callaghan could [also] do that, and they used to call each other 'comrade' [and] talk about our 'movement'. They used to use that word 'socialism' all of the time. Clement Attlee did it ... even the most right-wing people in former Labour periods said they were socialists ... Every Labour administration that we've had has disappointed its base as socialist base [but] even these compromised administrations achieved some things. The Wilson administration, and of course the Attlee administration ... all achieved a tremendous amount. Some of the established pillars of our society come from that administration ... if the working class is to get better off to some extent the ruling class has got to be worse off, that's what Attlee believed in by taxing them in the right way.[38]

People forget how right-wing people like Harold Wilson, Jim Callaghan and Clement Attlee were, but they achieved profound things because they were bold.[39]

With portent for the RMT's political strategy (see below), he suggested Labour should return to 'what used to be called

"Old Labour": you believed in some fairly traditional values, communitarian values, but you also weren't ashamed of being patriotic because I don't think there's anything wrong with that',[40] and Labour being radical 'does not mean being ultra-left – [Clement] Atlee was a radical but not from the left of the party. [Harold] Wilson was a radical but not from the left of the party ... we need a traditional socialist agenda about the redistribution of wealth.'[41]

All this served to delimit the extent to which Lynch was radical, with the *Jacobin* underlining this: 'Yet nothing Lynch asks for is radical. If anything, he reflects the mainstream popular outlook [over, for example, renationalisation].'[42] Consequently, and like Corbyn, Lynch is best characterised as a social democrat because he advocates reforming capitalism rather than abolishing it, using the state, directed by Labour when in office, to ameliorate the consequences of free market capitalism. According to Lynch, unions, affiliated and not, are key mechanisms by which to transmit workers' wishes into Labour.

For Lynch, there is another part of the puzzle that led him to social democratic politics. This was his belief that communism was a dangerous dead end for workers. In an exchange with Senior Assistant General Secretary and Communist Party member Eddie Dempsey for *PoliticsJOE*, recounting the gulags, mass executions and mass famines, Lynch argued that the problem with communism was that there were 'too many dead Russians' – an inversion of the popular phrase 'What can we learn from dead Russians?' such as Lenin, Trotsky and Stalin. Thus, he stated: 'I think the dead Russians killed too many Russians.'[43] In another interview he made clear he favoured the politics of Julius Martov – one of the leaders along with Lenin of the Russian Social Democratic Labour Party and then after the 1903 party congress, the leader of the Mensheviks – over those of Lenin and the Bolsheviks.[44] He also told the *Guardian*: 'I condemned the Soviet Union; I thought it was a murderous death cult. I never played with any of the symbolism of red stars and hammers and sickles. All oppressive regimes, without exception, are oppressive of workers and peasants.'[45]

Workerism not wokeism

For a former student of the LSE, which was set up by Beatrice and Sidney Webb, key propagators of the Fabian form of social democracy as well as being from wealthy backgrounds, there was a noticeable workerist streak in Lynch:

> We've got to develop socialist ideas that a trade union idea is not delivered by academics and ideologues from outside the movement ... but [they] come from within ... some of them come from the Methodist Church ... from Catholic social thinking ... from Baptist thinking ... from secular thinking within the working class but they're not delivered by vanguard politicians which is what we've had a lot of problems with, which ... just leads to sectarianism. It's got to be working-class struggle and working-class ideas that bring the movement forward.[46]

Another part of this was:

> What we can't allow is people who are parachuted into our communities to try to say you need to do this, you need to buy this paper, you need to follow this narrow sectarian line and somehow that will change society, because the lesson is that will never work.[47]

This perspective also led Lynch to bemoan the lack of working-class MPs, especially in Labour: 'Working-class people cannot relate to [Labour's front bench] ... [in part because they have] never actually worked in any of these industries. They come out of PR and law, communications, finance or whatever. They've never worked in a factory or in a supply centre.'[48] But he also lamented that even non-Labour MPs and those 'running the country' were not from businesses (where they would have been senior managers and chief executives) but instead from public relations, accountancy, finance and communications.[49] Later, at the fourth Eric Heffer Memorial Lecture in Liverpool on 6 October 2022, Lynch commented: 'I think people are desperate for leadership, leadership from within our class, not leadership from on high ... we have to have working-class people from our working-class communities representing us.' As highlighted before (see pp. 118–19), working-classness at best can be seen as necessary but not sufficient in itself for radicalism.

Disdain for the far-left

Unlike his predecessor, Bob Crow, and though Lynch had experienced an internal baptism of fire (see pp. 82–83), it is clear that his disdain for what he called 'the traditional ideological left'[50] was not just reserved for far-left activists in the RMT. This was part and parcel of his anti-intellectual workerism. According to one branch officer, Lynch made 'no secret of his contempt for the organised far-left, although he has obviously been able to overcome this contempt to a sufficient degree to run the union in alliance with the Communist Party and its fellow travellers'. For the far-left outside the RMT, Lynch derided and disparaged 'boring left-wing activists with a plastic bag ... stuffed full of papers', stating: 'I've always stood out against the people that just want to say you're either in this group or you're nothing.'[51] He was more forthright in a Cardiff speech: 'You're not going to get this struggle from a pamphlet or from a theoretical class. It's got to be about what we do amongst our own people in the pub, at the football ... the problem with the theoretical people ... people that sell a lot of newspapers outside meetings and people ... selling people a pamphlet or organising a meeting of the ideologically pure is not going to cause a turnaround ... [instead] working-class people educate each other all of the time.'[52] In a prediction concerning the response to the deals he sought to negotiate to end the two national rail strikes, Lynch lambasted the far-left: 'What I'm sick of is the critics who keep saying you didn't get every-thing you asked for or demanded in that strike. Well, no shit ... yeah that's how it goes ... and there'll be all sorts of people in newspapers on the left waiting to pounce on, you know, mistakes we've made.'[53] *Socialist Worker* would no doubt have been one of these, according to Lynch, after it variously argued the RMT leadership was 'desperate to throw in the towel after doggedly pursuing a strategy of lim-ited action doomed to failure from the start'; 'RMT leaders [pursued a] failed strategy'; 'the '[RMT] leaders' strategy of one of two days of strikes – punctuated by long pauses in action – has failed'; and 'The strategy of short periods of action – punctuated with long gaps between strikes – has failed to break the Tory government and rail bosses'.[54]

Labour – an unrequited labour of love?

Recalling that Labour prime ministers and ministers such as Harold Wilson and Dennis Healey were, according to Lynch, 'quite important and dynamic people in our society, and there seemed to be more balance in society [then], things seemed to be progressing, in spite of all the problems'[55] is key for understanding his diagnosis of the Labour Party today. Frequently, he argued Labour needed to shift to the social democratic left to connect with working-class voters. Among his frequent forays on this topic were:

> If we just get this bland democratic party sitting in the centre of politics and not actually getting behind workers' struggles, you have to ask yourself, why do they call themselves the Labour Party?[56]

> [Labour] must be more radical. It should ride what is going to be a massive strike wave and a set of campaigns that are going to change the country. Sir Keir Starmer needs to identify his party with working people who can then have their say at a general election and remove the current Conservatives for something much more progressive.[57]

> Starmer has got to find a way to identify with everyday working-class people's problems and if [he] can't do that he's gonna fail and that's what I fear ... if he wants to win an election [then] ... he's got to find a way back to working-class people. At the minute, he's not able to do it and that's a shame because we need him to win ... We want to kick the Labour Party into a position where they have to follow Enough is Enough![58]

> In fact, [Labour] could be another version of the Conservative Party ... They're not saying anything about anything.[59]

> I just want [Labour] to be effective and reflect what working-class people need, and if they don't do that, they won't get the chance because they won't get voted for. We need a Labour Party, and we need a Labour Party to win but that doesn't mean we should be shackled to it and just a bit like some kind of lapdog while they set the policies, and we just immediately give them money.[60]

> I just wish that the people that are meant to be representing us were as bold and radical as [the Tories] ... [This government] is all about redistribution of wealth, unfortunately it's

going the wrong way ... If Starmer can't understand that, he needs to wake up and get another job! We have to tell the Labour Party, you have to put your shoulder to our wheel as working-class people, and if you can do that we will support you, and if you can't you need to get out the way, and let someone else who can.[61]

I want the Labour Party to win the next election because it's in the class interests of our people to have a Labour government.[62]

Labour needs to support people in their struggle, they need to identify with their values that are socialist, that founded the Labour Party. They need to identify with the actual struggles that are going on today.[63]

The Labour Party has to sort out its own agenda. But Keir Starmer and the leadership will have to show that they identify with this growing movement for change and that they understand our demands.[64]

We need on the front page of the next Labour manifesto, one word: redistribution. Redistribution is the fundamental of what Keir Hardie believed in, it's the fundamental of what Nye Bevan believed in. It's the fundamental of what Jeremy Corbyn believed in. It ought to be what Keir Starmer stands up for and believes in, because it doesn't matter if you're from the left of the party, the middle of the party, the right of the party, or our movement, you must believe in fundamental change in favour of working-class people.[65]

It is fully clear that it is in our class interest and the direct interests of our members to get rid of this Tory government and replace it with a Labour government.[66]

[Starmer] needs to deliver for working people – that's his job and he needs to show that he is going to get on with it.[67]

[Starmer's] got to show that he's on the side of working people and progressive politics, and I don't think we're seeing that.[68]

When it came to strategising about how to achieve political change, Lynch fell back on generalities of 'fight back', 'rise up', 'mobilise', 'build up' and 'broaden out' the struggle.[69] Thus, he asserted: 'We need an uprising. We need a whole wave of synchronised, coordinated action.'[70] In various interviews, he argued:

We're going to have to respond in kind. But this will need a union-wide response. It needs the Labour Party, because they are the movement. We're going to need the support of the community and the whole of Britain's public opinion. It's got to be bigger than my trade union, because we're not able to do this on our own.[71]

[What] we've got to do out there – including in social-media land – is not only ask how we are going to respond as the working class, but, beyond that, how we are going to respond as a country, a population, that is interested in civil liberties and human rights. We will be calling on the TUC next week to get a campaign going. The actions that we are already seeing rising up in the communities has got to be built on. We've got to get people on the streets, we've got to get people taking community action, including collective action that we maybe haven't even thought of yet, in all sorts of ways – traditional demonstrations, but also all sorts of other direct action if we can get it going, coupled to industrial action, on a rolling, synchronised, co-ordinated basis.[72]

Though he then went on to say 'But I can't have all the answers and the RMT can't have all the answers',[73] he then continued: 'I am fairly tired of campaigns, or small political entities, that say "let's form this pure group, let's identify our favourite lefty, or our favourite issue, and pursue that until the nth degree". It has got to be a broad brush – like the five demands of Enough is Enough! and the People's Assembly demands, which are roughly the same – and we've got [to] allow everyone to identify behind them ... We've got to find a few banners that we can all get behind, and make concrete demands.'[74]

Most often, Lynch came out with platitudes devoid of much in the way of strategy, such as: 'The only way we can fight back is to make sure this is a movement for change';[75] 'We will fight the government in parliament, in the workplace and in the streets';[76] 'We're fighting for terms and conditions for ourselves but also for everyone else';[77] and 'If we are united, this movement and our class is unstoppable.'[78] Whatever the failings of his political imagination, allied to the RMT's disproportionate but still small political weight, Crow did try to advance a new strategy for the working class, beginning with the RMT holding a series of 'crisis of working-class representation' conferences which led to the formation of the National Shop Stewards' Network, TUSC and No2EU.[79] These were more sustained and specific initiatives than EiE!, which launched itself with many very well attended rallies in mid-2022 but then did little more than hold small numbers of infrequent protests in different towns and cities. This was no more than the People's Assembly was able to achieve, and which duplicated its efforts. Moving into 2023, EiE! became inactive nationally with the exception of its social media accounts. The *Morning Star* characterised it as having 'stalled for want of a discernible strategy'.[80] This meant Lynch's intention to 'continue to build the broadest possible alliances'[81] and wish to see unions make themselves into 'an independent working-class movement'[82] were no more than wishful thinking.

As already alluded to, for Lynch the point of extra-parliamentary campaigning was to pressurise Labour into action by, as he often put it, 'poking, prodding and pushing':

And the key demand, to put it plainly, is that we've got to move this Labour Party into a position where they identify openly, overtly, consistently, loudly ... with the struggles that all of us, and our friends, work colleagues, neighbours and family, are experiencing. And that might sound very old fashioned – we've got to make the Labour Party move. But we've got to kick them to our position. All these campaigns have got to coalesce around the idea that we need an opposition, and that opposition is the same stuff that it used to be – the trade unions have got to be oppositional, and so have the Labour Party politicians, and politicians from other parties if they want to get on board.[83]

Lynch continued:

I don't expect people like Keir Starmer and Rachel Reeves to come down to the picket line. But what they shouldn't do is stop people who want to come to the picket lines from coming ... He doesn't have to have my politics or my views or my detailed agenda, but he's got to identify with this wave, this groundswell, that's developing across the country, and show that he understands where working people are.[84]

However, at a rally at Parliament Square in London on an RMT strike day, Lynch told the crowd: 'I'm saying to Starmer and Reeves and anyone else who seeks to represent working people: whose side are you on?', and challenged Starmer to 'come over here and get on our picket line'.[85] A few weeks later he reversed this: 'It doesn't matter that he doesn't turn out with us on a picket line.'[86] He then changed his tune again, at the anti-Strikes (Minimum Service Level) Bill demonstration outside Parliament, calling out all the Labour front bench for their absence when he believed they should have been there.[87] Much earlier he had stated: 'I don't care if Keir Starmer comes on a picket line ... but what he's not doing is saying he supports us.'[88] This indicates that Lynch was not always consistent in his approach to Starmer and Labour on this particular issue.

The emphasis on extra-parliamentary campaigning to influence Labour took on an added significance as Lynch argued:

> We won't be affiliating [to Labour] ... I don't want to affiliate to anyone. I like the idea that we can support people when they do good things [and not when they do not] ... I want [Labour] to be successful ... It is in the class interests of our people to have a Labour government even if they just turn around some of the most egregious things that the Tories are doing – that would be a success and then if they can set out their own agenda ... about what they want to do that would be good too.[89]

and

> We're not affiliated and one of the reasons we are not affiliated is that Labour politicians since Blair have not identified with the working-class people, and failing to do that is one of the problems they have in working-class communities ... The Labour Party is about supporting working people, or it should be ... [It's] got to sort out [its] identity and come up with a set of policies that will relieve working-class poverty; that will give us a stable workplace with good conditions and minimum standards, that's what the Labour Party should be about. I welcome anyone who wants to support us on the picket lines, and show us messages of support; if Keir Starmer can't do that, it's a problem for him, not for us.[90]

But Lynch's political perspective foundered on the rocks of realpolitik. Thus, for the vast majority of 2020, the Tories were well ahead of Labour in the polls following their victory in the 12 December 2019 general election. This began to change towards the end of 2020 and into 2021, though while the Tory lead shrank, it was still notable. But from the end of 2021, Labour overtook the Tories in the polls, with the lead increasing into double digits from the late summer of 2022 and continuing at those levels well into 2023 (even if this lead showed something of a decline from

20 per cent+ to 10 per cent+ from late 2022). The implications of this for Lynch's left perspective were grave, and confounded what Lynch believed: 'I want Labour to win the next election. It's in the interest of our people that we replace this government with an alternative government but what I think might happen is that he [Starmer] is so bland and so anonymous that he won't win that election so he's really got to find a way to identify with the struggles that are going on.'[91] Only belatedly, in October 2022, did he recognise the realpolitik: 'It seems to me that Labour's on a trajectory to form a government.'[92] Thus, not only was Starmer under no electoral pressure to move to the left, but his strategy of moving to the right was vindicated in as much as any major credible opposition to the Tories became increasingly popular as long as no missteps were made. Indeed, and outside of Scotland, Labour was able to benefit from what it had always periodically been able to benefit from, namely widespread, popular anti-Tory anger. This speaks volumes to the axiom: governing parties lose elections rather more than opposition parties win them. The additional problem was that still with a large majority, the Conservatives were in no hurry to hold an election before they were lawfully compelled to, the last date being 25 January 2025. Unfortunately for Lynch and the left, there was no earthly reason why Starmer would jeopardise Labour's lead by potentially alienating some of the support he had already amassed.

Then Lynch disarmingly remarked: 'but if we don't win the next election for working people – even if it's with a Starmer-led Labour Party – it will be to the detriment of working-class people. If we do win it and get rid of the Tories, it will be progress for working-class people. Because the worst Starmer government is going to be better than the best Tory government.'[93] He reiterated this in 2023: 'I want Starmer to win the election. He is the leader of the party that we're all going to be voting for ... his government will be better than the government we've got. It's in our class interests that Labour forms the next government now ... Even the worst Labour administration will do better than the best Tory administration.'[94] This echoed some of his other thinking on politics being about pragmatism: 'I don't think you're going to win an election by having your favourite lefty';[95] 'I will be supporting the election of a Labour government because I haven't got time to wait for my favourite lefty to lead the Labour Party and then win the Labour Party around and then win a general election';[96] and 'I can't have my ideal left-wing candidate. I've got to go with the candidate who is going to oppose the Tories.'[97]

In this period, Starmer had been explicitly lowering public expectations of what an incoming Labour government was prepared to do in terms of righting the wrongs of Tory governments since 2010, and particularly where spending was involved.[98] Starmer sought to reassure vested interests of the lack of likely change a Labour government would entail. And yet, at the Edinburgh Festival Fringe on 5 August 2023, Lynch articulated his notion that Starmer must reveal his true yet still hidden values when it was plain that Starmer had already revealed what his true values were. So this essentially meant that no matter what Labour did under Starmer's leadership, Lynch would urge people to vote Labour even if they had to 'hold their noses' to do so. For Starmer, it meant that by shifting to the right there was not much danger that this would drain support away from Labour come the general election. Given the emasculation of the left in Labour by Starmer, there was no groundswell of opposition within Labour and no potential leadership candidates for the left in Labour to pin its hopes on. The likes of Rebecca Long-Bailey had long since been defenestrated. This was 'Groundhog Day' of 2015 and before for the left. It had policies it believed were radical and popular, but no way of imposing them on a reluctant leadership. But in another way, the situation was worse for there were no significant figures on the left who could challenge the party leader (as McDonnell had sought to do in 2007 and 2010) and thousands of those on the left had either been expelled or left in disgust. In this situation, it was no surprise that, for Lynch, strike action remained a central and critical tool in the union armoury. Meantime, the TUSC strategy remained stillborn as ever.[99]

Striking generally

During the national rail disputes, Lynch commented: 'I would prefer it if ... Labour... fully reflected what the unions want to do and win elections on that basis, but we can't wait for that to happen.'[100] Consequently, he often turned back to the industrial arena: 'Now we've got a situation where some trade unions are overtly saying, "We're not that bothered about what the Labour Party is saying. It's not going to change the landscape politically – but we can do it industrially." Dave Ward, Sharon Graham, Gary Smith, and myself, to some degree, are saying that';[101] 'We will progress the issues industrially if Labour does not do so politically';[102] 'Unions can only be based on industrial power. Political power comes from industrial strength';[103] and 'unions are the only thing that stand in the way of endless austerity and poverty'.[104] But later in that year, he argued:

> We haven't got the ability to call a general strike ... The TUC
> is the organisation that traditionally has had the power to
> call a general strike, but it would probably be illegal under
> current industrial legislation. What we have to do is gener-
> alise the discontent, generalise the industrial and political
> response. So, I will be speaking to ASLEF, and to CWU, and
> to UNITE whenever we can, about either going out on the
> same day, or doing a rolling programme.[105]

This reiterated his earlier position that calling such action
was the TUC's job: 'The TUC can call a general strike, not
me. If they call it, we'll support it, absolutely',[106] and 'It's
not in my power, it's up to the TUC. It's the TUC's job to
call a general strike, not ours, but we'd support it if they
did',[107] with Lynch predicting: 'What you are going to get is
a wave of solidarity action, generalised strike action, syn-
chronised action'[108] and 'What we will get through things
like Enough is Enough! ... is a generalised approach ...
and synchronised, organised industrial action ... so gener-
alised [strike action] not a general strike.'[109] Lynch main-
tained this position into 2023.[110] But this ignored the role
the RMT could have played in getting the TUC to adopt
such a stance – as it had done under Crow, and especially
that having a general strike was union policy in 2022[111] –
and it ignored the RMT's minimal involvement in the two
mass strikes of 1 February and 15 March 2023, suggesting
again (see pp. 131–33) that it might have struck too early. It
also belied Lynch's earlier notion that 'We need the big bat-
talions of our movement alongside us in this fight on these
platforms.'[112] But this merely brought the situation full
circle – back to its unresolved state – and refuted Lynch's
perspective: 'I think the moment is upon us when we can
effect long-term change.'[113]

The politics of striking

Very seldom did Lynch try to deny that there was a political nature to the RMT's strikes. One of these instances was on *GB News*, when he argued: 'This is not a political strike. The people behind me are not politicians, they're ordinary men and women that want a decent day's pay for a decent day's work and that's what we're after. So, the idea that this is some kind of political strike ... [is] nonsense and I'm sick and tired of hearing it ... when have we ever said [we want to bring down the Tory government]?'[114] That did not mean the question of the politics of striking went away. Yet the possibility of the strikes and their associated struggles generating socialist and class consciousness amongst workers was keenly limited by their overwhelmingly economistic and instrumental nature.[115] Though the strikes of mid-2022 onwards were primarily about the 'pounds and pence' of wage rises during the cost-of-living crisis, other issues of redundancy, workload, staffing levels and job satisfaction did exist and were more prominent for some than others. But that did not mean that they were necessarily capable of generating socialist and class consciousness. The strikes themselves remained primarily sectional in nature and constituted union consciousness focussed on workplace issues. This was still true in the public sector, where governments (Westminster, Holyrood, Cardiff) were the ultimate employer.

Unfortunately, the sense of workers being awoken into their collective power during their coordinated days on strike was not detectable in any significant way. Here, an added factor was that the majority of the larger strikes (by striker numbers) were long-drawn-out affairs which seemed more like wars of attrition (than Blitzkriegs) and had no imminent prospect of victory.[116] Had the strikes had a more overtly political nature (for instance, against the Tory government or one of its key policies), had they been conducted en masse by the vast majority of the then 6.5m union members and been victorious, the prospects for generating socialist and class consciousness would have been substantially improved. Lynch's contribution here was two-sided, where the two sides were not of equal weight and size. He was at pains to state plainly and frequently that his primary allegiance was to his members, and his priority was to achieve acceptable deals with Network Rail and the TOCs. Alongside but always after that – and never trumping it – was the wider social democratic message. Such an approach again stressed the limitations to socialist and class consciousness amongst workers, whether they be RMT members and rail workers or not.

Fox's 'frames of reference'

Lynch's world view (see pp. 167–72) is patently social democratic. Recalling the sociologist Alan Fox's 'frames of reference' helps establish the connection between wider world views and matters of industrial relations.[117] Consequently, Lynch's social democratic world view can best be characterised as 'radical pluralist' in the arena of industrial relations. This is because he accepts, albeit grudgingly and in testament to their power and influence, the legitimate existence of rail employers.[118] He does not dispute their right to operate, but does challenge the grounds on which they operate as well as how they operate. And though he does not call for their abolition per se, he does advocate a change in the format and purpose of those TOC employers by returning their operations to the public sector. Alongside this, and in the meantime, he also wishes to impose restrictions on their actions, whether that be the state-owned Network Rail or the privately owned TOCs, in order to curtail their power to pursue cost savings and profit respectively, through collective bargaining, government policy or legal means. Evidently, he is not a radical of a Marxist type in as much as he does not advocate rail workers directly controlling their 'industry'[119] as part of a project of self-management and workers' power throughout all of the economy and society. He argues for public ownership via the state where there is some kind of worker representation so that a reborn 'British Rail' would not be run by Whitehall mandarins in a high-handed Morrisonian way.[120] Clearly, while he recognises the ideology of unitarism amongst employers, he does not subscribe to it, rejecting it completely. Philosophically and fundamentally, Lynch views the employment relationship as a bargaining 'problem' where outcomes as 'solutions' are to be jointly negotiated. 'Radical pluralism' is then synonymous with his social democratic world view, in terms of his analysis of diagnosis and prognosis. So he believes in capitalism continuing to exist but being reformed through the state regulation of capital so that unions play a more influential role, as they did in the post-war period up until the mid-1970s.

James Connolly

In late June 2022, as media attention honed in on him, Lynch was asked who his political hero was, responding that it was Scots-born but Irish-bred republican socialist, James Connolly.[121] For example on the Robert Peston programme, Lynch said Connolly was 'a' hero of his, being 'An Irish socialist Republican. He educated himself and started non-sectarian trade unionism in Ireland, and he was a hero of the Irish Revolution.'[122] Later, Lynch confirmed Connolly was still his 'political hero'[123] but also mentioned another hero of the Irish national liberation struggle, Countess Markovitz.[124] Connolly was a revolutionary socialist who led the most militant forces in the Easter Rising in 1916, so this may seem an odd choice given Lynch is a social democrat. However, the reason for this is less to do with the socialism, whether from above or below, and more to do with not just Connolly's fight for national liberation for Ireland from the clutches of British imperialism but also Connolly's union organising work, as Lynch made clear on LBC.[125] In particular, it was also the respect Lynch had for Connolly in doing so as a self-educated, working-class socialist who lived in abject poverty most of his life as part of the sacrifice he made to be a full-time socialist organiser, and that he was also an organic intellectual. It is possible Lynch saw a kind of connection between himself and Connolly in regard to this, even though Lynch went to the LSE later in life. For example, Lynch told the *Sunday Independent*:

> [James Connolly is] inspirational. It's not just his involvement in 1916, but the stuff before then. His trade union activity is what mainly interested me. This is a man who was born in absolute destitution, another Irish exiled family from a different generation. His family in Edinburgh virtually had to teach themselves to read and write, and he had to go on and form his own view of socialism and his own view of the national struggle – and try to blend those things together. He went out to America for eight or nine years and tried to form unions there, start a movement. He ended up in Belfast trying to get the Loyalists, if you want to put it like that – the Protestant community – to join unions. I think he was just a remarkable character ... We would hear [about Connolly via] all the songs and then you'd have to go off and read up about him yourself.[126]

Lynch's respect for the non-sectarian initiatives of Connolly influenced his attitude towards the Provisional IRA, for he did not believe the IRA (and other armed militant republicans) only targeted so-called 'military targets' but were more like the Loyalists (who attacked Catholics for being Catholics) in being more indiscriminate. A fellow LSE student also attributed this perspective to the influence of where Lynch's mother came from – Crossmaglen – where Republican politics were 'not only sectarian and tribal but also violent and brutal'.

Come the death of Queen Elizabeth II on 8 September 2022, the RMT Press Office released a statement the same day saying: 'RMT general secretary Mick Lynch said: "RMT joins the whole nation in paying its respects to Queen Elizabeth. The planned railway strike action on 15 and 17 September is suspended. We express our deepest condolences to her family, friends and the country."'[127] This was a strange turn of events given that Lynch was a follower of Connolly, the RMT was a self-ascribed militant union and that the RMT's rulebook sought a 'socialistic order of society'. Though the action was taken to prevent a backlash, internally and externally, it suggested the RMT's leadership thought public opinion was important to winning its dispute. But this itself created a backlash within the RMT on account of the loss of strike momentum and the suggestion of cross-class unity.[128] The tweet containing the text of the press statement was deleted and a number of members were angered.[129] This also allowed *Socialist Worker* to put forward the opinion that Lynch:

> declared that the Irish socialist James Connolly is his political hero. [But it] was Connolly who said: 'A people mentally poisoned by the adulation of royalty can never attain to that spirit of self-reliant democracy necessary for the attainment of social freedom'; 'Neither in science, nor in art, nor in

literature, nor in exploration, nor in mechanical invention, nor in humanising of laws, nor in any sphere of human activity has a representative of British royalty helped forward the moral, intellectual or material improvement of mankind'; [and] 'The mind accustomed to political kings can easily be reconciled to social kings – capitalist kings of the workshop, the mill, the railway, the ships and the docks.' Connolly was right, and his words apply particularly to union leaders.[130]

Brexit

Left-wing comedian Stewart Lee characterised Lynch as a 'Brexit arse made good' because of Lynch's support for Brexit but then subsequently becoming a voice for social justice and economic equality.[131] This seeming pivot, however, did not stop media and public interest in, and scrutiny of, Lynch's views on Brexit – due to Lynch's continued high profile and the growing sense of 'Bregret'. Recalling the debates of the time in and around the LSE and the London left in the late 1980s and early 1990s, a fellow LSE student reflected that Lynch's hostility to the European Union was not one of 'Johnny come lately'. So, in the late 1980s and early 1990s Lynch was a 'Eurosceptic', meaning that he was critical of the project for the creation of the European Union, which was established in 1993, as well as the prospect of further integration of Britain into the European Union despite the introduction of the 'Social Chapter', the shorthand term for the 'Protocol on Social Policy and the Agreement on Social Policy' annexed to the Maastricht Treaty of 1991. This chapter covered employment conditions like minimum wages and consultation rights but only some were covered by qualified majority voting, meaning that British government opposition could be overruled. Lynch believed that the capture of the European Union by neo-liberal forces would mean that labour would be increasingly vulnerable to being forced to acquiesce to the diktats of capital. This was far in advance of the particular criticism that the RMT would develop with regard to the deregulation and privatisation of the railways under the European Union.

Under Crow's general secretaryship, a number of members of the Communist Party came to work for the RMT and some of these were prominent figures in the likes of the Campaign against Euro-federalism (which was established in 1991 and to which the RMT was affiliated). In 2004, the RMT also helped launch Trade Unionists against the EU Constitution, which then became Trade Unionists against the EU.[132] And so, like most leading lights in the RMT in the run-up to the 2016 referendum and afterwards, Lynch was a vocal Brexiteer because of the belief that the capture of the European Union by neo-liberal forces led to the privatisation of rail services and other public services, as well as being an obstacle to them being taken back into public ownership. But there is ambiguity, however, as rail services are still state-owned in France, Germany, Italy and the Netherlands. Lynch argued that 'the European Union has privatisation embedded in its constitution ... [and] I don't like the idea that you give your sovereignty and democracy away to a load of bureaucrats and bankers'.[133] He continued: 'The free movement of labour I don't think helps anyone because it means the countries that people are coming from have lost some of their most able people ... and it didn't help the labour market in Britain.'[134] So his assessment of the vote to leave in terms of the 'take back control' dictum was the aspiration that 'people wanted a bit of nationalism but they also wanted a bit of public ownership and traditional Labour and trade union values'.[135] Lynch contested that the nature of post-Brexit Britain was the consequence of Brexit per se, and believed this was rather the result of the way the Tories had chosen to implement it.[136] For example, he argued: 'If ... we'd voted for a different government which I campaigned for we wouldn't be making these changes ... any government could do those things outside the European Union because you have sovereign power ... [Any] future government is free to make any legislative changes that it wants and can enhance what we do, and can indeed nationalise public sector services, which you cannot do inside the European Union.'[137]

Earlier, in an extensive interview, Lynch laid out his position in some detail: 'It's [now] up to the government at Westminster whether they want to change those laws. All of the laws that we had inside the EU are now written in, copied straight into British legislation so if you want to change any of those laws for better or worse you now have a sovereign right to do that. If you're in the EU you can't. But if you take the last Corbyn manifesto, which I obviously support, it's likely that that manifesto was illegal under the European Union because you cannot [take in]to public ownership ... the leading parts of the economy.' He went on to observe: 'In the Viking Laval case ... Lithuanian workers were posted into Scandinavia ... [on] Lithuanian wages which obviously undermines the local [labour] market so there are problems [with] ... a free movement of labour ... that undermine collective agreements' and 'In terms of the most of the legislation that we've got, that is not inherited from the EU ... Our employment laws don't sit in EU legislation so the anti-trade union laws ... are not anything to do with EU legislation.' Asked whether he regretted what had happened since the Brexit referendum, he replied: 'I do regret that there is a Conservative government bringing [in these changes] ... we were asked in principle ... do you approve of the European Union and do you want to remain a member of it? My position is the traditional left position going back to Peter Shaw and Michael Foot. If we'd had the European Community, the EEC, I would have voted to stay in the EC. I don't personally and many people in my union don't believe that Europe should be a sovereign country. I don't believe that we should give up much of our fiscal policy to a European state.'[138]

But, unfortunately for the left-wing exit – 'Lexit' – argument, it remains the case that the promise of Brexit to mean 'taking back control' would result in the economy and politics in Britain becoming fairer and more democratic was 'pie in the sky'. From the outset, the Brexit campaign was almost entirely dominated by reactionary forces, and as a result further 'control' has passed on to those who were already in control, so there was no upending of the various elites that currently dominate society for their own benefit. Lexit was, therefore, in this period a major and predictable, even inevitable, strategic miscalculation. Such Brexit forces as existed wanted to leave the European Union in order to further deregulate the economy, allowing private capital to operate with even fewer constraints. There was only one way to have had a meaningful Lexit, and that was for a left-wing Labour government to take measures such as renationalising key sectors of the economy, which would then have led to expulsion from the European Union – measures which would likely garner mass support for such a government to stand its ground and maintain such sectors in public ownership.[139] But even with the credible election result of the Corbyn-led Labour Party in the 2017 general election, this expulsion option-cum-strategy was far from being in prospect, not least because there was considerable opposition to Corbyn from within the ranks of Labour itself.

Conclusion

Lynch did not envisage a world without capital and capitalism, for he believes social democracy is the hope for humankind. He is, in his own words, a 'pragmatic ... reformist'.[140] The sense of this can be seen in his statements that workers should not gain all the wealth that they create as would be the case with revolutionary socialism: '[Workers] have got to get their share';[141] 'Workers make the wealth of the world and all that we want is a fair share of that wealth';[142] 'All of the wealth in our society is created by workers ... What we need in this country, in all other countries, is a distribution of wealth so that those that do the work and create the wealth get a fair share of the fruits of their labour';[143] and 'Labour produces all wealth in the society and the role of a ... union is to get a fairer share of that or a better share of the wealth.'[144] However, his moderate radicalism took on an added significance on account of his ability to articulate it and the attention he was given due to the rail strikes in a peculiar period of political instability where the right became more rampant and reactionary. These are among the factors that produced the phenomenon of Lynch as a working-class hero. Based as they were more on 'words' than 'deeds', he was a powerful propagandist. And despite his unsuccessful search for political representation via Labour, for many Lynch's world view remained no less compelling for that.[145]

Conclusion

The relatively unknown figure of Mick Lynch burst into people's consciousness in the summer of 2022. In the process, for many he became their working-class hero, whereby people projected onto him their values and aspirations which they believed he embodied and would advance. While it was logical to do so given the emasculated state of the radical left, this was done in ignorance of much existing – and future – knowledge about Lynch, with the outcome that other parts of his make-up were ignored or downplayed. Subsequently, Lynch revealed himself not to be quite as radical and militant as many had thought or hoped. For example, he was vehemently critical of Labour but also extremely pro-Labour, while not a Labour Party member and the RMT remain unaffiliated. Moreover, he often had surprisingly low aspirations, saying: 'All I want from life is a bit of socialism',[1] 'We hope for a little bit more than nothing'[2] and 'You know we're gonna get something out of this [dispute] ... but what we've mainly got is our dignity and the ability to strike and the ability to inspire some other people.'[3] Ironically, this chimed with Bryan Garman's belief that a working-class hero should 'be radical [but not] too damn radical'.[4] But this is not to suggest he was a 'shill' as one former RMT senior national officer believed.

To the extent that Lynch became a working-class hero, he was something of an accidental as well as a reluctant one, making him an all the more intriguing figure. This is to recollect the sequence of events that led him to become RMT General Secretary during the time of the fight against the cost-of-living crisis and the programme of rail 'modernisation' reforms. And, recalling that 'fighting the good fight' was a fundamental foundation for a working-class hero, the RMT could not have hoped for a better frontperson to lead their dispute in the media. Had Lynch been cut from the same cloth as Mick Cash, he would not have stood out as he did, for he is a very astute and skilled public performer with a pronounced willingness to often discuss the class nature of capitalist society (unlike Cash). Referring back to the different layers of the framework for analysis, this gives some indication of the relationship between factors which were alternatively deemed 'necessary but not sufficient' and 'both necessary and sufficient'. But words not deeds could only carry a working-class hero so far. For a union leader as a working-class hero, outcomes mattered. Indeed, 'soft power' did not necessarily mean there was also the 'hard power' needed for delivering satisfactory outcomes or that 'soft power' could be combined with 'hard power' to produce 'smart power'.

This final chapter examines the phenomenon of the widespread perception of Lynch as a working-class hero in terms of the earlier criteria (see Chapter 2). For example, how credible was a working-class hero that did not win their bargaining demands; for how long can an individual be a working-class hero without winning their bargaining demands; and how credible was a working-class hero who was only seen to have the courage and determination to 'fight the good fight', without winning something significant? Previous working-class heroes like Reid and Scargill[5] did win some or all of their bargaining demands at particular points in time – even if these were not lasting victories. For some, this is the key component that maintains their status as working-class heroes decades later. Others from the past – like Dessie Warren and Jayaben Desai – are still seen as working-class heroes even though their struggles were not victorious. So where is Lynch placed in this pantheon? He showed some awareness of the issues involved when he ventured: 'We're in a better position than if we hadn't fought but it's not as good as we would have wanted at the beginning.'[6]

Leadership and followership

In examining Lynch's leadership of the RMT, contrasts and comparisons with other leaders and unions were necessarily made. This was not just a question of constructing a critical assessment of Lynch's leadership but also focussing on other unions and their leaders in order to address the wider issue of union power: what it is and how it can be generated and utilised? Specifically, the issue of translating 'power to' into 'power over' was the key aspect, along with differentiating between 'soft' power and 'hard' power. Indeed, in the summer of 2022, it seemed easy for many to conclude that with Lynch winning the media war at a time of traumatic Tory turmoil, the RMT's bargaining demands would be quickly won.[7] As this did not turn out to be so, investigating such issues is crucial to addressing the question of whether unions can be remade in the present period by being renewed and revitalised, both qualitatively and quantitively. Lynch's winning the media war showed that discursive power through framing was very far from enough. In this way, the issues of power, material interests and ideology were not obscured by the focus on the making of Lynch as a working-class hero. Rather, they were illuminated.

At first sight, this study has been about public perception and media mores, spanning the range from pleasing plaudits to brutal brickbats but with a focus on the phenomenon of the 'working-class hero'. But scratch beneath this surface and it becomes clear the central concerns have been power, material interests and ideology, on the one hand, and labour, capital and the state, on the other. Connecting these two troikas together, like two circles in a Venn diagram, are unions and union leadership. Lynch was the literal link here. This gives the first clue as to why the perception of Lynch as a working-class hero arose. In the context of the evisceration of the radical and revolutionary left, he was not just an oppositional voice for the sullen and voiceless who wished to make their opposition known. He was also a tribune for those that were tentatively shedding their timidity. More specifically, he was seen as a working-class voice for the voiceless working class and a champion for union members who were becoming more collectively assertive. The elongated nature of the two national rail strikes meant this phenomenon continued, albeit at a lower intensity, even when the nature of the disputes progressed from predominantly mobilisation to predominantly negotiation. In other words, the shock and awe of the new did decline somewhat as the disputes dragged on without satisfactory resolution, but Lynch was still provided with ample opportunities to cement his reputation for consistent critique of the Conservatives and capitalism. Indeed, it was a particular peculiarity of the period of politics in Britain that Lynch was first and most frequently called a working-class hero when the strikes were very much in their infancy, and this appellation was given for what he said rather than what he did. It is all the more so when, boiled down, just a small handful of television interviews in late June 2022 were the foundation for this designation. Compared to others like Reid and Scargill, their appellations as working-class heroes were far more based on their organising actions rather than their rhetoric.

Strategy and circumstance

The study has also shown that union strategy and political circumstance – albeit where there is no Chinese Wall between them – are the two key factors helping to explain the fertile environment which led to Lynch becoming a hero *for* the working class. Contrast the impact of Lynch's fulminations against P&O's brutal actions in March 2002 with those over the rail strikes. Although the RMT was unable to take industrial action in the former case as it did in the latter, a key difference, nonetheless, was the Westminster Tory government's voluble criticism of P&O. It talked of its moral outrage and let it be known it would change the law in order to stop recurrences of such actions. The resultant Seafarers' Wages Act 2023 was, however, very limited in its reach. Fast forward to the summer rail strikes and the tables were turned because the same Tory government became the main body not only causing the strikes – over limiting pay rises and insisting on efficiency savings via job cuts – but also preventing the resolution of the disputes. In this situation, the RMT was able to implement a strike strategy. And yet, strategy for unions is problematic, given their positions as 'secondary' or 'intermediary' organisations, having been created after the establishment of the capitalist employment relationship so that they are quintessentially after-the-fact, reactive organisations.[8] Given the power imbalance under capitalism between capital and labour, developing effective strategy which can deliver unions' bargaining demands is challenging to say the least.[9] Though unions are not entirely 'victims of history', to paraphrase Marx, neither do they make history in circumstances of their own choosing.

Militancy

Many in the RMT saw their union not only as militant but the most militant of unions. Lynch's take on this issue was: 'We're assertive – we're not afraid to use our power'[10] and 'The RMT has been at the forefront of the current wave of industrial action',[11] saying it had been 'the spark in 2022 for the strikes in many other sectors'.[12] He then added to this saying: 'Even though we have not sought a leadership role, by the actions of our members, we have led the labour movement. We are the most active and high-profile union in the country. Where we lead, others follow.'[13] And, since at least Crow's tenure as General Secretary, the tenor of RMT language had been about doggedly and determinedly opposing and fighting cuts and profits without any room for compromise, partnership or mutual gains. This continued under Lynch[14] but, as before, the nature and forcefulness of the opposing and fighting was often less than the tenor of the language suggested, indicating that the ability to create the 'power to' (disrupt) was less than expected and 'power to' did not easily generate the 'power over'. Consequently, and in this context, it is useful to consider industrial relations scholar John Kelly's definition of militancy as the use of extensive collective mobilisation through industrial action to gain ambitious bargaining demands, based on the premise of an incompatibility between the interests of capital and labour.[15] Matched against this, it is not clear-cut that the RMT's attitudes and behaviours in the case of the two rail disputes were militant – or, indeed, were especially militant when compared to other unions – because they sought to defend, rather than advance, the status quo in terms of the real value of pay, jobs, and terms and conditions, and do so through limited mobilisations even with an oppositional ideology. However, the context of the forces ranged against the RMT suggests this view should be tempered somewhat, with some emphasis put on members' determination to sustain a lengthy dispute over many months in terms of repeatedly rejecting employer offers, reballoting for industrial action and the number of days of strikes taken.

Striking outcomes: the unmaking of a working-class hero?

On strike settlements, Kelly noted: 'an issue that has been seriously neglected in the strikes literature ... is their outcomes', continuing 'we need to know more about the processes and *outcomes* of these strikes, particularly in the face of neo-liberal governments ... [W]e know relatively little about the pattern of outcomes of collective action, both strikes and non-strikes, and their explanation. The term "outcomes" should be used broadly to refer to the impact of collective action on substantive union goals, on the organizational capacity of ... unions, such as membership and finances, and on the labour movement more generally.'[16] Earlier, Kelly observed: 'Astonishingly, there is no reliable data on strike outcomes in Britain after 1935.'[17] Where the limited number of studies do examine strike outcomes,

most examine workers' cost–benefit calculations of the pro-
posed *future* actions prior to their commencement (should
the analysis suggest acting is credible and rational in these
terms[18]). But very few examine workers' cost–benefit analy-
ses *after* the action has been taken and how these impact on
their future willingness to take collective action.

Although representing only two cases,[19] the examina-
tion of the processes and outcomes of the two national rail
disputes in this study – through the prism of the figure of
Lynch and with foregrounding in previous RMT strikes –
has gone some way to highlight the complex and sometimes
contradictory dynamics involved. At best, the final agree-
ment made with Network Rail was presented, not unlike
the practice of other unions, in a somewhat generous light
by Lynch and the RMT. At worst, it was misleading, indicat-
ing a whiff of 'sharp power'. The action taken was enough
to gain limited movement but it was not enough to gain
any more – that is, an inflation-proof pay deal that was not
self-financing, a satisfactory job security agreement and the
maintenance of current terms and conditions. The TOC dis-
pute was similar but also different. Even more extensive but
still limited industrial action had not brought about a deal
that was acceptable to members. Along the way, there was
another whiff of 'sharp power' over the two RDG documents
and Lynch's role as a 'deal maker' (see pp. 111, 128–30).
Both disputes questioned, especially when no strike pay was
paid, the well-known line from the Strawbs' song, 'Part of
the Union' (1973): 'And I always get my way if I strike for
higher pay.'[20] In doing so, they also raised the quintessential
questions about whether striking works in itself, or whether
it is a matter of the means being appropriate for the ends.
Whatever conclusions may be drawn, the starting point
must be to create criteria by which to judge the issues – what

are the union's demands or objectives – and set them against what is achieved (when also factoring in loss in pay from striking) before then turning to look at the issue of whether the strategy and tactics were appropriate and proportional.

For certain sections of the left, the Network Rail agreement and the attempt to negotiate another with the TOCs unmade Lynch as a working-class hero. For other sections of the left, the agreements called into question whether it was sensible to see Lynch as a working-class hero in the first place. And yet amongst the wider populace, the perception of Lynch as a working-class hero was unlikely to have been significantly tarnished by the making of these agreements, primarily because they were not given the same media exposure that Lynch received in the early summer of 2022. Consequently, the deals' details and how they were arrived at was not in the possession of these people. The mere passage of time since the early summer of 2022 was more likely to have dulled Lynch's image as a working-class hero, where not gaining speedy and satisfactory resolutions played out against the resilience to carry on fighting and, in the context of the continuation of righteous anger against the Tories and Labour's absence of support, 'fighting the good fight' still paid dividends.[21] Indeed, the more the TOCs dispute dragged on without satisfactory resolution, the more Lynch stated the RMT would not be 'bowed' or 'cowed' and would continue the dispute no matter what. This appeared to be in inverse relationship to the effectiveness of further striking to gain any additional concessions.[22] Nonetheless, the extent of contestation of Lynch as a working-class hero increased as the disputes dragged on and assessments were made of the revised offers and the processes by which they were arrived at. That said, projection onto Lynch of working-class herodom was still possible but highlighted several aspects.

One was that the expectations of herodom were high. Another was that dissonance emerged between expectations and behaviour so that as the disputes dragged on and became more concerned with negotiation than strike mobilisation, Lynch moved from the externally viewed 'tribune' to the internally revealed 'deal-maker'.

Leadership lessons from Lynch

What lessons can other union leaders learn from Lynch? One concerns public persona. Calmness and calculation are required. This may come about through combinations of training, psychological preparation and particular person-alities. Particular personas can be especially helpful in reinforcing members' morale via public performances. Another is understanding that 'context is king' when thinking about whether members will be seen as 'villains' or 'heroes'. This means it is harder for some union leaders to develop the same kind of traction, depending on which goods and services their members provide and whether they are strategically important or funded or subsidised by the public purse. Another is that strong, effective leaders can only exist on the foundation of strong followers, namely their union members. Here, members need to willingly and actively choose to be led where tactics have to be creatively thought out and fine-tuned to create maximum disruption with the minimum sacrifice of wages, and people's lives not put at risk by such actions. For those union members whose jobs are in health, prisons, social care and the fire and rescue service, they will be politically attacked for putting people at risk. Lastly, there is knowing whether and how a political 'hot potato' can be created. Private sector strikes seek to hurt employers in their pockets. Public sector strikes seek to create political embarrassment. Here, only a few public sector workers like refuse collectors, teachers and border security guards have the ability to create safe and immediate disruption.

Innovation and inertia in ideas

One of the hallmarks of a working-class hero – who is a union leader – is innovation in ideas, especially in working out how to generate leverage in new situations. For the RMT, this was all the more vital after the introduction of the Strikes (Minimum Service Levels) Act 2023.[23] Lynch did not offer in words or deeds a new form or strategy for labour unionism. Whilst highlighting the need for more effective organising based upon greater knowledge and directed centrally by national officers, his internal paper on the need for the RMT to become an industrial union was an indication of this.[24] Previous examples of people who did innovate are Teamster union organiser Farrell Dobbs, who pioneered inter-state organising as a shift away from intra-state organising;[25] former union organiser, now union educator, Jane McAlevey, who formulated the 'whole worker' and 'deep organising' approaches;[26] former *Labor Notes* co-founder Kim Moody, who identified opportunities arising from the new fragility of the organisation of production, distribution and exchange under contemporary capitalism;[27] and Jimmy Reid, who developed the work-in strategy and tactic.[28] The need for such types of thinking was at least partially recognised in Lynch's report.[29]. Yet, by contrast, union organiser, Nigel Flanagan, did attempt to put detailed 'meat on the bones' of a more effective decentralised, grassroots organising approach.[30] But it remains the case that the RMT has not satisfactorily resolved the conundrum of turning 'power to' into 'power over', as Unite has managed to achieve in some cases in some sectors.

As outlined earlier and notwithstanding a number of factors like the effective indemnification for strike losses, the 2022–23 national disputes with Network Rail and TOCs highlighted in stark terms that though the RMT's campaign of industrial action could shift the bargaining opponents from their initial offer positions, this still fell significantly short of the union's bargaining demands. This implied not only that the 'power to' (disrupt) did not generate sufficient 'power over', but that a process to develop capacity for organisational learning had not taken place other than to mainly avoid TOC strikes taking place in isolation from those on Network Rail and increasing the disruption by having two one-day strikes a day apart rather than two-day strikes. Even taking into account that strikes are often a response to developments in negotiations (as much as developments in negotiations are a response to strikes), such advances were undone by the extended start–stop nature of the strikes and the lack of prior preparation in order to provide strike pay. The latter meant members could not afford to sustain a greater financial loss over a shorter period, which may have generated greater 'power over'. It may also be ventured that the Trade Union Act 2016 compelled the RMT to spend more energy on winning the ballots than thinking about what to do with them once gained, in terms of strategy and tactics. But this would be a generous interpretation given the hold of previous traditions of action.

Lynch's role in accounting for the long-drawn-out industrial disputes is less than self-evident. First, and as already highlighted, there is the existing, established tradition of RMT strike action which is primarily based on one-day actions. Second, there are the wishes of the strikers themselves, who often make their views forcefully clear to their union leadership as to the type of action they wish and are prepared to take.[31] This relates primarily to the loss of income in the absence of strike pay.[32] Third, NEC members and the union's other national officers have a role to play in influencing the union's actions. Trying to disentangle each from the others is a fraught business – one would have had to have been many flies on many walls to be privy to the many discussions and decisions. But what can be said with certainty is that Lynch did not have the unilateral power – much less the right – to decide on the tactics deployed or always have the last say on the deals prior to any membership referenda or consultation. Indeed, the *Guardian* observed: 'Rail bosses ... note[d] ... on three occasions the RMT's national executive ... rejected deals that ... Lynch and ... Dempsey ha[d] reached in the negotiating ... room.'[33] That said, and despite Lynch not having a vote on the NEC or at the union's annual (AGM) conference, the general secretary did have the right to speak at length at both so that the force of personality of the general secretary was important, as it had been under Crow.

Revisiting Sun Tzu's fifth-century BC Chinese treatise on the art of war and its methods is useful, as he observed: 'All men can see the tactics whereby I conquer, but what none can see is the strategy out of which victory is evolved'; 'Do not repeat the tactics which have gained you one victory, but let your methods be regulated by the infinite variety of circumstances'; and 'He who can modify his tactics in relation to his opponent and thereby succeed in winning, may be called a heaven-born captain.'[34] Such insights may help to reformulate strike strategy in terms of the elements of time, form and outcome, where time concerns the length of period the strikes take place over, form the type of strike (one-day, two-day, etc.) and outcome the extent of winning or losing where a cost–benefit analysis is conducted. Sun Tzu's insights are more apposite than those concerning the role of politics and ideology in war derived from German military theorist Carl von Clausewitz,[35] as per his para-phrased pronouncement: 'war is the continuation of poli-tics by other means'. Sun Tzu's observations suggest such a dominant, articulate and insightful figure as Lynch could have been expected to break out of the RMT habitus to develop new thinking on strategy and tactics.[36] For exam-ple, the idea of a 'smart strike' which seeks to maximise disruption with minimum costs to members could have seen RMT TOC members paying a levy for RMT Network Rail signallers to stay out on strike indefinitely, given that signallers are a relatively small group of members with much more strategic power than conductors and other TOC staff (even though technically speaking the Network Rail and TOCs are separate disputes with two sets of sepa-rate negotiations, but in practice the Conservative govern-ment is the ultimate arbiter).[37] Another example is that a specific strike 'war chest' could have been built up prior to the strikes, knowing well in advance that – in addition to the *de jure* strike loss indemnification for the TOCs and the *de facto* strike loss indemnification for Network Rail – the coming battle would be long and hard where striking members would lose considerable sums of wages, and the Conservative government wanted to face down and beat the RMT for electoral advantage. As stated earlier (see p. 257), the RMT had considerable assets to drawn upon in order to do so and latterly Lynch acknowledged that without strike pay 'we have to be careful with what we ask our members to do ... The people saying we should escalate are usually not the ones taking the action.'[38] Instead, platitudes were usually fallen back on, with Lynch, for example, saying before the summer of 2022: 'Unity in the struggles ahead are [sic] the union's strength ... You may lose if you fight [but] you will never win if you don't fight.'[39] Only on a couple of occasions did he allude to the need for new thinking:

> You're really petrified about being without four, five, six days' pay. If you get into a situation where you're losing a month's pay or more that's a real challenge so we've got to find ways of supporting each other and ... tactically doing different forms of industrial action.[40]
>
> We need the right strategies and systems so we deliver an effective political and industrial punch when required.[41]

Tactical torpor

In the first flushes of success with the first strikes, Lynch told an RMT rally outside King's Cross station in London on 25 June 2022: 'You have the power. A wheel doesn't turn and a light doesn't go on without us.' But, as highlighted before and paradoxically by Lynch here, the RMT has not resolved the long-standing issue of translating 'power to' into 'power over' even when the power to disrupt has been effective in closing down 80 per cent of the rail network. Effective disruption has not led to effective bargaining power over the bargaining opponents. In this connection, sometimes a 'revenue strike' or 'fare strike' as a form of industrial action short of striking was suggested, whereby members go to work but open all the ticket barriers and refuse to check tickets, thereby allowing passengers to travel for free in order to reduce company revenue, lessen disruption for passengers and avoid loss of pay for striking. The rub is that pay can be docked for partial performance of duties, with suspension and/or dismissal for breach of contract also possible. The last attempt to use this very seldom tried tactic was in early February 2014 on London Underground.[42] Moreover, as *Off The Rails* outlined, there were many other problematical issues.[43]

A situation of effective indemnification for TOCs' strike losses requires new thinking, and this could have been expected of a working-class hero who was capable of leading a union through a process of organisational learning. And in Network Rail there were criticisms of strikes being called in periods of additional income opportunities[44] as well as calling off an overtime ban.[45] Moreover, lessons from France, Greece, Italy and Spain could have been learnt in terms of the application of direct action through blockading, barricading and occupying signalling hubs, depots, tracks and other strategic points in the rail network. Lynch only ever advocated occupying lobbies of cleaning contractors (see p. 167). This kind of thinking was all the more necessary when the government engaged in a 'major reforming confrontation' as part of its attempt to resuscitate its electoral fortunes. A major reforming confrontation is a stage-managed conflict which seeks to radically reset the balance of power in industrial relations in favour of management.[46] The comments of Peter Wilkinson, a senior official in the Department for Transport, in 2016 about wishing to break the RMT (see p. 230)[47] still held true in 2022–23, with Network Rail's Chief Executive, Andrew Haines, saying the RMT being told 'you don't hold us to ransom and ... [you] don't have a right of veto' was 'a seismic moment'.[48]

But the translation of 'power to' into 'power over' is not solely or mainly predicated on industrial action or labour market scarcity via the ability to disrupt employers' operations, the economy and society. It also is predicated on political power through a political party.[49] Though the RMT had long been critical of Labour prior to its disaffiliation in 2003 and continued not to be affiliated, it had not resolved the issue of how to exercise political influence on the scale that was required. This meant it could not add the political *je ne sais quoi* to its potential industrial prowess. Ultimately, this explains why the 2022–23 dispute with Network Rail, TOCs and the Conservative government could not be won on sufficiently favourable terms for the RMT.

Transformational leadership

Leadership which is transformational is often participative and democratic, possessing strategic vision. In other words, new and effective ways of doing things are developed and deployed in order to achieve goals. Most often the crux of the matter is perceived in the following way: how does a small cog – the transformational leader – turn the wheel of, or even create, a much larger body of an engaged, active and mobilised membership which comprises an ideologically committed followership? Though issues of the outside environment – being more or less conducive – are important, the focus here is on the issue of agency, specifically self-agency. By contrast, the transactional leader uses patronage and pay (and other forms of remuneration and status) to gain an instrumental followership.

Lynch has not offered much in the way of transformational leadership within or beyond the RMT. Though he is much more representative, in demographic terms, of his own union membership, he is less so of unions' wider membership. But this has little direct bearing on the issue at hand because transformational leadership is about more than being said to be 'inspirational' to members and non-members as a result of delivering dramatic speeches or having considerable charisma. Rather, it is about creating an organisational culture which develops individuals and their capabilities for the purpose of advancing the interests and influence of that organisation. The often robust and contested nature of the RMT's internal organisational culture along with its democratic processes, which can provide the latitude for independent positions of influence among lay officials, and the manifest importance of its rule book mean there are organisational constraints on the ability of any RMT general secretary to effect transformational leadership. In this regard, it may be seen as a triumph, though falling short of transformational leadership, that Lynch has been able to re-establish the authority and influence of the office of the general secretary. As alluded to earlier (see pp. 89–90), the context of a major external threat to the RMT and its members was conducive in allowing 'peace to break out' in terms of uniting – or at least toning down – fractious factions. However, Lynch's style of internal leadership at the highest levels in the RMT is seen as somewhat authoritarian and autocratic by some, given his emphasis on doing deals where he is the deal-maker and where he wields his political capital to gain implementation of his agenda. This also indicated more of a servicing than mobilising approach. A former NEC member ventured that 'power has gone to his head'. There were also indications of a continuing 'toxic' culture within the RMT as an employer, with accusations of bullying by superiors against inferiors, when many believed the bullying was taking place the other way round and such alleged bullying was intended to suppress criticism and dissent.[50] One former NEC member believed Lynch:

combines being a great public speaker with a command of using the internal structures and the administration (including employed administrators) of the union to pursue his agenda in RMT ... through fair and foul means such as debate in meetings or in the [union's] boardroom along with false claims of mental health problems attributed to false accusations of bullying by opposing union members and subverting the union's democratic processes through those vulnerable to manipulation, [namely], employed staff and dependent elected officials. He comes across as reasonable until he knows you aren't going to go along with what he wants. Then the gloves come off.

And one branch officer noted Lynch had 'a tendency to denounce all criticism and dissent as bad-faith factional attacks with ulterior motives'. Lynch continued with predecessors' practice of having non-union bodies (RMT staff association, Unity House Staff Movement) alongside recognising the GMB union for representing RMT employees. He argued against a motion to establish a machinery of negotiation for lay tutors at the 2022 AGM. While the motion was passed, it had yet to be implemented.

That said, the bigger – if not biggest – contribution Lynch has made has been to reboot social democracy, where his contribution has been ideational through articulating a counter-narrative and counter-discourse which when pieced together amounts to an alternative ideology and world view to that of neo-liberalism. This stands in the context of the curtailing of Corbyn and Corbynism. And part and parcel of this contribution has been to reassert that unions are a critical part of social democracy. Lynch recognised this, saying the RMT had 'rekindle[d] the fire of trade unionism in Britain' by putting 'bigger ideas back on the table'.[51] Another big contribution, one RMT branch officer believed, was that Lynch had 'galvanised the working class and shown that they can fight', so imparting collective self-confidence.

'Trade union bureaucracy' thesis

Given that Lynch was no longer of the working class, what light did the course of the two national rail disputes and the RMT's conduct throw on the thesis of the 'trade union bureaucracy', especially in respect of the absence of an escalation of the action, and particularly a quicker escalation? Drawing on recent articulations of the 'bureaucracy' thesis,[52] it becomes apparent that the purchase of this thesis for these disputes is thin. Explaining and understanding the course of the disputes and the conduct of the RMT revolves around negotiating tactics and NEC strategy rather than the material basis of union officers' salaries, social position, ideological beliefs and functional intermediate positions.[53] In particular, the two aspects that stand out in the issues of negotiating tactics and NEC strategy are that 'power to' (disrupt) did not generate the necessary amount of 'power over' to win the union's bargaining demands, and that without strike pay there was a limit to how far union members were prepared to suffer loss of wages as a result of striking. Even if more striking through escalation could have led to generating more 'power over', the matter of members self-financing the strike would still have been critical, and the issues of union officers' salaries, social position, ideological beliefs and functional intermediate positions did not have a bearing on this.

Portent and potential

Lynch's assessment was: 'I think the ... union movement ... has certainly been reinvigorated. There's new leadership at all levels, not just the general secretaries. There is renewed energy at the workplace level, at local and regional levels.'[54]

Conclusion

So, what were the prospects for union renewal and revitalisation? And where did the figure of Lynch fit into this? In other words, and notwithstanding the possible denting of his working-class herodom, did the making of a high-profile working-class hero offer the prospect of helping to remake unions and the union movement? The emergence of Lynch as a working-class hero can be taken to pose the question of whether he might have helped herald the arrival of a new kind of union leader, capable of inspiring membership militancy and challenging the reheated 'Blairite' policies of Labour as part of a path towards the overall renewal and revitalisation of the unions. These are issues not just of left-wing politics but also of transformational types of leadership.

These questions of progressive political change and organisational transformation were posed over twenty years ago, and in very similar terms, by Andrew Murray when writing about – compared to Lynch – the then newer, younger, more left-wing union leaders designated 'the awkward squad', and including the likes of Crow and Serwotka.[55] To most, they held out the promise of transforming their unions and the union movement because they focussed on radical left-wing politics which railed against 'new Labour' and Blairism, on the one hand, and encouraged self-reliance and membership mobilisation, on the other. In retrospect, while the critiques of 'new Labour' were often compelling and the alternatives put forward were credible, the degree of traction for them was limited, particularly because there were a range of views about what relationship to take with Labour. The differences concerned working within Labour or setting up a new party of labour, as well as whether to concentrate on the industrial struggle in a quasi-syndicalist manner. And while some significant and progressive internal changes in unions were instituted by 'awkward squad' leaders – with regard to union organising, internal democracy and representation of under-represented groups – and many of these unions became more collectively combative for a time, there was no overall upturn in membership levels or in membership activity (union participation, strike action). This can be attributed not only to the hostile environment within which unions continued to operate, but also the fact that the sheer scale of the task of renewal and revitalisation was beyond that which could be orchestrated from national leaderships.[56]

This somewhat sobering assessment highlights all the more that whatever outcomes the 'Lynch effect' produced were likely to be much less (even at time of a relative uptick in strikes) as well as taking a while longer to detect. But there are also several additional obstacles to such a desired outcome. First, the notion of the working-class hero saying or doing things for others that they cannot or will not do for themselves has to be factored in. Some may have been inspired into activity and greater activity by Lynch – as per the transformational effect – but it is likely many more will have continued to look skywards for representation and prosecution of their views and interests by others. Second, Lynch was pretty much a lone player here, rather than part of the emergence of a collective phenomenon (as per the 'awkward squad'). Earlier, the absence of other working-class heroes and heroines amongst the current crop of union leaders was noted. Third, while Lynch supported and called for broadening out and diversifying the composition of union membership and the activists within it,[57] being the leader of a small union with a limited time as RMT General Secretary – due to his age – restricted the extent to which he could effect change. So there were some idiosyncratic issues which meant Lynch was unable, despite his best intentions and efforts, to spearhead union renewal and revitalisation.

The only other new union leader of significance has been Sharon Graham, given her advocacy and implementation of 'leverage' campaigns as a Unite-wide turn of strategy (see pp. 135–36). Even though the leverage strategy seeks to empower Unite members, Graham's role in this – as an individual providing inspiration and any sense of transformational leadership – is less central in this sense than Lynch's role was to the RMT in its 2022–23 disputes with Network Rail and the TOCs. Put another way, it is a case of 'comparing apples and oranges' because though Graham crucially championed the leverage strategy as part of her 'back to the workplace' orientation, her persona and politics were less central to the strategy's outcomes. By contrast, and where Lynch was judged by the criteria of a working-class hero, his persona and politics were far more critical. Moreover, whether through her personality and/or focus on 'back to the workplace', Graham was less willing to engage with the bigger political issues of the day compared to Lynch. This means Lynch attracted more attention from the media and, in turn, the wider public.

The *i* noted that the existence of the 'Mick Lynch effect' helped stimulate greater interest in joining unions,[58] but membership levels for 2022 did not indicate that the overall impact of the strikes was positive, with density falling to 22.3 per cent (from 23.1 per cent in 2021) and the loss of 200,000 members.[59] This confounded the example of the NEU being in any way representative: 'Since announcing its strike ballot results in January, the NEU [with 457,143 on 1 January 2022] ... gained around 50,000 mostly teaching members, with 7,000 of those joining over the five weeks since the first national strike day at the beginning of last month.'[60] The same can be said of PCS and Unite, respectively, 'membership grew more rapidly in the last four months of 2022 than during the rest of that year, ... in 2022, 30,758 new members join[ed], increasing the total by 4.3%', and '4,5000 members were joining us in a week', with a net gain of 30,000 members since Graham became general secretary.[61] The RMT's membership increases were necessarily much smaller in absolute terms. They were also smaller in relative terms. In the course of the Network Rail dispute, RMT membership rose from 20,070 to 20,700 (+3 per cent) in the company between the two ballots in 2022 but rose and then fell in the TOCs between the three ballots in 2022 and 2023 (21,036 to 21,636 to 20,476), representing a 3 per cent decrease overall. Moreover, by the end of 2022, the RMT's net membership increase was just 346, barely 0.5 per cent. In the case of the election for a new NEU general secretary, held between February and March 2023, the turnout was just 9 per cent, indicating membership participation remained highly problematic. Previous elections for general secretaries routinely saw between just 5 per cent and 10 per cent of members voting. Turnouts for elections to unions' national executives showed no discernible uptick in 2023 after the beginning of the cost-of-living crisis fightback. For the NEU, PCS, Unison and Unite unions, turnouts remained very low at between just 5 per cent and 7 per cent. Indeed, Flanagan questioned the extent, depth and permanence of union revival, especially with regard to the quantity and quality of members and their participation.[62]

Final remarks

To understand why a straight, white, 60-year-old male became a working-class hero in terms of subjective social construction and public perception, this study has shown that context was king. In other words, recalling the process and timing by which Lynch became RMT General Secretary, it was clear there were quite a few pieces of the jigsaw that might not necessarily have fallen into place. The most obvious of these was the resignation of his predecessor. This provided the opportunity for Lynch to become RMT General Secretary at a time of the biggest proposed onslaught on the RMT rail membership's terms and conditions of employment. Another obvious one was that had Labour been led by Corbyn rather than Starmer at the time, Lynch would not have scaled the heights of public recognition and importance that he did. A further one is that the RMT was by far and away the first union into battle with national strike action against the cost-of-living crisis. But at this 'royal court', the 'king' comprised not just the environment that Lynch and the RMT had to operate within but also their own agency. Here, Lynch showed himself to be a very able public political operator – a necessary if not sufficient component in becoming a working-class hero. The components that were sufficient included, among other things, the historically low level of collective self-confidence and class consciousness of workers, notwithstanding some uptick in both from the summer of 2022 onwards. On this basis, the phenomenon of Lynch as a working-class hero was used to open up crucial issues about power, material interests and ideology for unions and the working class in Britain. The crux of the matter was to consider using associational and structural resources of power to transform the 'power to' (disrupt) into 'power over' (bargaining opponents). In this context, analysis of the RMT's two national disputes somewhat belies Lynch's belief that 'The RMT is sound, robust and in good shape to meet the challenges ahead'[63] if meeting the challenges implies effectiveness and success in gaining the union's bargaining objectives. This was because the RMT had not yet identified 'the right strategies and systems ... [to] deliver an effective political and industrial punch when required'.[64]

Appendix 1: materials and sources

Writing a sociologically informed biography of Lynch has been made much easier not only because of the large number of interviews he undertook with mainstream (or traditional) media but also by the large number of interviews with the alternative and left-wing media. In those latter interviews, there has been a much greater interest in his personal and working life as well as his politics prior to the summer of 2022. And, critically, Lynch willingly acceded to these requests to explain not just his background and life experiences but also his world view. Consequently, he described and explained his views about issues well outside the remit of the RMT and unions in general. Among these interviews were the *Guardian* and LBC as examples of the mainstream media and *Jacobin*, *PoliticsJOE*, *Soundings* and *Tribune* as examples of the alternative and left-wing media. Even where Lynch was not interviewed, such as Radio 4's *Profile* programme,[1] considerable biographical material was still unearthed. Of course, it still remained the case that the questions asked in either the mainstream or alternative media interviews were not those drawn up specifically for this study.

This brings into view the issue of seeking Lynch's cooperation for this study. On 23 August 2022, Lynch was approached to be interviewed for the writing of this book via the RMT Press Officer, John Millington. Even though there was no opportunity to explain what the book would be about, as the initial request was merely to 'see if he'd consent to participate in a series of interviews for [the book]', the response on 2 September was that 'he is not interested in participating in this project'. Shortly afterwards, at a public event on 7 September, Lynch indicated that he would be willing to cooperate. But subsequent attempts to gain formal agreement were met with silence. On the eve of the Labour conference later that month, the ASLEF Press Officer, Keith Richmond, asked Lynch about the interview on my behalf, to be told: 'No, I'm not doing it ... I have neither the time nor the inclination.' Then on 5 October, after further fruitless attempts to make contact, John Millington emailed, saying: 'I spoke to Mick about this, and he is very sorry that he is not able to commit to this project while there is an industrial dispute on.' No further contact was made with Lynch as the national rail disputes continued well into 2023. Indeed, the TOCs dispute continued on after the completion of the writing of this book. However, it should also be noted that in late December 2022 a request was made to ASLEF General Secretary, Mick Whelan, to provide some comments on his assessment of Lynch. On contacting Lynch, Whelan was told by Lynch that 'he'd rather he did not'. And yet it should also be noted that before and after these overtures and requests, Lynch agreed to be interviewed by countless journalists and broadcasters during the national rail disputes and appeared to enjoy the opportunity to put his case and speak about his politics. Indeed, he agreed to extensive access for the making of the BBC2 two-part documentary shown on 25 May and 1 June 2023 called 'Strike: Inside the unions'. As a result of the absence of Lynch's cooperation, the approach taken in this study has been to let Lynch speak in his own words as often as possible, using the many media interviews he did consent to, rather than to paraphrase or summarise what he said.

Nonetheless, testimonies about Lynch were gained from RMT members. A limited number of testimonies were gained from branch secretaries but many more were gained through personal contacts. With the continuing absence of Lynch's cooperation, on 1 March 2023 all 212 branch secretaries were contacted individually by email to request testimony (which would be used anonymously) (see Appendix 2). The email addresses were those publicly available from the RMT website, being '...@rmt. org.uk' addresses. Before many could respond, acting on instruction, RMT Information Technology Officer, Paul Simonds, sent out an email to the RMT branches entitled 'Unauthorised email', saying 'please can you delete [this email] from inbox and delete from deleted items, **please do not ... reply to the email**'.[2] Despite this obstruction, more fulsome testimony was gained through personal contacts with branch secretaries, former presidents, former Council of Executives (CoE) and National Executive Committee (NEC) members, current and former regional organisers, and senior national officers and branch activists. Given the sensitivity of asking for testimony about a sitting general secretary, the offer of anonymity (see Appendix 2) means that a list of testimony givers is not possible as it was for the posthumously published biography of Crow.[3]

To supplement these sources, various RMT publications, press releases and documents like the monthly *RMT News* and annual AGM reports were also used, along with reports on the RMT in left-wing newspapers like the *Morning Star*, *Socialist Worker*, *Solidarity* and *The Socialist*. And while the Office for National Statistics provided only limited salient statistics, the only silver lining of the dark cloud that is the Trade Union Act 2016 was that unions from 2018 onwards are obliged to provide data in their annual returns to the Certification Officer on the number of ballots they organise for industrial action, their outcomes and the number of instances of industrial action that follow from these.

Appendix 2: questions for testimony givers

1) Since the summer of 2022, many in the media – as well as many 'ordinary' people on social media – have called Mick Lynch a 'working-class hero'. Would you agree that Mick Lynch has become or still is a 'working-class hero'?

   If yes, why are they right?
   If not, why are they wrong?

2) If yes, why do you yourself think Mick Lynch has become or still is a 'working-class hero'?

3) If yes, what are the attributes that Mick Lynch has for being a 'working-class hero' that others do not have? Put another way, what makes Mick Lynch be able to be a 'working-class hero' when others are not?

4) What are the essential traits, characteristics and skills of being a 'working-class hero'?

5) What are the strengths and weaknesses of Mick Lynch as a leader?

6) Is Mick Lynch more than just an able frontperson/ media spokesperson for the RMT? And, how influential

is Mick Lynch in the leadership of the RMT (National Executive, other employed officers) in setting its agenda and strategy?

7) Does he come across the same away from the camera as he is in front, that is, reasoned and reasonable?

Notes

Introduction

1 Lynch went bald in the mid- to late 1990s. He has often joked about it: 'My hairdresser had to pursue other interests – he's had to go into another field of work' (Cardiff, 26 January 2023). For 2022, Lynch shared only two of the dominant demographic characteristics of union membership: older (50+) workers were the most unionised, with a density of just under 30.0 per cent, with 16–24 year olds being the least unionised, at a 5.6 per cent density; white ethnic workers had a density of 23.3 per cent and Black or Black British workers a 22.8% per cent density; women (25.6 per cent) had a higher density than men (19.1 per cent), and London (17.6 per cent) had the lowest union density of all nations and regions, with Northern Ireland (32.3 per cent) having the highest. Statistics from ONS, *Trade Union Membership, UK 1995–2022: Statistical Bulletin* (London: Office for National Statistics, 2023). For further details on union demography in 2022, see pp. 49–50.
2 For pen portraits of these and others see P. Routledge, *Bumper Book of British Lefties* (London: Politicos, 2003).
3 *Independent*, 22 June 2022. Lynch's comment, 'If you're not bargaining, you're begging. The British working classes should not have to beg', could be bought alongside an image of his face on coasters for coffee cups at Left Store.
4 Harriet Williamson, *Independent*, 23 June 2022.
5 See https://twitter.com/Rachael_Swindon/status/15393429696140 82049?s-20 (accessed 18 May 2023).

227

Chapter 1

1 Hansard HC Deb., vol. 365, col. 510, 22 March 2001.
2 S. Lukes, *Power: A Radical View* (London: Macmillan, 1974).
3 J. Nye, *Soft Power: The Means to Success in World Politics* (London: Oxford University Press, 2004).
4 See E. Batstone, 'The frontier of control', in D. Gallie (ed.), *Employment in Britain* (Oxford: Blackwell, 1988), pp. 218–47; E. O. Wright, 'Working-class power, capitalist-class interests and class compromise', *American Journal of Sociology*, 105/4 (2000): 957–1002; B. Silver, *Forces of Labor: Workers' Movements and Globalization since 1870* (Cambridge: Cambridge University Press, 2003); C. Lévesque and G. Murray, 'Understanding union power: Resources and capabilities for renewing union capacity', *Transfer: European Review of Labour and Research*, 16/3 (2010), pp. 333–50; S. Schmalz, C. Ludwig and E. Webster, 'The power resources approach: Developments and challenges', *Global Labour Journal*, 9/2 (2018): 113–34; J. Holgate, *Arise: Power, Strategy and Union Resurgence* (London: Pluto, 2021).
5 Wright, 'Working-class power'; Silver, *Forces of Labor*.
6 Batstone, 'The frontier of control'.
7 Lévesque and Murray, 'Understanding union power'.
8 See A. Fox, *Industrial Sociology and Industrial Relations*, Research Papers No. 3, Royal Commission on Trade Unions and Employers' Associations (London: HMSO, 1966); A. Fox, *Beyond Contract: Work, Power and Trust Relations* (London: Faber & Faber, 1974).
9 They had attempted to essentially stage occupations of the ships. This was the same issue as for the OILC rig occupations in 1990. See G. Gall, 'Organising in the offshore oil and gas industry in Britain, c. 1972–1990: A long flame burning or spark that has gone out?', in G. Gall (ed.), *Union Organising: Campaigning for Trade Union Recognition* (London: Routledge, 2023), pp. 39–55; G. Gall, 'Union organising in the offshore oil and gas industry: Retrospection on possibilities and probabilities', *Scottish Labour History*, 41 (2006): 51–69. The OILC merged into the RMT in 2008. See G. Gall, *Bob Crow: Socialist, Leader, Fighter: A Political Biography* (Manchester: Manchester University Press, 2017), pp. 98–9.
10 The battle against the sackings was not helped by the fact many of the seafarers' employment contracts were not based in British law, or by the refusal of the Johnson-led Conservative government to act swiftly on its condemnation of P&O. Just one seafarer refused to

accept the enhanced redundancy terms, taking P&O to an employment tribunal and winning more than the redundancy package he was offered (*Guardian*, 17 March 2023). This seafarer believed: 'If several hundred people were willing to hold P&O up in a tribunal for years, they may well have thought again' (*Guardian*, 17 March 2023). The RMT undertook token protests at ports used by P&O but these did not amount to blockades. While Lynch acknowledged the exploitation of the seafarers, some RMT activists were unhappy about his use of the terms, 'foreign labour' (*PoliticsJOE*, 27 November 2022) and 'migrant labour' (*Novara Media*, 16 December 2022) to describe the replacement agency workers.

11 The 1919 strike by the NUR was a nine-day continuous strike which was successful in its objective of maintaining pay levels. The first national rail strike in 1911, during the period of the 'Great Unrest' of 1911–14, lasted two days and was successful. See A. Gordon, '1911: The first national railway strike and the rail union amalgamation movement', *Historical Studies in Industrial Relations*, 33 (2012): 127–47.

12 M. Berlin, *Never on our Knees: A History of the RMT, 1979–2006* (London: Pluto Press, 2006), pp. 115–16.

13 *Ibid.*, p. 81.

14 *Morning Star*, 23 June 2022 [emphasis added].

15 T. Morris, 'Annual review article 1994', *British Journal of Industrial Relations*, 33/1 (1995): 117–35, at 122–4; Berlin, *Never on our Knees*, pp. 117–22.

16 Gall, *Bob Crow*, p. 201.

17 J. Rose, *100 Years of Kings Cross ASLEF: Solidarity Forever* (London: Kings Cross ASLEF, 1986), p. 37.

18 See G. Gall, 'Three decades on, the 1982 flexible rostering dispute', *ASLEF Locomotive Journal*, April 2012, pp. 12–13; M. Humphrys, 'We're still as proud today as we were then', *ASLEF Journal*, July 2022, pp. 8–9.

19 T. Haines-Doran, *Derailed: How to Fix Britain's Broken Railways* (Manchester: Manchester University Press, 2022), pp. 156–7.

20 *RMT News*, February 2023. See p. 247 for the change in contractual status during the pandemic and after, but where the effective strike indemnity was maintained.

21 RMT press release, 29 July 2023.

22 RMT press release, 7 January 2023.

23 RMT press release, 16 March 2023. The RMT also produced the report, *Parasitic bodies: The business model of the private train operating companies who are wrecking our railways* (London: RMT, 2023), which highlighted that between 2006 and 2022

TOCs invested just 1 per cent of the money spent on the railways but saw a 126 per cent pre-tax return on this.

24 See, for example, R. Darlington, 'Leadership and union militancy: The case of the RMT', *Capital and Class*, 33/3 (2009): 3–32; R. Darlington, 'Organising, militancy and revitalisation: The case of the RMT', in G. Gall (ed.), *Union Revitalisation in Advanced Economies: Assessing the Contribution of 'Union Organising'* (Basingstoke: Palgrave Macmillan, 2009), pp. 83–106; *Guardian*, 13 August 2016; *Red Pepper*, 25 June 2022; *The Social Review* 3 July 2022; *Anti-Capitalist Resistance*, 23 August 2023; *Socialism Today*, October 2023; Holgate, *Arise*, p. 172; N. Flanagan, *Our Trade Unions: What Comes Next after the Summer of 2022?* (London: Manifesto Press, 2023), p. 7.

25 Gall, *Bob Crow*, pp. 200–1.

26 The RMT believed DOO trains would reduce passenger safety and its own industrial influence.

27 Haines-Doran, *Derailed*, p. 69.

28 The Trade Union Act 2016 also doubled the period of notice a union must serve an employer with before any industrial action is taken, from seven days to fourteen days, and compelled unions to reballot every six months if they wished to continue to have a lawful mandate for action.

29 In this regard, it is interesting to note that at a public meeting in February 2016 in Croydon, Peter Wilkinson, a senior official in the Department for Transport, told the audience that 'The [RMT] can't afford to spend too long on strike and I will push them into that place.' Haines-Doran, *Derailed*, p. 68.

30 Gall, *Bob Crow*.

Chapter 2

1 *Mirror*, 24 June 2022; *i*, 24 June 2022; *Evening Standard*, 26 June 2022; *TaketoNews*, 28 June 2022; *New Statesman*, 29 June 2022; *National*, 4 July 2022; *Nevermind Media*, 26 August 2022; *Standard*, 25 June 2022.

2 *Independent*, 25 June 2022.

3 *Daily Express*, 22 June 2022; *Daily Mail*, 8 June 2022, 19 June 2022; *Daily Telegraph*, 24 June 2022, 22 December 2022. Alongside these were the usual slurs of being 'Marxist' (TalkTV, 17 June 2022; ITV, 21 June 2022) and 'hard-left' (*Evening Standard*, 26 June 2022).

4 See https://twitter.com/hearmeplaypiano/status/1540000317676437504?s=20 (accessed 11 May 2023).

Notes

5 See www.fangrrrl.com/collections/mick-lynch (accessed 11 May 2023); https://etsytees.com/product/mick-lynch-youre-a-working-class-hero-shirt (accessed 11 May 2023). T-shirts, hoodies and tote bags can also be bought with 'Lynch for PM' and 'Mick Lynch 4 Prime Minister' emblazoned upon them. The comments sections of videos of Lynch's speeches made at the time of the TUC 2023 congress were littered with congratulatory comments such as 'Lynch for PM!'.

6 *Joe.co.uk*, 24 June 2022. The band The Hanging Bandits recorded a song called 'The Trials of Mick Lynch'.

7 Cf. Anne Graziano on Raymond Williams's textual analysis. A. Graziano, 'The death of the working-class hero in "Mary Barton" and "Alton Locke"', *Journal of Narrative Theory*, 29/2 (1999): 135–57.

8 *Financial Times*, 23 July 2022, 28 August 2022.

9 *The Times*, 15 December 2022.

10 *Sunday Independent*, 26 June 2022; *National*, 28 August 2022; *Christian Science Monitor*, 22 August 2022.

11 *The Times*, 29 June 2022; *Dazed*, 23 June 2022; *Scotsman*, 24 June 2022; *Herald*, 26 June 2022.

12 *New York Times*, 8 December 2022.

13 *National*, 21 June 2022, 27 January 2023; *Herald*, 23 June 2022; *Guardian*, 24 June 2022, 23 August 2022; *Independent*, 2 July 2022; *Irish News*, 27 August 2022; *Challenge*, 28 August 2022; *Irish Times*, 18 March 2023.

14 See, for example, *Metro*, 23 June 2022; *Birmingham Evening Mail*, 29 June 2022.

15 *Morning Star*, 21 June 2022.

16 *Herald*, 18 December 2022; *Mirror*, 26 December 2022.

17 See www.tiktok.com/@thereluctantaccountant/video/7193811943893847302 (accessed 11 May 2023).

18 This TikTok vlogger has posted eighty-three videos since her first one on 16 December 2022, the video on Lynch being the third most watched one, with some 20 per cent of all the nearly 350,000 views by 3 February 2023. Some 350 overwhelmingly supportive comments about Lynch were made in response to the vlog along with nearly 8,000 likes.

19 LBC, 4 January 2023.

20 *Socialism Today*, May 2023.

21 *Joe.co.uk*, 24 June 2022; *Jacobin*, 6 October 2022.

22 *The Times*, 28 June 2022.

23 *Big Issue North*, 25 July 2022.

24 *Tortoise Media*, 19 December 2022.

25 *Hardtalk*, 15 February 2023.

26 *Metro*, 18 January 2023.

27 *Solidarity*, 8 February 2023.

28 *Mail on Sunday*, 14 May 2023.

29 *i*, 24 June 2022.

30 A tentative agreement was reached in April 2023 but this did not end the dispute until early July 2023 (*Guardian*, 22 April 2023; *Guardian*, 24 May 2023; *BBC News* online, 12 July 2023).

31 See G. Gall, *The Meaning of Militancy? Postal Workers and Industrial Relations* (Aldershot: Ashgate, 2003).

32 The *Guardian* noted: 'While his primary objective is to defend rail workers from further real-terms pay cuts and job losses, Lynch has assiduously used his platform to make a wider case, damning a society defined by an "imbalance between the people that do the work to keep this country going, who create the wealth of our civilisation and don't get a fair share of that wealth because it's going to people who are vastly wealthy"' (*Guardian*, 28 June 2022).

33 This was despite accusing Royal Mail of wishing to turn workers' pay and working practices into those used by the likes of Amazon, Deliveroo and Uber.

34 Sharon Graham address to TUC congress, 11 September 2023.

35 Where strikes took place, Unite paid strike pay of around £70 per day out of its dispute fund (see pp. 135–36).

36 This suggests that issues of gender are not in any way significant.

37 With a bent towards a younger audience than the likes of Facebook. See p. 143 for the issue of weighting to create a representative sample for polling.

38 *Guardian*, 25 June 2022.

39 By contrast, the RMT's Facebook page had less than half (40 per cent) the followers it had as RMT members while the FBU's Facebook page had 90 per cent of followers it had as FBU members.

40 US pop-punk band Green Day recorded its own version of the song in 2009.

41 See J. Foster and C. Woolfson, *The Politics of the UCS Work-In: Class Alliances and the Right to Work* (London: Lawrence and Wishart, 1986) and W. Knox and A. McKinlay, *Jimmy Reid: A Clyde-Built Man* (Liverpool: Liverpool University Press, 2019).

42 When in Glasgow at a public event on 9 March 2023, Lynch quoted extensively from Reid's 'alienation' address, made when Reid was installed as Rector of the University of Glasgow on 28 April 1972 (*Herald*, 12 March 2023).

43 Later, through acting and other television work, Tomlinson became wealthy enough to be able to donate in excess of £1m to

hospitals and health care in Liverpool, and to provide substantial donations to the Socialist Labour Party, led by Scargill.

44 The film *Unsung Hero: The Jack Jones Story* (2018) was made about him and the *Guardian* (25 September 2000) carried an extensive interview with him entitled 'Working-class hero'.

45 Of course, some countered that he was, rather, a 'working-class zero' as a result of the belief about his role in accounting for the defeat of the strike. M. Adeney and J. Lloyd, *The Miners' Strike, 1984–1985: Loss Without Limit* (London: Routledge and Kegan Paul, 1986).

46 Cora Kaplan referred to 'the firefighter – [as] symbolically, perhaps, the nation's last working-class hero'. C. Kaplan, 'The death of the working-class hero', *New Formations*, 52 (2004): 94–100, at 94.

47 See R. Smith, *James Connolly: Working-class Hero* (Dublin: Poolbeg Press, 2016).

48 To these may be added the likes of union organiser Joe Hill, film-maker Michael Moore and singer-songwriter Bruce Springsteen. Some other union leaders in North America like Walter Reuther of the United Automobile Workers and Bob White of the Canadian Auto Workers were also called working-class heroes. See B. Garman, *A Race of Singers: Whitman's Working-Class Hero from Guthrie to Springsteen* (Chapel Hill: University of North Carolina Press, 2000).

49 See Gall, *Bob Crow* and *Tommy Sheridan: From Hero to Zero?: A Political Biography* (Cardiff: Welsh Academic Press, 2012).

50 This was not the case for Jeremy Corbyn, John McDonnell or Len McCluskey. Former 'Red Clydeside' MP John Wheatley was, and so too for a time was Labour MP John Prescott, even though the basis for that is very slim indeed.

51 M. Metcalf, *Betty Tebbs: A Radical Working-Class Hero* (London: UNITE Education, 2019).

52 See, for example, S. Aronowitz, *Working-Class Hero: A New Strategy for Labor* (New York: Adama Books, 1983); Graziano, 'The death of the working-class hero'; Kaplan, 'The death of the working-class hero'. S. Burns, *Archie Green: The Making of a Working-Class Hero* (Champaign: University of Illinois Press, 2011); A. Daw and X. Zhou, 'Working-class heroes: Intraspeaker variation in General Secretary Len McCluskey', *Lifespans and Styles*, 3/2 (2017): 20–8; M. Callahan and Y. Moore, *Working-Class Heroes: A History of Struggle in Song: A Songbook* (Oakland, CA: PM Press, 2019); H. Harrison, *The Beast of Bolsover! Dennis Skinner: Working-class Hero!* (Morrisville, NC: Lulu, 2020); B. Reade, *Diamonds in the Mud: A Working-Class Hero is*

Something to Me (London: Mirror Books, 2021); Smith, *James Connolly*.

53 Garman, *A Race of Singers*, pp. 41, 167, 178, 188, 257.

54 This perspective is at odds with that of the likes of the Socialist Equality Party (which is affiliated to the International Committee of the Fourth International (ICFI) and its World Socialist Web Site) and the Spartacist League (affiliated to the International Communist League (Fourth Internationalist)) that all national union leaders are innately traitorous to the interests of their members because of the corrupting influence of incorporation and corporatism. This perspective is not synonymous with the thesis of the 'trade union bureaucracy' (see p. 214). Some Trotskyist groups like Socialist Appeal (affiliated to the International Marxist Tendency) have been fulsome in their praise of Lynch.

55 ONS, *Trade Union Membership, UK 1995–2022*.

56 See J. Kelly, *Trade Unions and Socialist Politics* (London: Verso, 1988).

57 Provisional data shows there were 2.518m days not worked due to strikes in 2022.

58 BBC, *Political Thinking*, 28 May 2022.

Chapter 3

1 It was somewhat ironic then that the term 'Sparks Fly' was the title of the autobiography of right-wing EEPTU union leader Frank Chapple. See F. Chapple, *Sparks Fly: A Trade Union Life*, updated edition (London: Michael Joseph, 1985).

2 His brothers' and sister's work concerned painting and decorating, teaching, plastering and nursing/midwifery (LBC, 29 July 2022; *Guardian*, 23 August 2022).

3 *Sunday Independent*, 26 June 2022.

4 *Ibid.*

5 *Guardian*, 8 May 2021.

6 *Irish Examiner*, 8 May 2023.

7 *Jacobin*, 6 October 2022.

8 *Soundings*, 'The spirit of resistance: Mick Lynch in conversation with Gary Younge', *Lawrence Wishart Blog: Soundings*, 6 December 2022. Available at https://lwbooks.co.uk/the-spirit-of-resistance-mick-lynch-in-conversation-with-gary-younge (accessed 11 May 2023).

9 *Sunday Independent*, 26 June 2022.

10 *Ibid.* ASLEF General Secretary, Mick Whelan, also attended
    the same primary school as Lynch but was two years his senior
    so they did not meet until the 1990s through union gather-
    ings (*Observer*, 7 May 2023). *Jacobin* (15 August 2023) noted
    the presence of many other current union leaders of Irish
    descent in Britain including Eddie Dempsey, Sharon Graham and
    Jo Grady.
11 *Sunday Independent*, 26 June 2022.
12 *Soundings*, 'The spirit of resistance'.
13 *Jacobin*, 6 October 2022.
14 BBC, *Political Thinking*, 28 May 2022.
15 LBC, 29 July 2022.
16 *Ibid.*
17 *Financial Times*, 23 July 2022.
18 LBC, 29 July 2022.
19 Radio 4, *Profile*, 25 June 2022.
20 *Soundings*, 'The spirit of resistance'.
21 *Irish Examiner*, 8 May 2023.
22 *PoliticsJOE*, 11 August 2022.
23 *Jacobin*, 6 October 2022.
24 *The Journal*, 13 August 2022.
25 *Soundings*, 'The spirit of resistance'.
26 *New Statesman*, 17 August 2022.
27 *Soundings*, 'The spirit of resistance'.
28 *Ibid.*
29 *Ibid.*
30 *Irish Examiner*, 8 May 2023.
31 *Irish Examiner*, 8 May 2023.
32 LBC, 29 July 2022.
33 *Big Issue North*, 25 July 2022.
34 BBC, *Political Thinking*, 28 May 2022; *LBC*, 29 July 2022.
35 LBC, 29 July 2022.
36 There was no mention of the EPIU or its leader John Aitkin in the
    extensive official history of the EEPTU written by then EEPTU
    National Officer, John Lloyd, in 1990. Volume 2 of the *Historical
    Directory of Trade Unions*, covering electricians, was published in
    1984 and so did not cover the EPIU, although volume 6, published
    in 2009, did make a brief mention of the EPIU. See J. Lloyd, *Light
    and Liberty: The History of the EETPU* (London: Weidenfeld and
    Nicolson, 1990); A. Marsh and V. Ryan, *Historical Directory of
    Trade Unions*, Volume 2 (Aldershot: Gower, 1984); J. Smethurst
    and P. Carter, *Historical Directory of Trade Unions*, Volume 6
    (London: Routledge, 2009).

37 See E. Hammond, *Maverick: The Life of a Union Rebel* (London: Weidenfeld & Nicolson, 1992).

38 W. Maksymiw, J. Eaton and C. Gill, *The British Trade Union Directory* (London: Longman, 1990), pp. 112–13. See also P. Bassett, *Strike Free: New Industrial Relations in Britain* (London: Macmillan, 1986); J. McIlroy, *Trade Unions in Britain Today* (Manchester: Manchester University Press, 1988).

39 Maksymiw, Eaton and Gill, *The British Trade Union Directory*, pp. 112–13.

40 See A. Murray, *The T&G Story: A History of the Transport and General Workers Union, 1922–2007* (London: Lawrence and Wishart, 2008), p. 177.

41 Maksymiw, Eaton and Gill, *The British Trade Union Directory*, p. 113.

42 *EPIU Bulletin*, September 1992

43 BBC, *Political Thinking*, 28 May 2022.

44 *Financial Times*, 23 July 2022.

45 BBC, *Political Thinking*, 28 May 2022.

46 See D. Smith and P. Chamberlain, *Blacklisted: The Secret War Between Big Business and Union Activists – The Fully Story*, revised second edition (Oxford: New Internationalist Publications, 2016).

47 *Herald*, 17 December 2022.

48 *Guardian*, 8 May 2021.

49 *Jacobin*, 6 October 2022.

50 *Ibid.*

51 BBC, *Political Thinking*, 28 May 2022.

52 For example, Lynch featured only once in the photos of the BSG Facebook group, while Hedley featured more than ten times; Lynch did not feature in the group's blog while Hedley did; and in Smith and Chamberlain's definitive account of the anti-blacklisting campaign, Lynch was only mentioned once while Hedley had over ten entries. See Smith and Chamberlain, *Blacklisted*.

53 There were no student fees at this time and student maintenance grants were available, and it was possible to claim unemployment benefit and housing benefit in non-term times.

54 *PoliticsJOE*, 11 August 2022.

55 *The Journal*, 13 August 2022.

56 *Irish Times*, 18 March 2023.

57 *RMT News*, March 2016.

58 *Morning Star*, 16 May 2021.

59 LBC, 29 July 2022.

60 *Morning Star*, 5 July 2006.
61 *RMT News*, July/August 2006.
62 *Evening Standard*, 26 June 2022.
63 *The Times*, 21 June 2022.
64 BBC, *Political Thinking*, 28 May 2022.

Chapter 4

1 The Council of Executives became the NEC in 2015 as a result of the union's internal structures review.
2 *Jacobin*, 6 October 2022. See also *New Statesman*, 17 August 2022; *Guardian*, 23 August 2022.
3 RMT, *RMT as an Industrially Organised Union*, 20 January version (London: RMT, 2022).
4 These figures are taken from the annual returns provided by the RMT to the Certification Officer. The figures on ballots on the RMT's website are higher because they also include ballots on the likes of pay offers. Thus, 2022 saw 158, there were 211 in 2021, 85 in 2020, 136 in 2019, 120 in 2018, 108 in 2017, 76 in 2016, 113 in 2015 and 89 in 2014.
5 Figures for the number of days of IASOS for the four previous years were 592, 941, 365 and 92 respectively.
6 In a declining number of cases in the new millennium, employers pay for unions' national executive members to be on full facility time. The Tory Trade Union Act 2016 put further pressure on public sector employers to reveal the extent to which this practice continued, in an attempt to reduce its extent.
7 Later, he became a Trustee Director of the £30bn Railway Pension Scheme.
8 *New Statesman*, 26 February 2015.
9 *Morning Star*, 24 June 2014.
10 *RMT News*, January 2013 [emphasis added].
11 *Morning Star*, 25 June 2014.
12 *RMT News*, May 2015.
13 G. Gall, *Bob Crow: Socialist, Leader, Fighter: A Political Biography* (Manchester: Manchester University Press, 2017), pp. 233–4.
14 *New Statesman*, 17 August 2022.
15 *Solidarity*, 30 May 2018.
16 *Socialist*, 13 July 2022.
17 *Socialism Today*, 12 December 2023.
18 *Yorkshire Post*, 20 August 2022.
19 *RMT News*, October 2020; *Rail News*, 10 November 2020.

20 Radio 4, *Profile*, 25 June 2022.
21 *RMT News*, October 2020.
22 *Evening Standard*, 3 November 2020.
23 CFDU press release, 30 September 2020.
24 This included Cash himself in his subsequent editorial column in *RMT News* (November/December 2020) and his Twitter account (@MickCashexRMTGS) headed as 'retired rmt [*sic*] general secretary ...', as well as many in the general and specialist railway media including *Off The Rails* (10 November 2020). Cash was 60 when he announced his 'retirement'.
25 *RMT News*, November/December 2020.
26 See M. Berlin, *Never on our Knees: A History of the RMT, 1979–2006* (London: Pluto Press, 2006), pp. 35–41.
27 *Union News*, 8 September 2020.
28 Press Association, 7 September 2020.
29 BBC, *Political Thinking*, 28 May 2022.
30 See www.rmt.org.uk/about/rmt-structure/council-of-executives (accessed 11 May 2023).
31 *Newsletter*, 8 November 2020.
32 Gall, *Bob Crow*.
33 One such member was Alex Gordon, who some opponents have characterised as, thus, moving from syndicalism to Stalinism.
34 *Newsletter*, 3 August 2020.
35 *Newsletter*, 10 September 2020.
36 *Newsletter*, 8 November 2020.
37 BBC, *Political Thinking*, 28 May 2022.
38 *Off The Rails*, 10 December 2021.
39 *Off The Rails*, 4 July 2022.

Chapter 5

1 *Irish Examiner*, 8 May 2023.
2 On 22 September 2014 Cash was elected, receiving 8,938 votes, with Pottage gaining 4,006, Hedley 1,885, Leach 1,428 and Gordon 1,176 on a 23 per cent turnout.
3 The context of the importance of these two factors was that in RMT material and publications (such as press releases, *RMT News* and circulars), the figure of the general secretary dominates.
4 BBC, *Political Thinking*, 28 May 2022.
5 *Morning Star*, 16 May 2021.
6 *Guardian*, 8 May 2021.
7 *Morning Star*, 16 May 2021. See also *Guardian*, 23 August 2022.

8 *RMT News*, May 2021 [emphasis added].
9 *Morning Star*, 16 May 2021.
10 Meaning their three-year term of office had come to an end. This led Lynch to emphasise the point: 'They rotate through and rotate out' (BBC, *Political Thinking*, 28 May 2022).
11 *Guardian*, 8 May 2021.
12 Just before Lynch went off on sickness absence himself in September 2020, a staff member in the union's Organising Department was dismissed due to a long-term mental ill health absence even though the staff member and his union representative put forward a schedule for his return to work and which was approved by his line manager. The dismissal was reversed on appeal. There was another case of disciplinary that led to dismissal when Lynch was Senior Assistant General Secretary or Acting General Secretary.
13 In one of the few public statements on the matter, Lynch wrote in his *RMT News* (February 2022) editorial: 'With the industrial fights hotting up across rail, buses and maritime I'm sorry to have to report that a small group of people and their outside supporters have chosen this moment to try and cause maximum disruption to our organisation. These actions at Unity House have provoked serious complaints from our staff and their trade unions GMB and NUJ [National Union of Journalists] regarding a frankly sickening campaign of abuse, harassment and bullying targeting our loyal and hardworking staff and others using our head office. This has now led to a formal industrial dispute by the GMB and NUJ declared against us based on workplace safety. I make this clear as your general secretary. You elected me to do a job of work to deliver for you on the workplace issues that impact on you, your colleagues and your families. I intend to do just that no matter what a small group intent on damaging our union throw at me and the organisation. We face a level of cuts and attacks unprecedented in a generation. Anyone who tries to deflect us from the massive task that confronts us to defend jobs, pay and pensions will get short shrift from me.'
14 Mihaj claimed he was bullied and victimised by the RMT and its officers over raising allegations of misuse of union funds, refusing to support Cash's re-election campaign and campaigning for an independent union, the GMB, to represent RMT staff as an alternative to the RMT staff association. He took the RMT, Cash and five others to an employment tribunal, with the decision on 12 October 2022 that the claim of race discrimination under the Equality Act 2010 was struck out, and all claims against five of the respondents (other than the RMT and Cash) were also struck

out. No strike out or deposit orders were made on claims under disability discrimination or victimisation, trade union detriment, unfair dismissal or breach of contract.

15 Eddie Dempsey was elected as Assistant General Secretary on 25 October 2021, beating Alan Pottage by around 600 votes on a 14 per cent turnout. Previously an RMT regional organiser, Dempsey was supported by the RMT Broad Left. He then became Senior Assistant General Secretary in April 2022 following Hedley's retirement on ill health grounds. This created a vacancy for assistant general secretary, which John Leach won on 9 June 2022. The CFDU supported Pottage and Leach in these elections as it had often done before when the two candidates had previously stood for other elected officer positions.

16 RMT, *RMT as an Industrially Organised Union*, 20 January version (London: RMT, 2022).

17 *Ibid.*, p. 4.

18 *RMT News*, November/December 2020.

19 See E. Heery and J. Kelly, 'Professional, participative and managerial unionism: An interpretation of change in trade unions', *Work, Employment and Society*, 8/1 (1994): 1–22.

20 LBC, 26 May 2022; BBC, *Political Thinking*, 28 May 2022.

21 *New Statesman*, 17 August 2022.

22 *Guardian*, 23 August 2022.

23 *Newsletter*, 3 July 2022.

Chapter 6

1 *Guardian*, 23 June 2022.
2 *Herald*, 23 June 2022.
3 *Scotsman*, 24 June 2022.
4 *New Zealand Standard*, 25 June 2022.
5 *Evening Standard*, 25 June 2022; *Guardian*, 28 June 2022.
6 *Observer*, 26 June 2022.
7 *Sunday Independent*, 26 June 2022.
8 *Guardian*, 20 July 2022.
9 *New Statesman*, 28 July 2022.
10 *Agence France-Presse*, 9 January 2023.
11 *RMT News*, September 2022.
12 *Evening* Standard, 26 June 2022.
13 *The Spectator*, 22 June 2022, 26 June 2022. Lynch's mild bemusement at the questions asked only departed him on the odd occasion. On Radio 4's *Today* programme (13 December 2022), he

became somewhat bad-tempered and a little rattled on the issue of members' loss of wages due to striking and the implications of this for their support for continued striking. Later that morning on ITV's *Good Morning Britain* with Richard Madeley, he was clearly exasperated and irritated – but did not become visibly angry or walk out – when he told Madeley: 'You're just ranting now. You're just talking to yourself, now, Richard. Why don't you just interview yourself?'

14 *Scotsman*, 24 June 2022.
15 *Guardian*, 23 June 2022.
16 *Observer*, 26 June 2022.
17 *Financial Times*, 23 July 2022.
18 Lynch seldom wrote articles or papers, given that he was an 'old school' influencer and operator whose stock-in-trade was the spoken word. One such occasion was a page-length review of a book on London transport in *RMT News* (February 2016) and another was the twelve-page internal paper, RMT, *RMT as an Industrially Organised Union*, 20 January version (London: RMT, 2022). As is common practice, articles written by union general secretaries in, for example, the *Morning Star*, are not necessarily actually written by them.
19 See *New Statesman*, 25 June 2022, 28 July 2022.
20 *Financial Times*, 23 July 2022.
21 *Ibid.*
22 *Green Left Weekly*, 12 October 2022.
23 *Metro*, 18 January 2023.
24 *Wigan Today*, 12 January 2023.
25 *Sun on Sunday*, 18 December 2022.
26 SWP, *Class Struggle is Back: Strikes, Why Labour Fails and the Fight for Socialist Revolution* (London: Socialist Workers Party, 2022).
27 *Guardian*, 23 August 2022.
28 *Jacobin*, 6 October 2022.
29 *New Statesman*, 17 August 2022.
30 Cardiff, 26 January 2023.
31 LBC, 29 July 2022.
32 *Ibid.*
33 *Jacobin*, 6 October 2022.
34 *Sunday Mirror*, 8 January 2023.
35 *Irish Examiner*, 8 May 2023.
36 *Journalist*, August/September 2022.
37 *Soundings*, 'The spirit of resistance: Mick Lynch in conversation with Gary Younge', *Lawrence Wishart Blog: Soundings*, 6

December 2022. Available at https://lwbooks.co.uk/the-spirit-of-resistance-mick-lynch-in-conversation-with-gary-younge (accessed 11 May 2023).

38 *Irish Times*, 18 March 2023.
39 BBC, *Political Thinking*, 28 May 2022.
40 *Morning Star*, 21 June 2022.
41 *Morning Star*, 23 June 2022.
42 Cardiff, 26 January 2023.
43 BBC, *Political Thinking*, 28 May 2022.
44 *Irish Independent*, 26 June 2022.
45 *Financial Times*, 23 July 2022.
46 *Irish Independent*, 6 May 2023.
47 *Irish Examiner*, 8 May 2023.
48 *Observer*, 26 June 2022.
49 LBC, 29 July 2022.
50 LBC, 4 January 2023.
51 BBC, *Newscast*, 21 July 2022.
52 *Sunday Independent*, 26 June 2022.
53 BBC radio, *Hardtalk*, 15 February 2023.
54 *Morning Star*, 24 February 2023.
55 *Agence France-Presse*, 9 January 2023.
56 *Sunday Mirror*, 8 January 2023.
57 LBC, 29 July 2022.
58 *Guardian*, 23 August 2022.
59 House of Commons Transport Select Committee, 11 January 2023.
60 *PoliticsJOE*, 11 August 2022.
61 For example, Crow's portrait was taken down from a prominent position in RMT headquarters and replaced by one of former NUR General Secretary, Jimmy Knapp.
62 *Morning Star*, 23 February 2023.
63 *Sun*, 5 June 2009.
64 *Guardian*, 9 June 2009; *Mirror*, 9 February 2014.
65 G. Gall, *Bob Crow: Socialist, Leader, Fighter: A Political Biography* (Manchester: Manchester University Press, 2017).
66 *Spectator*, 26 June 2022.
67 *Big Issue North*, 25 July 2022.
68 *Guardian*, 11 March 2014.
69 *Sky News*, 16 March 2023.
70 *Guardian*, 20 June 2009.
71 *The Times*, 21 June 2022.
72 *Daily Mail*, 21 June 2022.
73 Gall, *Bob Crow*.

74 See, for example, *Telegraph*, 21 June 2022; *Evening Standard*, 26 June 2022; *Huffington Post*, 18 August 2022; *BBC News* online, 13 December 2022; *Spectator*, 13 December 2022; *Daily Express*, 24 December 2022; *Herald*, 12 March 2023; *Belfast Telegraph*, 18 April 2023.

75 Gall, *Bob Crow*.

76 *Evening Standard*, 8 November 2017.

77 *RMT News*, November/December 2017.

78 *Evening Standard*, 26 June 2022.

79 See *Irish Independent*, 6 May 2023, on Lynch and Gall, *Bob Crow*, p. 141.

80 BBC, *Political Thinking*, 28 May 2022.

81 *Morning Star*, 2 November 2022.

82 *Novara Media*, 9 December 2022.

83 *BBC News* online, 13 December 2022.

84 Gall, *Bob Crow*, pp. 45, 54.

85 *Morning Star*, 3 March 2021.

86 Gall, *Bob Crow*, p. 224.

87 Radio 4, *Profile*, 7 December 2019.

88 LBC, 29 July 2022.

89 *Guardian*, 31 September 2014. This undermined the veracity of the claim of the RMT Broad Left (*Newsletter*, 8 November 2020) that Cash was a 'militant trade unionist and socialist … Our union registered more disputes than any other [union] under [his] leadership.' This statement took no account of the issues of the number and size of bargaining units (see also Gall, *Bob Crow*, pp. 193 and 200) and it is worth recalling that Cash opposed Crow on an anti-militant basis for the post of assistant general secretary in 1999 (see *ibid.*, p. 43).

90 *Ibid.*

91 *Novara Media*, 16 December 2022.

92 *Ibid.*

93 *Double Down News*, 16 December 2022.

94 A. Nunns, *The Candidate: Jeremy Corbyn's Improbable Path to Power* (London: OR Books, 2018).

95 *Guardian*, 8 October 2017.

96 *New Statesman*, 17 August 2022.

97 BBC, *Political Thinking*, 28 May 2022.

98 LBC, 29 July 2022.

99 *BBC News* online, 13 December 2022.

100 *Spectator*, 17 December 2022.

101 *New Statesman*, 26 January 2023.

102 Gall, *Bob Crow*, pp. 154–5.

103 *BBC2*, 'Strike: Inside the unions', 25 May 2023.
104 *Guardian*, 29 July 2023. Lynch could have chosen to say 'RMT members' and not 'we'.
105 *PoliticsJoe*, 12 September 2023; *Spectator*, 7 August 2023.
106 See R. Darlington and M. Upchurch, 'A reappraisal of the rank-and-file/bureaucracy debate', *Capital and Class*, 36/1 (2012): 73–91; R. Darlington, 'The rank and file and the trade union bureaucracy', *International Socialism*, 142 (2014): 57–82.
107 Liverpool, 6 October 2022.
108 *Soundings*, 'The spirit of resistance'.

Chapter 7

1 BBC, *Newscast*, 21 July 2022.
2 LBC, 26 May 2022.
3 *Novara Media*, 28 July 2022; *Herald*, 17 December 2022.
4 BBC, *Newscast*, 21 July 2022.
5 Members' communication, 20 February 2023.
6 *Guardian*, 8 March 2023.
7 *Guardian*, 10 February 2023, 12 December 2022.
8 RMT staff were awarded a below inflation, 3.6 per cent pay increase in 2022.
9 RMT press release, 8 March 2023.
10 LBC, 4 January 2023.
11 *Guardian*, 11 March 2023.
12 RMT press release, 20 March 2023. The subsequent issue of *RMT News*, which was published on 22 March 2023, carried the same traits.
13 LBC, 26 May 2022; BBC, *Political Thinking*, 28 May 2022.
14 Cardiff, 26 January 2023.
15 *BBC2*, 1 June 2023.
16 *Morning Star*, 21 March 2023.
17 *Socialist Appeal*, 23 March 2023.
18 For example, *Off The Rails*, 20 March 2023, 25 March 2023; *Socialist*, 30 March 2023.
19 *Guardian*, 21 March 2023.
20 *BBC2*, 1 June 2023.
21 *BBC News* online, 20 March 2021. Subsequent to the end of the Network Rail dispute, the company announced that no strikers would be eligible for the performance-related annual bonus, which was worth around £300 (*Guardian*, 30 August 2023).

22 As most signallers struck, a relatively small number of managers and members of other unions (like the Transport Salaried Staffs' Association (TSSA)) worked.

23 *Observer*, 28 May 2023.

24 See https://www.rmt.org.uk/news/public-document-library/offer-letter-from-the-rdg-130423/ Strangely, the *Off The Rails* (17, 23, 28 April 2023) did not pick up upon this 'no-strike' stipulation. Neither did it identify the Lynch's *volte face*. The same was true of other socialist journals like the *Morning Star, Socialist Worker, The Socialist* and *Socialist Appeal*.

25 RMT testimony giver (see Appendix 1 for details).

26 RMT press release, 27 April 2023. While the 22 March 2023 RDG letter to Lynch summarising where discussions had got to by that day did not mention a 'no-strike' clause, it cannot be credibly stated that its insertion – unlike that of the instance of DOO's last-minute insertion before Christmas 2022 – into the 13 April RDG offer was either an act of reneging or torpedoing given that Lynch was lead for the RMT negotiating side.

27 *Guardian*, 28 April 2023.

28 *Ibid.*

29 ASLEF train drivers struck on 12 May 2023 so there were two days of disruption.

30 ASLEF train drivers struck on 3 June 2023 so there were two days of disruption.

31 *Guardian*, 3 June 2023.

32 *Observer*, 28 May 2023.

33 *Guardian*, 1 June 2023.

34 *Tribune*, 6 June 2023.

35 *BBC News* online, 22 June 2023.

36 RMT press release, 1 September 2023. A second RMT press release on 1 September 2023 then indicated that the RDG had formally rejected the RMT's proposals.

37 RMT press release, 4 September 2023.

38 The South Eastern trains and the East Coast mainline franchises were returned to the private sector after short periods in the public sector, following the Westminster government being forced to act as an 'operator of last resort'.

39 RMT press release, 8 June 2023.

40 *Ibid.*

41 *RMT News*, July/August 2022, February 2023.

42 *Tribune*, 27 July 2022.

43 LBC, 4 January 2023.

Notes

Sunday Mirror, 8 January 2023.

45 LBC, 26 May 2022.

46 LBC, 4 January 2023.

47 Good Morning Britain, 18 August 2022.

48 Cardiff, 26 January 2023.

49 Double Down News, 24 December 2022.

50 When Trotsky coined the phrase at the talks that led to the Treaty of Brest-Litovsk – which ended Russia's participation in the First World War – on 3 March 1918, it signified a strategy which was ultimately unsuccessful, as Soviet Russia ceded massive swathes of territory which endangered the October 1917 revolution even further.

51 Irish Times, 18 March 2023.

52 PoliticsJOE, 11 August 2022.

53 The same has been true for ASLEF's strikes amongst train drivers in the same period since the summer of 2022.

54 Guardian, 19 January 2023.

55 Ibid.

56 Novara Media, 9 December 2022.

57 Novara Media, 15 December 2022.

58 LBC, 4 January 2023.

59 This position softened somewhat in the summer of 2023 when the Tories accepted the recommendations of the pay review bodies for pay rises for 2023–24 – without any significant movement on pay rises for 2022–23 – for groups like teachers. By the late summer of 2023, junior and senior doctors and university staff were two of the few remaining large groups of workers still taking national industrial action. In late June 2023, RCN nurse union members effectively accepted a pay offer that was significantly below its claim after failing to renew their industrial action mandate. Then in late July, members of the NEU and three other teaching union members in England accepted their improved pay offer after the NEU renewed its strike mandate in May. In late August, PCS members in the civil service then ended their industrial action in order to take stock and prepare for their next pay bargaining round. The Tories also increasingly used the issue of migrants crossing the English Channel as another means of trying to whip up electoral support.

60 See, for example, RMT Broad Left Newsletter (8 November 2020), London Review of Books (24 June 2022) and Flanagan, Our Trade Unions, pp. 47, 77.

61 LBC, 26 May 2022.

62 Tribune, 5 January 2023.

Notes

63 RMT press release, 2 June 2023.
64 *Sophy Ridge on Sunday* programme, 16 July 2023.
65 *Morning Star*, 11 September 2023.
66 *BBC2*, 25 May 2023.
67 *Guardian*, 21 March 2023.
68 The situation is a little more complex where the employer is a private (profit-seeking) one working in the public sector as the result of the contracting out of service provision (see pp. 23–24).
69 So long as TOCs abide by their 'management fee' contracts, which stipulate the extensive powers of the Secretary of State in their industrial relations (including remuneration, redundancies, restructuring, terms and conditions and negotiating strategies for these), their effective indemnities are maintained. Post-pandemic, this resulted from TOCs being placed on 'management fee' contracts where there is no revenue-associated risk. Prior to the pandemic, TOCs were free to negotiate as they wished with the RMT and other unions but with indemnity for losses occasioned by industrial action. During the pandemic, emergency measures agreements (EMAs) and then emergency recovery management agreements (ERMAs) provided TOCs with a management fee for running the railways regardless of revenue. One of the consequences of this is that if TOCs wish to increase the relative value of their 'management fee', they can only do so by cutting costs and not by increasing revenue. In practice, this has meant mainly downward pressure on staff costs.
70 See, for example, *Guardian*, 24 June 2022.
71 It should also be noted that polling by YouGov for its 2019–2023 tracker on 'In principle, do you think train and underground drivers should or should not be allowed to go on strike?' showed that 53–59 per cent responded 'Yes'.
72 *Guardian*, 7 January 2023.
73 *Novara Media*, 15 September 2022.
74 *Novara Media*, 28 July 2022.
75 G. Gall, *Bob Crow: Socialist, Leader, Fighter: A Political Biography* (Manchester: Manchester University Press, 2017), p. 121.
76 *PoliticsJOE*, 11 August 2022.
77 Gall, *Bob Crow*, pp. 162–5; G. Gall, 'Injunctions as a legal weapon in collective industrial disputes in Britain, 2005–2014', *British Journal of Industrial Relations*, 55/1 (2017): 187–214.
78 See Gall, 'Injunctions as a legal weapon' for the period 2005–14.
79 These ballots were conducted on a company-by-company basis. Those RMT members voting for strike action and IASOS were in Chiltern Railways, CrossCountry Trains, Greater Anglia, LNER,

East Midlands Railway, c2c, Great Western Railway, Northern Trains, South Eastern, South Western Railway, TransPennine Express, Avanti West Coast and West Midlands Trains. Initially, RMT members on Govia Thameslink Railways, including Gatwick Express, only voted for industrial action short of a strike.

80 Less than a month later, RMT members in Network Rail rejected the latest offer by 64 per cent on an 83 per cent turnout in an RMT e-referendum where there was a 'reject' recommendation. The offer comprised a 5 per cent and 4 per cent pay rise over a two-year period with thousands of job losses, 50 per cent cut in scheduled maintenance tasks and a 3 per cent increase in unsocial hours.

81 The intended Network Rail reballot did not take place due to the settlement of the dispute in March 2023.

82 In April 2023, the second day of the RCN's two-day strike was injuncted (*Guardian*, 28 April 2023) for the same reason as Royal Mail threatened the CWU, namely the expiry of the six-month strike mandate.

83 LBC, 4 January 2003; *Tribune*, 5 January 2023; *Morning Star*, 1 February 2023. For further analysis of the draconian effects of the Bill, provided by Keith Ewing and John Hendy, see *Morning Star*, 15 January 2023, 24 January 2023 and *Red Pepper*, 5 February 2023.

84 See Gall, 'Injunctions as a legal weapon'.

85 This included Parliament's own Regulatory Policy Committee deeming the Bill 'not fit for purpose' and its own Joint Committee on Human Rights stating the Bill to be 'not justified'. See *Financial Times*, 17 February 2023; *Guardian*, 17 January 2023, 6 March 2023.

86 See, for example, *Independent*, 23 May 2023.

87 See *Guardian*, 25 March 2023.

88 The sliding wage scale was introduced in France in 1952 and removed in 1982, while in Italy it was introduced in 1945 and removed in 1992.

89 As of 2022, Belgium, Spain, France, Cyprus, Luxembourg, Malta and Slovenia have wage indexation systems for public and private sector workers.

90 *Guardian*, 23 August 2022.

91 *Independent*, 22 June 2022.

92 There are different types of arbitration. Conventional arbitration allows the arbitrator to determine a settlement after taking submissions from both sides once the issue in dispute has been agreed on. Meanwhile, pendulum arbitration requires the arbitrator to

choose either the union or the employer proposal, meaning the difference cannot be split as under conventional arbitration. The intention here is to make the two sides come closer together in their proposals, given its Russian roulette nature.

93 See T. Gourvish, *British Rail 1974–1997: From Integration to Privatisation* (Oxford: Oxford University Press, 2002).

94 I. Beardwell, 'Annual review article 1989', *British Journal of Industrial Relations*, 28/1 (1990): 113–28, at 123.

95 Gall, *Bob Crow*.

96 G. Gall, *The Meaning of Militancy? Postal Workers and Industrial Relations* (Aldershot: Ashgate, 2003).

97 *Guardian*, 20 October 2022.

98 *PoliticsJOE*, 11 August 2022.

99 *Ibid.*

100 *Guardian*, 20 October 2022.

101 See A. Murray and L. German, *Stop the War: The Story of Britain's Biggest Mass Movement* (London: Bookmarks, 2005).

102 As the Palestine Action network has been able to since the mid-2010s with regard to arms manufacturers supplying Israel.

103 See S. Hannah, *Can't Pay, Won't Pay: The Fight to Stop the Poll Tax* (London: Pluto, 2020).

104 BBC, *Political Thinking*, 28 May 2022.

105 *RMT News*, March 2016. There were obvious cases in other unions where even the general secretary – quite apart from other senior officers – was from the 'rank and file'. In 2019, Jo Grady was elected UCU General Secretary from the grass roots without having previously held any (employed) officer position. This was similar to Mark Serwotka being elected PCS General Secretary in 2000 (and John Moloney in 2019 as PCS Assistant General Secretary).

106 *Jacobin*, 6 October 2022.

107 *Double Down News*, 4 August 2022.

108 *PoliticsJOE*, 11 August 2022.

109 *Guardian*, 23 August 2022.

110 *BBC 2*, 1 June 2023.

111 *LBC*, 29 July 2022. One former NEC member believed: 'The survival of "the union" is of paramount importance and Mick [Lynch] will use all means at his disposal to stop anything or anyone he believes is threatening "the union" as an institution.'

112 *BBC2*, 25 May 2023.

113 *LBC*, 29 July 2022

114 *Soundings*, 'The spirit of resistance: Mick Lynch in conversation with Gary Younge', *Lawrence Wishart Blog: Soundings*, 6

December 2022. Available at https://lwbooks.co.uk/the-spirit-of-resistance-mick-lynch-in-conversation-with-gary-younge (accessed 11 May 2023).

115 See E. Heery and J. Kelly, 'Professional, participative and managerial unionism: An interpretation of change in trade unions', *Work, Employment and Society*, 8/1 (1994): 1–22.

116 *PoliticsJOE*, 11 August 2022.

117 M. Upchurch, R. Croucher and M. Flynn, 'Political congruence and trade union renewal', *Work, Employment and Society*, 26/5 (2012): 857–68.

118 Gall, *Bob Crow*.

Chapter 8

1 See, for example, *RMT News*, September 2020, September 2022, November/December 2022, January 2023; *Morning Star*, 16 May 2021; *Financial Times*, 23 July 2022; *Tribune*, 27 July 2022; *New Statesman*, 17 August 2022; *Guardian*, 20 October 2022; *Soundings*, 'The spirit of resistance: Mick Lynch in conversation with Gary Younge', *Lawrence Wishart Blog: Soundings*, 6 December 2022. Available at https://lwbooks.co.uk/the-spirit-of-resistance-mick-lynch-in-conversation-with-gary-younge (accessed 11 May 2023); *Wales Online*, 22 January 2023.

2 *Sky News*, 19 June 2022.

3 *RMT News*, November/December 2022.

4 *Guardian*, 13 February 2023.

5 BBC, *Political Thinking*, 28 May 2022.

6 *Soundings*, 'The spirit of resistance'.

7 *Jacobin*, 6 October 2022.

8 Cardiff, 26 January 2023.

9 *Jacobin*, 6 October 2022.

10 *Ibid.*

11 H. Draper, 'The twin souls of socialism', *New Politics*, 5/1 (1966): 7–84.

12 G. Gall, *Bob Crow: Socialist, Leader, Fighter: A Political Biography* (Manchester: Manchester University Press, 2017), pp. 154–5.

13 *Guardian*, 7 February 2014.

14 *Soundings*, 'The spirit of resistance'.

15 *Financial Times*, 10 September 2004.

16 *Soundings*, 'The spirit of resistance'.

17 *Solidarity*, 5 October 2022. This quote, from the *Novara Media* panel discussion at The World Transformed Conference in

Liverpool on 25 September 2022, was also reported elsewhere as 'pragmatic reform of our system'.

18 *RMT News*, March 2019.
19 *Morning Star*, 24 June 2019; *RMT News*, July/August 2019.
20 Asked about rail workers controlling the railways by an RMT member as a form of workers' power on LBC (26 May 2022), Lynch avoided giving a direct answer.
21 *Morning Star*, 28 June 2018.
22 *Morning Star*, 16 May 2021.
23 BBC, *Political Thinking*, 28 May 2022.
24 *LBC*, 29 July 2022.
25 *PoliticsJOE*, 11 August 2022.
26 Liverpool, 6 October 2022.
27 LBC, 4 January 2023. Lynch had not been a Labour member since the mid-1980s (Cardiff, 26 January 2023) and stated elsewhere: 'I'm not a communist' (LBC, 26 May 2022).
28 *PoliticsJOE*, 11 August 2022.
29 BBC, *Newscast*, 21 July 2022; *Sunday Mirror*, 8 January 2023.
30 *The Times*, 21 June 2022.
31 BBC, *Newscast*, 21 July 2022.
32 *The Times*, 21 June 2022.
33 *PoliticsJOE*, 11 August 2022.
34 BBC, *Political Thinking*, 28 May 2022.
35 *Jacobin*, 6 October 2022.
36 *Soundings*, 'The spirit of resistance'.
37 *Morning Star*, 24 February 2023.
38 Cardiff, 26 January 2023.
39 *Irish Times*, 18 March 2023.
40 *New Statesman*, 17 August 2022. In regard to patriotism, Lynch later stated: 'We're not part of any anti-growth coalition. We're not against the economy, we're not against the country, we want the country to succeed'; *Guardian*, 8 October 2022 [emphasis added].
41 Radio 4, 25 September 2022.
42 *Jacobin*, 6 October 2022.
43 *PoliticsJOE*, 11 August 2022.
44 *Big Issue North*, 25 July 2022; LBC, 29 July 2022.
45 Lynch continued: 'And then people tell me I'm a Putin apologist? I'm not. Putin should stop the war, get out of Ukraine and respect the sovereignty of that nation.' *Guardian*, 23 August 2022.
46 *PoliticsJOE*, 11 August 2022.
47 *Ibid.*
48 *New Statesman*, 17 August 2022.
49 LBC, 29 July 2022.

Notes

50 Liverpool, 6 October 2022.
51 *Ibid.*
52 Cardiff, 26 January 2023.
53 *Ibid.*
54 *Socialist Worker*, 4 April 2023; 9 May 2023; 31 May 2023; 6 June 2023. See also *Socialist Worker* 22 August 2023 and 29 August 2023. A more nuanced analysis was regularly provided by the *Off The Rails* blog (see, for example, 24 August 2023).
55 *Soundings*, 'The spirit of resistance'.
56 *Telegraph*, 29 May 2022.
57 *Big Issue North*, 25 July 2022.
58 *PoliticsJOE*, 11 August 2022.
59 *New Statesman*, 17 August 2022.
60 *Yorkshire Post*, 20 August 2022.
61 *Morning Star*, 26 September 2022.
62 *Liverpool Echo*, 26 September 2022.
63 *PoliticsJOE*, 27 November 2022.
64 *Tribune*, 5 January 2023.
65 *Morning Star*, 23 January 2023.
66 General Secretary's address to 2023 RMT annual conference (RMT press release, 27 June 2023).
67 *Peston* programme, 5 July 2023.
68 *Sophy Ridge on Sunday* programme, 16 July 2023.
69 See, for example, *Morning Star*, 3 October 2022, 1 February 2023.
70 *Guardian*, 19 October 2022.
71 *Guardian*, 23 August 2022.
72 *Soundings*, 'The spirit of resistance'.
73 *Ibid.*
74 *Soundings*, 'The spirit of resistance'.
75 *Morning Star*, 3 October 2022.
76 *RMT News*, November/December 2022.
77 *PoliticsJOE*, 27 November 2022.
78 Aberdare, 25 January 2023.
79 See Gall, *Bob Crow*.
80 *Morning Star*, 12 July 2023.
81 *Morning Star*, 26 June 2023.
82 General Secretary's address to 2023 RMT annual conference (RMT press release, 27 June 2023).
83 *Soundings*, 'The spirit of resistance'.
84 *Ibid.*
85 *BBC News* online, 13 December 2022.
86 *Sunday Mirror*, 8 January 2023.
87 *Evening Standard*, 16 January 2023.

Notes

88 *New Statesman*, 17 August 2022.
89 LBC, 29 July 2022.
90 BBC, *Politics Live*, 21 June 2022.
91 *Double Down News*, August 2022.
92 Liverpool, 6 October 2022.
93 *Soundings*, 'The spirit of resistance'.
94 Cardiff, 26 January 2023.
95 *Jacobin*, 6 October 2022.
96 Cardiff, 26 January 2023.
97 *Irish Times*, 18 March 2023.
98 See, for example, *Guardian*, 29 December 2022, 27 January 2023.
99 See Gall, *Bob Crow*, pp. 89–91.
100 *Yorkshire Post*, 20 August 2022.
101 *Tribune*, 7 July 2022.
102 LBC, 29 July 2022.
103 *Jacobin*, 6 October 2022.
104 *Guardian*, 5 October 2022.
105 *Soundings*, 'The spirit of resistance'.
106 BBC, *Newsnight*, 8 August 2022.
107 *PoliticsJOE*, 11 August 2022.
108 *Independent*, 18 August 2022.
109 *PoliticsJOE*, 11 August 2022.
110 See LBC, 4 January 2023.
111 Gall, *Bob Crow*, pp. 175–9.
112 *Morning Star*, 3 October 2022.
113 *PoliticsJOE*, 11 August 2022.
114 *GB News*, 8 October 2022.
115 Such instances are discussed at length in J. Kelly, *Trade Unions and Socialist Politics* (London: Verso, 1988).
116 To extend the military metaphor using the First World War, its trench warfare in western Europe can be seen as apt in that while the RMT was not advancing in gaining its bargaining demands, neither was the government in terms of its desired 'reform' of work practices on the railways. This is a more apt metaphor than the Second World War, where Germany's defeated six-month-long Operation Barbarossa against Russia could be compared to its previously victorious six-week Western Campaign that led to the fall of France.
117 See A. Fox, *Industrial Sociology and Industrial Relations*, Research Papers No. 3, Royal Commission on Trade Unions and Employers' Associations (London: HMSO, 1966); A. Fox, *Beyond Contract: Work, Power and Trust Relations* (London: Faber & Faber, 1974).
118 See LBC, 29 July 2022.

119 See *ibid.*

120 Herbert Morrison was the post-war Labour minister who oversaw the nationalisation of key industries where the key issue was to use state ownership to modernise the economy and improve the efficiency of domestic capital. Accordingly, worker representation was somewhat lacking.

121 The most recent biography of Connolly is L. McNulty, *James Connolly: Socialist, Nationalist and Internationalist* (London: Merlin Press, 2022).

122 *Peston* programme, 22 June 2023.

123 *Morning Star*, 19 October 2022.

124 *Big Issue North*, 25 July 2022.

125 LBC, 29 July 2022.

126 *Sunday Independent*, June 26 2022.

127 The ASLEF, TSSA and CWU unions also cancelled their strikes.

128 Similarly, in an RMT press release (5 September 2022) just before the death of the monarch, Lynch said: 'Liz Truss should act in *the national interest* and play a positive role in helping to settle the rail dispute. This means investment in the railway infrastructure, unshackling Network Rail and the rail companies so we can come to a negotiated settlement on job security, pay and working conditions' [emphasis added].

129 *Novara Media*, 15 September 2022.

130 *Socialist Worker*, 14 September 2022.

131 *Guardian*, 31 July 2022.

132 Gall, *Bob Crow*, p. 82.

133 *New Statesman*, 17 August 2022.

134 *Ibid.*

135 *Tribune*, 27 July 2022.

136 BBC radio, *Hardtalk*, 15 February 2023.

137 LBC, 4 January 2023.

138 LBC, 19 August 2022.

139 G. Gall, 'Taking back the power: Forcing the EU's hand', *Scottish Left Review*, 114 (November–December 2019): 12.

140 *Ibid.*

141 *Sunday Independent*, 26 June 2022.

142 Glasgow picket line, 10 October 2022.

143 *Double Down News*, 16 December 2022.

144 Cardiff, 26 January 2023.

145 If Lynch could be accused of naivety in his pleas to Starmer to be more radical, he was not alone. Sharon Graham (*Morning Star*, 16 July 2023; *BBC News* online, 15 July 2023, *Guardian*, 8 October 2023) also did so. At the July 2023 Labour Party National Policy

Forum, Starmer ignored such pleas and gained majority support for his 'no uncosted spending pledges' stance (*Guardian*, 24 July 2023). Graham's position was not dramatically changed by the watering down of policies on workers' rights at the National Policy Forum (*Guardian*, 18 August 2023).

Conclusion

1 *Guardian*, 8 May 2021.
2 Liverpool, 6 October 2022.
3 Cardiff, 26 January 2023.
4 B. Garman, *A Race of Singers: Whitman's Working-Class Hero from Guthrie to Springsteen* (Chapel Hill: University of North Carolina Press, 2000).
5 Lynch was compared to Scargill by the *Evening Standard* (9 December 2022).
6 *BBC2*, 1 June 2023.
7 See, for example, *New Statesman*, 28 July 2022.
8 See W. Müller-Jentsch, 'Trade unions as intermediary organizations', *Economic and Industrial Democracy*, 6/1 (1985): 3–33; C. Offe and H. Wiesenthal, 'Two logics of collective action', in C. Offe (ed.), *Disorganized Capitalism: Contemporary Transformations of Work and Politics* (Cambridge: Polity Press, 1985), pp. 170–220.
9 For an extended discussion see G. Gall, 'Union strategy and circumstance: Back to the future or forward to the past?', in A. Wilkinson and K. Townsend (eds), *Research Handbook on Work and Employment Relations* (Cheltenham: Edward Elgar, 2011), pp. 91–110.
10 LBC, 26 May 2022.
11 *Morning Star*, 21 February 2023.
12 *Morning Star*, 24 February 2023.
13 General Secretary's address to 2023 RMT annual conference (RMT press release, 27 June 2023).
14 See, for example, *Guardian*, 18 August 2022; *Morning Star*, 19 October 2022, 2 November 2022.
15 J. Kelly, 'Union militancy and social partnership', in P. Ackers, C. Smith and P. Smith (eds), *The New Workplace and Trade Unionism* (London: Routledge, 1996), pp. 41–76. For a consideration of the postal workers using this framework see G. Gall, *The Meaning of Militancy? Postal Workers and Industrial Relations* (Aldershot: Ashgate, 2003).

16 J. Kelly, 'Conflict: Trends and forms of collective action', *Employee Relations*, 37/6 (2015): 720–32, at 728–9 [emphasis added].
17 J. Kelly, *Rethinking Industrial Relations: Mobilization, Collectivism and Long Waves* (London: Routledge, 1998), p. 141.
18 *Ibid.*, pp. 33–4.
19 A third RMT dispute ran in parallel to those at Network Rail and the TOCs. This was on London Underground and concerned jobs, pensions and working conditions. However, it saw only five days of striking from June 2022 to March 2023. Strike action scheduled for the last week in July 2023 was stood down after negotiations the week before made progress (RMT press release, 21 July 2023). There were also a series of one- and two-day strikes in the same period of the two national rail disputes by other RMT members on the railways in catering, cleaning, maintenance and security functions including a first national strike cleaners' strike.
20 The line of the song was true for the 1972 miners' seven-week strike but not the 1971 postal workers' seven-week strike, which was then the longest and biggest strike since the 1926 General Strike. G. Gall, *'The Meaning of Militancy?' Postal Workers and Industrial Relations* (Aldershot: Ashgate, 2003) pp. 32–3.
21 For example, Lynch was awarded the 2023 'Spirit of Mother Jones' in Cork in late July 2023 (*Morning Star*, 29 July 2023). Born Mary Harris Jones in Cork in 1837, Mother Jones was an Irish-American union leader. Cork Mother Jones Committee spokesman, James Nolan, commented: 'We believe that Mick Lynch by his direct action, solid analysis, straight talking and plain speaking in defence of workers and union rights has won widespread support and respect among working people both in Britain and here in Ireland.'
22 See, for example, *Morning Star* (26, 29 June 2023), *RMT News* (June 2023) and General Secretary's address to 2023 RMT annual conference (RMT press release, 27 June 2023).
23 Whether and when Labour would repeal the Act remained to be seen.
24 *RMT as an Industrially Organised Union*, 20 January version (London: RMT, 2022).
25 See F. Dobbs, *Teamster Rebellion* (New York: Pathfinder Press, 1972).
26 See J. McAlevey, *No Shortcuts: Organizing for Power in the New Gilded Age* (New York: Oxford University Press, 2016).
27 See K. Moody, *On New Terrain: How Capital is Reshaping the Battleground of Class War* (Chicago: Haymarket, 2017); K. Moody, 'Motion and vulnerability in contemporary capitalism: The shift to turnover time', *Historical Materialism*, 30/4 (2022): 1–32.

28 See J. Foster and C. Woolfson, *The Politics of the UCS Work-In: Class Alliances and the Right to Work* (London: Lawrence and Wishart, 1986); W. Knox and A. McKinlay, *Jimmy Reid: A Clyde-Built Man* (Liverpool: Liverpool University Press, 2019).

29 RMT, *RMT as an Industrially Organised Union*, 20 January version (London: RMT, 2022).

30 Flanagan, *Our Trade Unions.*

31 In some cases, this has meant striking on a Saturday or Sunday in order to provide for an uninterrupted weekend, when rest days are often worked. However, in the TOCs dispute, there was some evidence the demand for Saturday striking had been ignored for some time (*Off The Rails*, 23 April 2023). The significance of striking on a Saturday was that after the end of the pandemic and with commuting not returning to its pre-pandemic pattern, Saturdays were often the busiest days for train usage.

32 As the RMT pays no strike pay, it has a hardship fund, currently called the National Dispute Fund, which members must apply for, as Lynch explained to LBC (4 January 2023). Members of the public were urged to donate to it in addition to the fund receiving donations from RMT branches (alongside the existence of their own dispute funds). In circular FIN/10/22-FIN/219 (1 February 2023), Lynch stated there was around £2m in branch and regional accounts which could be used to alleviate strike hardship. The value of the National Dispute Fund was £85,000 in 2021 and £585,000 in 2022. However, the RMT itself had – as its 2021 Certification Officer annual return showed – £27.477m of shares which paid dividends of £633,000, representing a vast increase from 2013 when it held £15.35m in shares (see Gall, *Bob Crow*, p. 63). The figures for 2022 were £26.25m and £548,000 in dividends. A strategic approach would have seen some of these much greater national assets realised in order to finance strike pay nationally in the two national disputes (see p. 208). In addition to Unite, the PCS and Unison unions also have strike pay. For Unison, it is £50 per day.

33 *Guardian*, 11 March 2023.

34 Sun Tzu, *The Art of War* (Atlanta: Dalmatian Press, 2007), p. 41.

35 C. von Clausewitz, *On War* (Princeton, NJ: Princeton University Press, 1984).

36 On Crow's limited attempt see G. Gall, *Bob Crow: Socialist, Leader, Fighter: A Political Biography* (Manchester: Manchester University Press, 2017), p. 163.

37 A levy on all members to sustain strikes by selected members was initiated in the PCS union in early 2023.

38 *Tribune*, 6 June 2023.
39 *RMT News*, October 2021.
40 Cardiff, 26 January 2023.
41 General Secretary's address to 2023 RMT annual conference (RMT press release, 27 June 2023).
42 *Ibid.*, p. 163.
43 *Off The Rails*, 28 September 2022.
44 *Off The Rails*, 25 March 2023.
45 *Socialist*, 30 March 2023.
46 A. Ferner and M. Terry, '"The crunch had come": A case study of changing industrial relations in the Post Office', Warwick Papers in Industrial Relations, No. 1, Industrial Relations Research Unit, University of Warwick, 1985, p. 11.
47 See also Gall, *Bob Crow*, p. 235; T. Haines-Doran, *Derailed: How to Fix Britain's Broken Railways* (Manchester: Manchester University Press, 2022), p. 68.
48 *Guardian*, 21 March 2023.
49 E. Batstone, 'The frontier of control', in D. Gallie (ed.), *Employment in Britain* (Oxford: Blackwell, 1988), pp. 218–47.
50 Additionally, some allegations relate to Cash's tenure but where Lynch was alleged to be complicit as a national officer.
51 *Morning Star*, 24 February 2023.
52 See R. Darlington and M. Upchurch, 'A reappraisal of the rank-and-file/bureaucracy debate', *Capital and Class*, 36/1 (2012): 73–91; R. Darlington, 'The rank and file and the trade union bureaucracy', *International Socialism*, 142 (2014): 57–82.
53 See also J. McIlroy, 'Marxism and the trade unions: The bureaucracy versus the rank-and-file debate revisited', *Critique*, 42/4 (2014): 497–526.
54 *Tribune*, 5 January 2023.
55 A. Murray, *A New Labour Nightmare: The Return of the Awkward Squad* (London: Verso, 2003).
56 G. Gall and J. Fiorito, 'The forward march of labour halted? Or what is to be done with "union organising"? The cases of Britain and the US', *Capital and Class*, 35/2 (2011): 231–50.
57 *Jacobin*, 6 October 2022; *Soundings*, 'The spirit of resistance: Mick Lynch in conversation with Gary Younge', *Lawrence Wishart Blog: Soundings*, 6 December 2022. Available at https://lwbooks.co.uk/the-spirit-of-resistance-mick-lynch-in-conversation-with-gary-younge (accessed 11 May 2023).
58 *i*, 24 June 2022.
59 ONS, *Trade Union Membership, UK 1995–2022*.
60 *TES*, 4 March 2023.

Notes

61 PCS press release, 19 April 2023; Unite press release, 13 July 2023, *Morning Star*, 14 September 2023.
62 Flanagan, *Our Trade Unions.*
63 General Secretary's address to 2023 RMT annual conference (RMT press release, 27 June 2023).
64 *Ibid.*

Appendix 1

1 Lynch's wife, Mary, was extensively interviewed for this programme.
2 Emphasis in original.
3 See G. Gall, *Bob Crow: Socialist, Leader, Fighter: A Political Biography* (Manchester: Manchester University Press, 2017), p. 240.

Selected bibliography

Adeney, M. and Lloyd, J., *The Miners' Strike, 1984–1985: Loss Without Limit* (London: Routledge and Kegan Paul, 1986).

Aronowitz, S., *Working-Class Hero: A New Strategy for Labor* (New York: Adama Books, 1983).

Bassett. P., *Strike Free: New Industrial Relations in Britain* (London: Macmillan, 1986).

Batstone, E., 'The frontier of control', in D. Gallie (ed.), *Employment in Britain* (Oxford: Blackwell, 1988), pp. 218–47.

Beardwell, I., 'Annual review article 1989', *British Journal of Industrial Relations*, 28/1 (1990): 113–28.

Berlin, M., *Never on our Knees: A History of the RMT, 1979–2006* (London: Pluto Press, 2006).

Burns, S., *Archie Green: The Making of a Working-Class Hero* (Champaign: University of Illinois Press, 2011).

Callahan, M. and Moore, Y., *Working-Class Heroes: A History of Struggle in Song: A Songbook* (Oakland, CA: PM Press, 2019).

Chapple, F., *Sparks Fly: A Trade Union Life*, updated edition (London: Michael Joseph, 1985).

Clausewitz, C. von, *On War* (Princeton, NJ: Princeton University Press, 1984).

Darlington, R., 'Leadership and union militancy: The case of the RMT', *Capital and Class*, 33/3 (2009): 3–32.

Darlington, R., 'Organising, militancy and revitalisation: The case of the RMT', in G. Gall (ed.), *Union Revitalisation in Advanced Economies: Assessing the Contribution of 'Union Organising'* (Basingstoke: Palgrave Macmillan, 2009), pp. 83–106.

Darlington, R., 'The rank and file and the trade union bureaucracy', *International Socialism*, 142 (2014): 57–82.

Selected bibliography

Darlington, R. and Upchurch, M., 'A reappraisal of the rank-and-file/ bureaucracy debate', *Capital and Class*, 36/1 (2012): 73–91.

Daw, A. and Zhou, X., 'Working-class heroes: Intraspeaker variation in General Secretary Len McCluskey', *Lifespans and Styles*, 3/2 (2017): 20–8.

Dobbs, F., *Teamster Rebellion* (New York: Pathfinder Press, 1972).

Draper, H., 'The twin souls of socialism', *New Politics*, 5/1 (1966): 57–84.

Ferner, A. and Terry, M., '"The crunch had come": A case study of changing industrial relations in the Post Office', Warwick Papers in Industrial Relations, No. 1, Industrial Relations Research Unit, University of Warwick, 1985.

Flanagan, N., *Our trade unions: What comes next after the summer of 2022?* (London: Manifesto Press, 2023).

Foster, J. and Woolfson, C., *The Politics of the UCS Work-In: Class Alliances and the Right to Work* (London: Lawrence and Wishart, 1986).

Fox, A., *Beyond Contract: Work, Power and Trust Relations* (London: Faber & Faber, 1974).

Fox, A., *Industrial Sociology and Industrial Relations*, Research Papers No. 3, Royal Commission on Trade Unions and Employers' Associations (London: HMSO, 1966).

Gall, G., *Bob Crow: Socialist, Leader, Fighter: A Political Biography* (Manchester: Manchester University Press, 2017).

Gall, G., 'Injunctions as a legal weapon in collective industrial disputes in Britain, 2005–2014', *British Journal of Industrial Relations*, 55/1 (2017): 187–214.

Gall, G., 'Organising in the offshore oil and gas industry in Britain, c. 1972–1990: A long flame burning or spark that has gone out?', in G. Gall (ed.), *Union Organising: Campaigning for Trade Union Recognition* (London: Routledge, 2023), pp. 39–55.

Gall, G., 'Taking back the power: Forcing the EU's hand', *Scottish Left Review*, 114 (November–December 2019): 12.

Gall, G., *The Meaning of Militancy? Postal Workers and Industrial Relations* (Aldershot: Ashgate, 2003).

Gall, G., 'Three decades on, the 1982 flexible rostering dispute', *ASLEF Locomotive Journal*, April 2012, pp. 12–13.

Gall, G., *Tommy Sheridan: From Hero to Zero?: A Political Biography* (Cardiff: Welsh Academic Press, 2012).

Gall, G., 'Union organising in the offshore oil and gas industry: Retrospection on possibilities and probabilities', *Scottish Labour History*, 41 (2006): 51–69.

Gall, G., 'Union strategy and circumstance: Back to the future or forward to the past?', in A. Wilkinson, and K. Townsend (eds), *Research*

Handbook on Work and Employment Relations (Cheltenham: Edward Elgar, 2011), pp. 91–110.

Gall, G. and Fiorito, J., 'The forward march of labour halted? Or what is to be done with "union organising"? The cases of Britain and the US', *Capital and Class*, 35/2 (2011): 231–50.

Garman, B., *A Race of Singers: Whitman's Working-Class Hero from Guthrie to Springsteen* (Chapel Hill: University of North Carolina Press, 2000).

Gordon, A., '1911: The first national railway strike and the rail union amalgamation movement', *Historical Studies in Industrial Relations*, 33 (2012): 127–47.

Gourvish, T., *British Rail 1974–1997: From Integration to Privatisation* (Oxford: Oxford University Press, 2002).

Graziano, A., 'The death of the working-class hero in "Mary Barton" and "Alton Locke"', *Journal of Narrative Theory*, 29/2 (1999): 135–57.

Haines-Doran, T., *Derailed: How to Fix Britain's Broken Railways* (Manchester: Manchester University Press, 2022).

Hammond, E., *Maverick: The Life of a Union Rebel* (London: Weidenfeld & Nicolson, 1992).

Hannah, S., *Can't Pay, Won't Pay: The Fight to Stop the Poll Tax* (London: Pluto, 2020).

Harrison, H., *The Beast of Bolsover! Dennis Skinner: Working-Class Hero!* (Morrisville, NC: Lulu, 2020).

Heery, E. and Kelly, J., 'Professional, participative and managerial unionism: An interpretation of change in trade unions', *Work, Employment and Society*, 8/1 (1994): 1–22.

Holgate, J., *Arise: Power, Strategy and Union Resurgence* (London: Pluto, 2021).

Humphrys, M., 'We're still as proud today as we were then', *ASLEF Journal*, July 2022, pp. 8–9.

Kaplan, C., 'The death of the working-class hero', *New Formations*, 52 (2004): 94–110.

Kelly, J., 'Conflict: Trends and forms of collective action', *Employee Relations*, 37/6 (2015): 720–32.

Kelly, J., *Rethinking Industrial Relations: Mobilization, Collectivism and Long Waves* (London: Routledge, 1998).

Kelly, J., *Trade Unions and Socialist Politics* (London: Verso, 1988).

Kelly, J., 'Union militancy and social partnership', in P. Ackers, C. Smith and P. Smith (eds), *The New Workplace and Trade Unionism* (London: Routledge, 1996), pp. 41–76.

Knox, W. and McKinlay, A., *Jimmy Reid: A Clyde-Built Man* (Liverpool: Liverpool University Press, 2019).

Selected bibliography

Lévesque, C. and Murray, G., 'Understanding union power: Resources and capabilities for renewing union capacity', *Transfer: European Review of Labour and Research*, 16/3 (2010): 333–50.

Lloyd, J., *Light and Liberty: The History of the EETPU* (London: Weidenfeld and Nicolson, 1990).

Lukes, S., *Power: A Radical View* (London: Macmillan, 1974).

Maksymiw, W., Eaton, J. and Gill, C., *The British Trade Union Directory* (London: Longman, 1990).

Marsh, A. and Ryan, V., *Historical Directory of Trade Unions*, Volume 2 (Aldershot: Gower, 1984).

McAlevey, J., *No Shortcuts: Organizing for Power in the New Gilded Age* (New York: Oxford University Press, 2016).

McCluskey, L., *Always Red* (London: OR Books, 2021).

McIlroy, J., 'Marxism and the trade unions: The bureaucracy versus the rank-and-file debate revisited', *Critique*, 42/4 (2014): 497–526.

McIlroy, J., *Trade Unions in Britain Today* (Manchester: Manchester University Press, 1988).

McNulty, L., *James Connolly: Socialist, Nationalist and Internationalist* (London: Merlin Press, 2022).

Metcalf, M., *Betty Tebbs: A Radical Working-Class Hero* (London: UNITE Education, 2019).

Moody, K., 'Motion and vulnerability in contemporary capitalism: The shift to turnover time', *Historical Materialism*, 30/4 (2022): 1–32.

Moody, K., *On New Terrain: How Capital is Reshaping the Battleground of Class War* (Chicago: Haymarket, 2017).

Morris, T., 'Annual review article 1994', *British Journal of Industrial Relations*, 33/1 (1995): 117–35.

Müller-Jentsch, W., 'Trade unions as intermediary organizations', *Economic and Industrial Democracy*, 6/1 (1985): 3–33.

Murray, A., *A New Labour Nightmare: The Return of the Awkward Squad* (London: Verso, 2003).

Murray, A., *The T&G Story: A History of the Transport and General Workers Union, 1922–2007* (London: Lawrence and Wishart, 2008).

Murray, A. and German, L., *Stop the War: The Story of Britain's Biggest Mass Movement* (London: Bookmarks, 2005).

Nunns, A., *The Candidate: Jeremy Corbyn's Improbable Path to Power* (London: OR Books, 2018).

Nye, J., *Soft Power: The Means to Success in World Politics* (London: Oxford University Press, 2004).

Offe, C. and Wiesenthal, H., 'Two logics of collective action' in C. Offe (ed.), *Disorganized Capitalism: Contemporary Transformations of Work and Politics* (Cambridge: Polity Press, 1985), pp. 170–220.

Selected bibliography

ONS, *Trade Union Membership, UK 1995–2021: Statistical Bulletin* (London: Office for National Statistics, 2022).

Reade, B., *Diamonds in the Mud: A Working-Class Hero is Something to Me* (London: Mirror Books, 2021).

RMT, *RMT as an Industrially Organised Union*, 20 January version (London: RMT, 2022).

Rose, J., *100 Years of Kings Cross ASLEF: Solidarity Forever* (London: Kings Cross ASLEF, 1986).

Routledge, P., *Bumper Book of British Lefties* (London: Politicos, 2003).

Schmalz, S., Ludwig, C. and Webster, E., 'The power resources approach: Developments and challenges', *Global Labour Journal*, 9/2 (2018): 113–34.

Silver, B., *Forces of Labor: Workers' Movements and Globalization since 1870* (Cambridge: Cambridge University Press, 2003).

Smethurst, J. and Carter, P., *Historical Directory of Trade Unions*, Volume 6 (London: Routledge, 2009).

Smith, D. and Chamberlain, P., *Blacklisted: The Secret War Between Big Business and Union Activists – The Fully Story*, revised second edition (Oxford: New Internationalist Publications, 2016).

Smith, R., *James Connolly: Working-Class Hero* (Dublin: Poolbeg Press, 2016).

Soundings, 'The spirit of resistance: Mick Lynch in conversation with Gary Younge', *Lawrence Wishart Blog: Soundings*, 6 December 2022. Available at https://lwbooks.co.uk/the-spirit-of-resistance-mick-lynch-in-conversation-with-gary-younge (accessed 11 May 2023).

Sun Tzu, *The Art of War* (Atlanta: Dalmatian Press, 2007).

SWP, *Class Struggle is Back: Strikes, Why Labour Fails and the Fight for Socialist Revolution* (London: Socialist Workers Party, 2022).

Upchurch, M., Croucher, R. and Flynn, M., 'Political congruence and trade union renewal', *Work, Employment and Society*, 26/5 (2012): 857–68.

Wright, E. O., 'Working-class power, capitalist-class interests and class compromise', *American Journal of Sociology*, 105/4 (2000): 957–1002.

Index

Index

Index

Trades Union Congress (TUC)
60, 61, 69, 154, 155, 163,
167, 177, 184
Trade Unionist and Socialist
Coalition (TUSC) 67, 77,
178, 183
Train Operating Companies
(TOCs) 17, 19, 23–24, 25, 26,
34, 35, 37, 51, 108–9, 121,
122–23, 126, 128, 130, 133,
134, 140, 141, 146, 147, 149,
157, 159, 186, 202, 203, 206,
208, 210, 211, 217, 218, 222,
230n23, 247n69, 254
Transport Salaried Staffs'
Association (TSSA) 245n22,
254n127
Trotsky, Leon 44, 119, 171,
246n50
Trotskyism 116, 234n54
Truss, Liz 132, 139, 149,
254n128
Tzu, Sun 207–8

union membership 48–49, 227n1
Unite, the union 2, 19, 37, 77,
134, 135–36, 206, 217, 218,
232n35, 257n32

University and College Union
(UCU) 36, 39, 249n105

Ward, Dave 34–36, 39, 183
Weighell, Sidney 79
working-class class
consciousness 32, 44, 50–51,
153, 185–86, 219
working-class heroes
charisma, role of 41, 46
class location 44
definition 9, 42–46
examples of 42–43
expectations of 52, 159, 203
folk hero versus working-class
hero 31–32
tensions within 46, 48–49, 52
the 'good fight', the role of
fighting 47–48
union leaders as working-class
heroes 34–37, 47
Whelan, Mick 36, 37, 222,
235n10
Wrack, Matt 36, 150

EU authorised representative for GPSR:
Easy Access System Europe, Mustamäe tee 50,
10621 Tallinn, Estonia
gpsr.requests@easproject.com

www.ingramcontent.com/pod-product-compliance
Lightning Source LLC
Chambersburg PA
CBHW010237100426
42813CB00034B/3447/J